Primary Religious Education – A New Approach

Conceptual enquiry in primary RE

By Clive Erricker, Judith Lowndes and Elaine Bellchambers

Routledge
Taylor & Francis Group

LONDON AND NEW YORK

This first edition published 2011
by Routledge
2 Park Square, Milton Park, Abingdon, Oxon OX14 4RN

Simultaneously published in the USA and Canada
by Routledge
270 Madison Avenue, New York, NY 10016

Routledge is an imprint of the Taylor & Francis Group, an informa business

© 2011 Clive Erricker, Judith Lowndes and Elaine Bellchambers

Typeset in Bembo by
Saxon Graphics Ltd, Derby
Printed and bound in Great Britain by
TJ International Ltd, Padstow, Cornwall

British Library Cataloguing in Publication Data
A catalogue record for this book is available from the British Library

Library of Congress Cataloging-in-Publication Data
Erricker, Clive.
   Primary religious education - a new approach : conceptual enquiry in primary RE / by Clive Erricker, Judith Lowndes and Elaine Bellchambers.
      p. cm.
   1. Religious education of children. 2. Education, Primary. I. Lowndes, Judith. II. Bellchambers, Elaine. III. Title.
   BV1475.3.E77 2011
   200.71--dc22
                         2010011853

ISBN13: 978-0-415-48066-6 (hbk)
ISBN13: 978-0-415-48067-3 (pbk)
ISBN13: 978-0-203-84294-2 (ebk)

Primary Religious Education – A New Approach

The role of Religious Education within the primary school and how it should be implemented has been the subject of worldwide debate. Responding to the delivery of the non-statutory framework for RE and the recent emphasis on a creative primary curriculum *Primary Religious Education – A New Approach* models a much needed pedagogical framework, encouraging conceptual enquiry and linking theory to its implementation within the wider curriculum in schools.

The book outlines this new conceptual approach to Religious Education and is based upon the Living Difference syllabus successfully implemented in Hampshire, Portsmouth, Southampton and Westminster. It demonstrates how to implement the requirements of the new curriculum and Ofsted criteria for effective RE and is rapidly gaining both national and international support. Through this approach, Religious Education is discussed within the larger context of primary education in the contemporary world. This book will help you to teach RE in a creative way in the primary classroom by providing:

- historical commentaries
- an overview of existing approaches
- case studies based upon developments in religious literacy
- connections to initiatives such as Every Child Matters and cross-curricular links to other areas of the curriculum, including PSHE.

With an all-encompassing global context, this book provides tutors, students and practicing teachers with a firm basis for developing their thinking about the subject of RE, how it is placed in the primary curriculum and how it may be successfully implemented in schools.

Clive Erricker was, until recently, Hampshire County Inspector for Religious Education. Prior to that he was a Lecturer in Religious Education at University College Chichester for over a decade. He began his career teaching English and RE in schools.

Judith Lowndes is a general inspector/adviser for Religious Education in Hampshire. She has extensive experience of teaching primary pupils and advising on Religious Education provision, she has also been a Lecturer for Religious Education to students and trainee teachers in higher education.

Elaine Bellchambers has worked as a teacher and as an Ofsted inspector. She is currently Senior Lecturer in Religious Education and Professional Studies at the University of Winchester and responsible for co-ordinating Primary Religious Education.

Contents

Acknowledgements

Acknowledgements are due to:

Hampshire County Council; Hampshire, Portsmouth and Southampton SACREs; and Hampshire, Portsmouth and Southampton teachers, especially those whose work has been cited or quoted in this book and those who contributed to the work of the Primary RE County Steering Group and Regional Development Groups. Any works included that were previously published by Hampshire County Council are under its copyright and are included with its permission, by licensed agreement.

Also, particular thanks to Kath Bagley and Georgie Mulhall for their work as primary RE ASTs in Hampshire and Portsmouth respectively; and the Hampshire Primary History Steering Group and Katherine Wedell for permission to include parts of her report on the implementation of Living Difference in specific chapters of this book.

Introduction
Making RE meaningful

This book provides an introduction to RE in the primary curriculum, both for students studying on degrees and PGCEs in education and for teachers on continuing professional development programmes in which RE is a component. Religious education is in a state of transition at a time when the primary curriculum is also undergoing radical changes in its underlying principles and delivery. How can RE contribute to a creative primary curriculum that develops young people as successful learners, confident individuals and responsible citizens? We hope this book will give you the guidance that makes you confident in teaching RE so that can happen. It presents a new conceptual approach to RE that makes links to other subjects obvious and meaningful. It focuses on the development of the learner. It emphasises the importance of skills development. However, the book goes further in suggesting that RE itself can become a more inclusive aspect of the curriculum, and thus more educationally valuable; that it can be more than 'religious' education, and that the generic conceptual enquiry approach advocated here can be the basis of a fully integrated curriculum that does not compromise the integrity of other subject disciplines.

About this book

The book is divided into three parts. The first addresses how RE can be important within the curriculum, what good RE looks like and ways in which effective learning can take place. It will introduce you to the subject and its contribution to the primary curriculum.

The second part focuses on conceptual enquiry as an effective way to ensure RE makes a meaningful contribution to children's development. It provides illustrations of how this can be done in the classroom and case studies of good practice. It also explains how, as a result, children's learning can be approached in a holistic and creative way through a process-oriented pedagogy that allows you to diagnose progression, combine with other subjects effectively, and ensure learners' engagement with and enthusiasm for the subject.

The third part offers practical ways in which you can transform the practice in your school. It addresses ways in which you can provide an enquiry-based and creative curriculum that emphasises personalised learning and pupil voice. It shows how this combines with assessment for learning, effective questioning and progressive key stage planning that incorporates diagnostic and formal assessment. It also shows how you can plan from the strengths you have as a teacher, both as an RE manager and subject leader, and in terms of contributing from differing subject expertise by incorporating engaging resources and appropriate learning strategies. It gives examples that extend across each year of the primary curriculum. It assesses how this way of working can transform your approach to the curriculum by suggesting ways in which these innovations can point to future developments in primary education by establishing democratic learning in classrooms and schools that takes account of the needs of children as they inherit a pluralised and globalised world.

The chapters

Chapter 1 deals with the way that both religion and religious education have been viewed in the past and are viewed now, in the present. It identifies the controversial nature of both religion and religious education in society today and arguments for and against them. This includes attitudes toward the growth of faith schools, the role multiculturalism has played and its impact, and why democracy and democratic education can be ill at ease with religion and religious education.

Chapter 2 asks, 'What is good RE?' It reviews government legislation and recent approaches to the subject. In particular, it analyses the new initiatives and previous shortcomings of the Qualifications and Curriculum Authority (now the Qualifications and Curriculum Development Agency) and the ambiguity in approach that has developed in RE. It presents the 'vital ingredients' that need to be present in the construction of good RE.

Chapter 3 is concerned with effective learning, the conditions that need to be in place beyond the classroom and the way learning needs to be constructed within a democratic classroom environment. This involves using a constructivist approach to learning and utilising community of enquiry techniques. It identifies the importance of inclusive relationships and affirming the rights of the child. It advocates that central to effective learning are both critical and creative thinking, and that religious education can play a crucial role in this respect.

Chapter 4 introduces conceptual enquiry as an approach to learning and, specifically, a methodology that ensures its effectiveness. The chapter begins with research undertaken with primary school children that informs this approach. It then presents the pedagogical principles employed, derived from Living Difference, the Hampshire, Portsmouth and Southampton Agreed Syllabus for Religious Education. The chapter provides examples of planning based on the approach and comments by teachers who have employed it.

Chapter 5 relates the conceptual enquiry methodology, which was introduced in Chapter 4, to holistic and creative learning. It identifies characteristics of holistic and creative learning and then draws on the research project that evaluated the impact of the conceptual enquiry methodology and presents its results, analysing how and why teachers found it effective in progressing pupils' learning, because they came to understand it holistically and creatively, and why some did not. It also illustrates how this approach can make addressing community cohesion provision successful.

Chapter 6 consists of case studies in good practice. It shows, in detail, how the conceptual enquiry methodology approach has been used by teachers in four primary schools to improve their practice and that of their colleagues and to enhance pupils' achievement. It shows how the approach can be effective in both the cognitive and affective domains of learning. It also shows how learning in religious education can enhance achievement in other areas of the curriculum.

Chapter 7 focuses on creating an enquiry-based curriculum and how that can be constructed in RE across the primary phase. It introduces planning within and across key stages with descriptions of specific cycles of learning (units of work) that combine to create progression and continuity in pupils' learning both with regard to concepts studied and material introduced from the main religions to be covered. It also provides advice on the RE manager's role and the responsibilities to be attended to in curriculum leadership.

Chapter 8 provides advice for the non-specialist in RE who has specialist knowledge in another subject. It shows how specialist knowledge and techniques in other subjects can be introduced into RE and enrich its delivery. The chapter provides examples of ways in which specialists in specific subjects can enhance the delivery of RE by virtue of the expertise they can bring and the techniques that are transferable from their own disciplinary expertise using specific strategies and resources. It also provides further understanding of the subject matter of RE.

Chapter 9 considers the future of RE and the primary curriculum. It does so by, first, analysing the recommendations of the Rose Report and the Cambridge Review and the implications and possibilities they offer. It then presents, through a review of previous contributions to this book and by offering a way in which the primary curriculum could be reconstructed, a way in which conceptual enquiry can provide a holistic and creative curriculum suited to the needs of pupils in the 21st century.

How to use this book

Of course we hope you will read this book from cover to cover; each section follows on progressively from the one before. However, it becomes practically relevant when we relate it directly to the tasks we have to undertake, in planning and teaching, on an everyday basis. Therefore it is not just a reference book but also a manual that you can turn to as and when you need specific guidance. In our experience, teachers grasp the approach we are advocating by degrees: it takes time to sink in and then to refine practice until it becomes second nature. A bit like riding a bike, learning to drive a car, or master a new sport or hobby: you get some bits before you get others and then, miraculously, it all comes together and you wonder what the fuss was about and why you made it such hard work! That is normal. So, return to the relevant chapters as and when you need them. We all usually start by flicking through and dipping into the bits that most interest us, relating them to what we already do, think and know; but eventually the idea is to hone a new and tested way of delivering the subject as an integral aspect of the whole of primary pupils' experience of learning.

Ultimately, it is necessary to understand this approach holistically, when all its parts come together. Again, in our experience, teachers start by seeing this approach as a new structure to work to before they recognise the importance of its underlying process. If you are an RE coordinator or subject manager in a primary school it will also be your responsibility to lead others forward and liaise with other coordinators or subject managers. This will prove invaluable, since the more you explain what you are trying to do the better you will understand it yourself. Also, planning with others is immeasurably easier and more rewarding than having to plan on your own. So, share sections of this book with others, as they are relevant, at the time, to the steps you are taking to transform your curriculum and pupils' learning. You can't create a joined-up curriculum without joined-up thinking amongst staff and a joined-up purpose as to what you want for your pupils. We hope this approach will enrich your vision for both RE and your school.

RE in the primary curriculum

1

Why is RE important?

Clive Erricker

Introduction

As a primary school teacher you will want to know how to teach good RE to your children. This chapter provides you with some background on religion and RE in our society, both historical and contemporary. This will give you a map or context for understanding the subject and the influence of and responses to religion. The aim is to give you confidence but not to shy away from controversy. To teach RE well you must do it with conviction. Really effective RE teachers have to believe it is an important aspect of their children's education.

This chapter seeks to convince you of the educational importance of RE and its place in the school curriculum. It starts by presuming you are not convinced of that or, if you are, asking you to consider your justifications for that. It presents some historical reasons for why RE is already a compulsory subject and goes on to question why we should consider teaching young people about religion and how that has been justified through to the present day. It poses some objections to this before, finally, suggesting we need to reconsider what RE is there for and how that has to focus on RE being part of the overall curriculum and the development of young people.

Religion and religious education – something to laugh about?

RE in an historical and contemporary context

> 'There is no religion in England... If one speaks of religion, everyone laughs.'
> (Montesquieu, *Oevres*, vol. vii:184; Barnard, 1961:xiii)

This observation by the French writer Montesquieu was made in the 19th century. Times have changed: in the 21st century religion is not such a laughing matter, nor just a private one. 'Religious education' could be substituted for 'religion' in the quotation since it does suffer from the image of being educationally anomalous as far as many parents, and even teachers, are concerned. The question persists: if you are not religious how is it useful? And, if you are religious, presumably school is not the place where you will get your education in religion; rather it would be in your own religious community. Certainly, if RE is to be understood as educationally worthy it needs some defending.

I can still remember parts of my own primary school experience. For some strange reason one of my memories is being given a bible, as all children were at that time and forever previously. I can't remember the talk that accompanied this but it would have been intended to be morally uplifting. I didn't go to a Church school so why did this event take place? What was it about the English education system that presumed religion and education should go hand in hand? Should such an assumption be made today? Religious education has been a part of the primary curriculum in England and Wales ever since public schooling began, but its role has changed. Elementary education was made compulsory under the 1870 Education Act, with arithmetic, basic literacy and religious education compulsory subjects. Why RE? Fast forward to today. Do we still think RE should be compulsory? If so, for what reason?

Religious education has always been controversial, but the reasons for this have changed over time. In 1870 comparatively few would have disputed that Britain was a Christian country. Also, the Christian churches were instrumental in bringing about compulsory education. It made sense that if you were intending to educate all young people for the first time, education in their religious heritage was essential. But what sort of Christianity should be taught? There was no love lost between the Church of England (the Established Church) and influential non-conformist groups such as the Methodists. The latter were instrumental in seeking the education of the poor and increasing literacy among the working classes, which was an important aspect of their seeking rights within an exploitative industrialised society. The right of children to be educated, rather than simply used as a cheap form of labour in factories, provides the backdrop within which religious education formed a part of state education. Education in religion, as part of providing literacy to the population, was controversial because it was highly politically charged. The wider social context was one in which radical reformists such as Robert Owen, and new democratic ideals were pitted against the traditional hierarchical ordering of society. If you taught children religion in elementary (primary) schools, to what purpose were you doing it? Was it to produce orderly and compliant citizens who knew both their catechism and their place, or to empower young people through making them literate and aware of the powerful teachings to be found in scripture? The former dominated, but many feared the latter being a result.

Today, for most primary school teachers, this historical context has been lost. Additionally, secularization has marginalized the importance of religion. Therefore, for many teachers, its purpose is unclear at best and for some its presence on the curriculum is viewed negatively if they themselves are not religious. As a result the subject is often badly taught and, to some degree, avoided or handed to a 'religious' member of staff to manage it.

There are many poor reasons for seeking to justify RE and, at worst, they echo some of the poor reasons for its justification in the earlier more religious age described above. Here are some historical attitudes to education and religious education that will alert us to the context into which we fit when thinking about them today.

In 1807 Samuel Whitbread was seeking to pass a Bill in Parliament to enable free schooling for children between the ages of 7 and 14. The opposition was strong. Education might make the lower classes discontented, as Davies Giddes observed:

'it would teach them to despise their lot in life, instead of making them good servants in agriculture and other laborious employments... It would enable them to read seditious pamphlets, vicious books and publications against Christianity.' (Barnard, 1961:55; *Hansard*, ix, 798, 13 July 1807)

With a contrasting perspective, but focusing on the same idea of what makes for educational effectiveness, Robert Owen said:

'Human nature is one and the same in all... by judicious training the infants of any one class in the world may be readily transformed into men (sic) of any other class.' (Barnard, 1961:58; Owen, 1813:72)

The Swiss progressive educationalist Pestalozzi (1746–1827) understood education to be religious but in a different way to most:

'The child must learn of the goodness of God or the rightness of truth and kindness from his actual experience; and the educator's job is not to inculcate or propagandise, but so to direct the child that he may obtain this experience.' (Barnard, 1961:38–9; Green, 1905:85)

For Pestalozzi this meant the school should have the atmosphere of the home and the teacher should behave with the same care as a parent.

From just these three historical quotations we can see that the idea of education is rooted in different understandings of human nature and experience, society and aspiration. This alerts us to thinking not first about subjects children should or should not be taught but ways in which schooling can develop or retard children. If we take this broader educational perspective it can help us determine the value or otherwise of RE and how the subject might be given a useful purpose in primary schooling today.

However, today there is significant division as to the value of religion, or God in particular. In our modern democratic society is God a help or a hindrance? The ground has shifted as far as the relationship between religion and society is concerned. Commentators discern different understandings, from wider perspectives, than those held historically in a society that we might regard as more religious and more mono-religious. We can observe this in the quotes below.

In *The Observer* Review section on 30 September 2007 we read, on page 9, the heading, 'Is God democratic?' Various replies follow this:

'What a question… Of course God is not democratic; if he is, exactly how long is a heavenly term of office?' Mark Thomas

'Since this question is so meaningless to me, I'll pretend that what you asked was, "Is there a place for God in a democracy?" One of the cornerstones of the democratic process is that discussion should be rational and that the bases upon which decisions are reached should be accessible to everyone. Religious beliefs do not fall into that category.' Brian Eno

'If God stands for tolerance, compassion, the equality of all mankind and moral accountability, then this is all in keeping with the democratic ideal.' Riz Ahmed

'God is above democracy. From a Muslim point of view, it is imperative that we take God out of politics.' Ed Husain

'All deeply held faith has the capacity to be anti-democratic, because it places the supposed laws of God against the real laws of free men and women.' Nick Cohen

So, are God and religion irrelevant within our modern world? Some would say the problem is not just religion's and God's irrelevance but its and His negative influence.

Summary

This section has explored historical reasons for RE being a subject on the primary curriculum related to the place of religion in English and Welsh society and the development of schooling to include all children and different views on the purpose of education and religious education in particular. We have also noted the tensions that exist today over the place of religion and the purpose of religious education in an increasingly secular but also plural democratic society.

Both historically and today religion and religious education are regarded with passion and suspicion. This poses some questions that we need to consider. For example:

- In a modern democratic society does teaching religion in state schools make sense or not?

- What sort of RE can you agree with, if any, and what could it achieve?

- What is your view? Is religion a serious matter and an appropriate subject for the primary curriculum or is it 'something to laugh about' or at least keep private?

Religion and religious education – something to worry about?

Against religion

'For years I have been pointing out that religions are likely to destroy human life as we know it now on this planet. Religions contribute to virtually all the intransigent and seemingly insoluble conflicts in the world.' (Bowker, 1996:3)

John Bowker is a religious man so this may seem a somewhat contrary statement. But it was prophetic in relation to events occurring at the beginning of our present century. There is now an understandable negativity toward religion amongst many who are not religious because of its recent association with violence, warfare, anti-democratic behaviour, abuses of children's, women's and human rights and its fundamentalism, exhaustively reported in the press and media. This largely but not exclusively is focused on Islam. Bowker's point is not that we shouldn't teach RE but that it is necessary to do so to inform young people of the threat religions pose.

Other atheist critics are just as virulent in relation to religion and religious education. Richard Dawkins, the scientist, quotes Victor Hugo: 'There is in every village a torch – the teacher: and an extinguisher – the clergyman' (Dawkins, 2006: 309). But whilst raging against the influence of religion and its negative, irrational influence he goes on to suggest that:

'A good case can indeed be made for the educational benefits of teaching comparative religion… Let children learn about different faiths, let them notice their incompatibility, and let them draw their own conclusions about the consequences of that incompatibility. As for whether they are "valid", let them make up their own minds when they are old enough to do so.' (Dawkins, 2006:340).

Dawkins is appreciative of the literary and aesthetic heritage of scriptures and traditions without wishing to buy into their beliefs (Dawkins, 2006:344). His educational point is made in relation to his own upbringing, 'I thank my parents for taking the view that children should be taught not so much *what* to think but *how* to think' (p. 327). By contrast, he suggests that children who are labelled as Catholic or Muslim, because that is what their parents are, are wrongly labelled. They are the children of Catholic or Muslim parents but that does not make it 'normal and right to indoctrinate tiny children in the religion of their parents, and to slap religious labels on them' (p. 339).

With this last statement Dawkins is, in particular, railing against the presence of faith schools in the state education system and many, not just Dawkins, are worried about them.

Faith schools: a growing problem?

In a recent polemic against faith schools, Roger Marples (2006) identifies the main concerns that are the focus of those who are sceptical of those institutions as educational sites within democratic societies. He begins: 'One of the major concerns shared by those of us with strong reservations about faith schools is that they may not attach sufficient importance to children's autonomy' (p. 22). The autonomy or own agency of young people is a principle concern because, it is feared, faith schools will wish to prevent or curtail this in accordance with the dogmas that underpin religious belief systems. This in turn, as Marples points out, affects the capacity for independent thought and their potential for growth as individuals: 'Those who would frustrate, either intentionally or unwittingly, a child's capacity for independent thought, are denying the child a right to flourish' (p. 23).

The matter of intention on the part of the educators, Marples makes clear, is not the main issue, but rather what is imbibed in an unquestioning faith school environment:

> 'If children do acquire religious beliefs unquestioningly, out of fear or undue respect of parents and teachers, then they may be said to have been indoctrinated whether or not there was any intention... and it is unrealistic to suppose that all faith schools would attach priority to ensuring that pupils are encouraged to *critically* reflect on their religious beliefs.' (p. 25)

It is not only those critical of religion, like Marples, who share his concerns. In a letter to the *Guardian*, an elderly Jewish man writes:

> 'By their nature, faith schools are prone to separate youngsters from the wider culture, and lead them to assume they are different and, by definition, superior to the rest of the population. That is bad for community relations in general and for their own co-religionists' real security in the long run... I feel this especially when I contemplate Jewish parents now, in my native Leeds, actually bussing their children daily to a Jewish school in distant Manchester. I cannot think of a more effective way of distancing children from the rest of their community – the quiet hostility this breeds amongst others is something I hate to contemplate.' (Walinets, 2008)

According to these arguments, faith schools, and perhaps by extension RE itself, have the effect of preventing critical thinking in young people and separating them off from others in their society who are not, religiously, the same as them. It is a form of social control and subservience. Contrastingly, Madeleine Bunting offers support for faith schools. She argues that state schools lack 'common values' and here faith schools have an advantage:

> 'They can fall back on a well-known religious narrative... For a faith school, the common values are familiar to all and easy to explain, and therein lies the possibility of a strong ethos. This is not to say that non-religious schools can't achieve this – of course they can, but it is harder. Secular ethical traditions are honourable but they lack the familiarity, the symbols, the narratives and histories that bring the abstract to emotional life.' (Bunting, 2008:31)

Faith schools are not new. 'Between 1870 and 1876 a million and a half new school places were provided; but of these two-thirds were due to the churches and only one-third to the new school boards' (Barnard, 1961:119). The school boards acted as the equivalent of today's local authority. Whilst religious instruction was part of the package in the church schools there was enough opposition to compulsory religious instruction in the schools run by the school boards to invoke the (in)famous 'Cowper-Temple Clause'. It goes like this:

> 'No religious catechism or religious formulary which is distinctive of any particular denomination shall be taught… It shall not be required, as a condition of any child being admitted into or continuing in the school… that he shall attend any religious observance or instruction in religious subjects…, from which observance and instruction he may be withdrawn by his parent.' (Barnard, 1961:118)

This Clause sought to overcome what was called at the time 'the religious difficulty', but it seems we still have 'the religious difficulty' in some ways today. Why create a compulsion to teach religion in schools and, at the same time, make it a subject that you can be withdrawn from, that you don't, by law, have to do? Educationally this is a very unsatisfactory state of affairs. Religious education is either an important educational part of children's development or it is not. However, historically its purpose was indoctrinatory in a way that did not apply to any other subject. Can that be said to apply today?

Summary

This section has acquainted us with the critics of religion and forms of religious education that are predisposed to present religion as a unifying and positive aspect of our society. It has also introduced us to the somewhat baffling status of religious education, compulsion and withdrawal, historically inherited. It raises a number of issues for us to consider:

- Is religion destructive and irrational? If it is, at least in part, is that what we should be teaching in RE or do we banish it from the curriculum?

- Does RE stop children thinking critically, or can it help them to do so?

- Should faith schools be banned because they are divisive, or fostered because they nurture children better than state schools?

- Should parents be allowed to withdraw children from RE on grounds of conscience or not?

Religion and religious education – something to change?

Religious diversity and multicultural RE

So far we have sketched out the early history of RE in state schooling to explain why it has its place in the curriculum and raised some issues pertinent then and today. Since then a lot has changed but some things have stayed the same. The key change has been the influence of multiculturalism. Especially, after the Second World War and increasingly in the 1960s and 1970s immigration into Britain increased and started to change the urban landscape. This was mainly as a result of de-colonisation, where subjects of countries colonised by Britain held British passports and rights. In countries in East Africa, for example Kenya, Zanzibar and Uganda, independence affected those Asians, originally from India, who had made their homes there and many now sought to escape the backlash brought about by independence and black rule. Therefore, many applied to enter Britain. For others Britain offered more prosperous lives, and still does today. The debate over immigration and migrants goes on. Multiculturalism was a positive affirmation of diversity with a liberal spirit. For RE it was an opportunity to embrace differing religious traditions or world religions as the new subject matter of the curriculum and give new relevance to the subject.

Added to this, since 1964 Religious Studies had appeared in higher education, and new graduates entered RE teaching with a knowledge of these religions, not just a knowledge of Christian theology or biblical studies. Ninian Smart was the inspiration behind this change in curriculum in higher education, starting the first Religious Studies degree as professor at Lancaster University. He also promoted the first RE Council project to produce new textbooks based on studying world religions in schools. Despite there being no change in the law at this time – the 1944 Education Act (the Butler Act) still expected Christianity to be the religion taught – the spirit of the times had changed. The law did not catch up with this until the 1988 Education Reform Act in which Christianity and the other main religions in Britain became the basis of the RE curriculum, but with Christianity given prominence in terms of curriculum time. However, multiculturalism and the idea of religions working for the common good was the expectation, as Smart observed:

> 'I personally consider that we need a new worldview for the world, which stresses their (religions') complementary values in helping to build a truly global civilization… a kind of spiritual democracy should eliminate inter-religious and inter-ideological violence… We are very far from achieving it: but I would consider that the study of religion can contribute to it.' (Smart, 1999:xiii)

This, Smart believed, could be achieved by studying religion phenomenologically, by emphasising the need to 'bring out the nature of believers' ideas and feelings… walking in the moccasins of the faithful' (Smart, 1999:xi) in order to generate empathy and common human understanding.

Multiculturalism still has a way to go to achieve Smart's goal and some believe it has failed and should be discarded. This is now debated in approaches to RE that we shall study later. Part of the problem lies in the possibility that people of different religions and cultures, whilst living in the same vicinity, do not actually wish to engage in getting to know one another so much as wishing to stay within their own groups.

Consider this experiment carried out in 2006 by Sanjay Suri, a journalist of Punjabi Indian descent brought up in England, recounted in his book *Brideless in Wembley* (Suri, 2007). In one of his studies for the book Sanjay Suri parked himself on a bench in Leicester's largest mall, The Shires, to conduct a study, between 12 pm and 5 pm concerning:

'what I dared to call myself a rough quantitative survey... I wanted to see how many came to The Shires with their ethnic own, and how many with others... the mall seemed a random enough place to see who might step out in mixed ethnic company.' (p. 23)

After five hours he reports:

'I scanned perhaps 12,000 to 15,000 people. Through this I counted only 44 people in 12 mixed groups... Most of these mixed groups were clearly university students... If this observation was valid we were talking zero point zero zero something by way of multicultural Leicester... Leicester did not appear a multicultural city, only a city of adjacent cultures. Perhaps not even that; just variously monocultural.' (p. 25)

Delving deeper into divisions in later chapters he gives various examples of how and why they occur. Based on traditions of caste and hierarchy he shows that what we are witnessing is the determination of a transplanted Indian culture to retain its traditional customs, structures and forms. He reveals that our idea of multiculturalism is too naïve to engage with deep-rooted social structures that do not recognise the liberal democratic ideals we present as amenable to their own traditional ways of ordering society. For example, in relation to marriage, what family you belong to, its place in the caste hierarchy, the occupation you have traditionally pursued and whether you are Punjabi or Gujarati are all significant in determining your suitability.

Suri's accounts affect the way in which we may think of Britain as a multicultural society and the way in which we think of *making* Britain a multicultural society. There are deep distinctions between social groups that those groups may wish to preserve as intrinsic to their sense of identity, belonging and separation. This applies across all sorts of divisions, it may have a religious aspect and it may not – it is a complex phenomenon involving class, caste, occupation, ethnicity, colour, gender, age, economic capital (income), education, traditional rites, expectations and customs and established or changing social conditions. It is significant that Suri equates mixed ethnic grouping with university education, suggesting that the latter can be a strong force for social change and that maybe it is those with middle-class liberal values for whom multiculturalism works.

It is one thing to live separately but another to attack those who are not like you. Following the London bombings of July 2005 Rageh Omaar, a British Muslim brought up on the Edgware Road, London, reflects on why one of the bomb sites chosen was Edgware Road tube station:

> 'Mohammed Sidique Khan chose Edgware Road as a target... because it was a symbol of something that he and his movement despised... it represented a relationship between Islam and the West, a cultural and ideological abomination... They were attacking the idea that Islam as a religion and Muslims as a community can thrive in the West... Al Qaeda is on the side of those who argue that multiculturalism has failed and should be abandoned.' (Omaar, 2007:36–7)

Omaar grew up on the Edgware Road, which has been a major settlement area for Arab and other Middle-Eastern Muslims from the professional classes. It is also a hub for many media connections with the Islamic and Arab world (the Saudis and Kuwaitis especially) that influence foreign policy (see Omaar, 2007:28ff). Sidique Khan, in Omaar's words, was himself 'a thirty year old bright and successful teaching assistant from Beeston in Yorkshire' (Omaar, 2007:36). The question remains as to why such a 'British Muslim' should resort to a fundamentalist and oppositional reading of Islam? Omaar concludes by affirming that:

> 'This pessimistic vision of a divided society, of people wishing to separate themselves from each other, whether it be Muslims from non-Muslims or the other way around, offers us nothing for the future of this country. That is why it has to fail.' (Omaar, 2007:237)

And yet he provides the graphic example of Dewsbury:

> 'The steady economic decline since the 1970s has lead to greater social polarisation and political tension between the Muslim and white communities; in 1989 Dewsbury experienced some of the worst race riots seen in Britain... In 2006 the BNP won a seat on the local council.' (Omaar, 2007:225)

He wishes to highlight the activity of extremist groups in exacerbating disaffection but we must ask what the conditions are that lead to disaffection and social fragmentation, and clearly lack of economic and social capital is one.

Omaar's is a straightforward defence of multiculturalism on the basis of the need of the host community to understand and accept differences within its citizens and their groups. He advises that such differences can be accommodated within a diverse, pluralist, democratic society. What has to be opposed is separatism and extremism based on religious bigotry and fundamentalism.

Whereas multiculturalism was largely uncontested as an approach to RE in the 1970s through to the beginning of the 21st century, it would now seem naïve to think that informing young people about different religions or introducing them to different cultural forms of expression is, in itself, likely to change their attitudes and opinions, let alone their behaviours. Also, for those children who do not live in urban areas populated by diverse ethnic groups their experience of those who belong to differing religions is going to be limited or non-existent.

Additionally, children who go to church schools, especially in village communities, may well receive a very different form of religious, social and cultural experience (itself an aspect of 'multicultural' Britain). It is true that multicultural RE has sought to do more than just attempt to get children to learn about religions but, as the Schools Curriculum and Assessment Authority (SCAA) report on primary RE in the 1990s revealed, in primary schools there is a preponderance of this. Also, the liberal spirit that has underpinned multiculturalism prevented any criticism of minorities, emphasising the need to understand and appreciate them, to empathise. This created a romantic, simplistic and incomplete reality of their humanness. As Hirsi Ali puts it, 'The adherents to the gospel of multiculturalism refuse to criticise people whom they see as victims' (Ali, 2006:xvii). At the very least, if we are involved in education, including primary schooling, we should have an interest in human and children's rights and scrutinise religious teachings and practices accordingly. If so, it is difficult to avoid the conflict that exists between the teachings of many religious groups (though not all) based on interpretations of their scriptures, that oppose certain rights for homosexuals, women and children, and United Nations declarations of these rights. Thus there is, at least, a need for critical dialogue with such groups.

Community cohesion

More recently a duty has been placed on schools and local authorities to promote community cohesion (DfES, 2007) and to combat extremism (DCFS, 2008). Although the former is not exclusively to do with RE the subject is meant to contribute to it. In a broad sense cohesion covers ensuring that groups in schools and local communities are not disadvantaged or marginalised. Combating extremism explicitly draws a distinction between terrorists or violent extremists, who are to be undermined, and mainstream voices, who are to be supported. In this there is explicit mention of Muslim communities in local and regional areas and the need to establish good communication with them. It makes sense that schools with local/regional Muslim communities would seek to establish good contact with them as part of their RE and community cohesion work. Nevertheless, this presumes that local Muslim communities would want to make contact with them. This would depend on the community: whether it feels fit, ready and equipped to do so, whether it really wishes to do so.

Here we reach a point at which we have to acknowledge that minority religious communities in Britain are at various stages of development, often consist of a number of factions, ethnic and national backgrounds, and may be more concerned about their insider development than contact with the society beyond themselves of which, nevertheless, they are a part. If they are originally migrant communities there are generations of work to do to adapt to their new situation. Often there is a fear of assimilation, losing their identity, their culture, their faith and their past, and a tendency to wish to remain separate, at least initially, to keep a hold on such things. It is this spectrum from assimilation through integration to separateness that these communities occupy that adds complexity to the whole question of the place of religion in our society and western society generally, and the question of the purpose of religious education. When the government calls for religions to 'modernise' it means take on the values of western, specifically British, democracy. The response to such a challenge has yet to be resolved.

Beliefs that clash

It is also the case that children who are part of religious communities attend our schools. They are nurtured in a specific faith and belong within a faith (in the sense of religious) community. To exclude their understandings from the classroom would be to exclude them, in much the same way as excluding non-religious understandings would exclude non-religious children. Inclusivity is essential, yet also controversial. Recently a top scientist, Professor Michael Reiss, at that time director of Education at the Royal Society, called for creationism or 'intelligent design' to be taught as an alternative to evolution in science lessons because, 'I realised that simply banging on about evolution and natural selection didn't lead some pupils to change their minds at all. Now I would be more content simply for them to understand it as one way of understanding the universe' (Reiss, 2008:3). He added that around one in 10 children came from families with creationist beliefs and, importantly, that good teaching meant respecting children's views: 'I do believe in taking seriously and respectfully the concerns of students' (Reiss, 2008:3).

In opposition to this, one critic suggested that 'It is perfectly acceptable for schools to include discussion of creationism but the appropriate place for this to happen is in religious education classes' (Reiss, 2008:3). This conjures up a vision of science teaching one thing and RE another. Why not link these up? In other words, within the primary curriculum where you have alternative views on any issue shouldn't the different views be taught, explained and discussed in tandem (even though you would not expect creationism and evolution as such to be introduced in the primary curriculum)? At the same time there should not be a rigid distinction between what religious people believe and what science states (after all evolution is not anathema to all religious believers and some scientists are religious, as is Professor Reiss himself). This does not just apply to creationism and evolution, science and religion, but also to simpler aspects of children's learning where their experiences and understandings may differ.

Summary

This section has presented a case for why RE should have a multicultural or pluralistic approach that positively affirms religious diversity in a plural society, and some objections to this based on different values. It has also addressed the question of how we approach community cohesion. Clearly there are some issues to consider in deciding whether a multicultural/pluralistic approach to RE is sufficient. The questions below highlight some of the main points to respond to:

- Do you think that Smart's idea of a 'spiritual democracy' is achievable and will multicultural RE help us towards that?

- Should we be presenting all religions empathetically in order to enrich the values of our children?

- How do we, and should we, teach children rights education for minorities and teach about religious and other groups who don't uphold them?

- Should we expect religious groups to affirm the values of our democratic society to enable community cohesion and should we teach children to affirm those values through RE?

- What should we do when some children come from religious families with beliefs that oppose scientific teachings? Is this something we should address in RE?

- When children have different beliefs should these be things we discuss in RE and beyond?

Religion and religious education – the good, the bad and the ugly

So far we have presented ways in which religion and RE have occupied a place in our society and our education system, ways in which they have both changed and in which our society has changed. We have tried to show that religion can be recognised as both good, promoting young people's development, and controversial, if not harmful, in disrupting society. The quotation below sums this up, at least in relation to the monotheistic religions (those believing in one God, which is usually meant to refer to Christianity, Judaism and Islam):

'Concerning monotheism, everything has been said – and its opposite. That it is a humanism and a form of barbarism. A liberation and a plague. The cure for our malaise and a substitute neurosis. A kind of operatic duet, with alternating voices has been composed on this theme. I choose not to get involved in that particular confrontation… Let it be noted that the thesis and the antithesis can simultaneously be true: the divine pharmacy, like every other, has its ambivalence. *Pharmakos*, as is well known, means both elixir and poison. No need to break swords, once again, over a familiar theme.'(Debray, 2004:4)

Debray's point is well made: anything powerful and potentially beneficial contains the capacity for harm. Education itself can do that as can natural elements like fire and water or what we call drugs (used in medicine and used illicitly). As we progress scientifically so the potential both ways is increased (for example: nuclear fuel, nuclear weapons). The point is not to support religion or reject it but to understand its influence, positive and negative, in our world and that of our children. Now I introduce an important caveat that has significant educational implications and will place the emphasis on learning and on the learner, not the subject that is taught.

Once you take this perspective, religious education has a highly significant role but not if it is restricted to the narrow prescription of religious. What we need to be concerned with is the development of the learner as a human being, this is a holistic endeavour and RE has to be seen, in this context, in the same light. How, whether religious or not, can this be understood?

Young people need more than subject-specific skills. They need to become literate and numerate but they also need a sense of their identity, belonging and relationship with the world that they are experiencing and of which they are a part. They need to be valued and value themselves. They need to express their opinions, feelings, thoughts and sense of self. Religions have traditionally found ways of supporting this through celebrations, festivals, rites of passage, doctrines and creeds (expressions of belief) and values statements. Also, they deal with significant experiences such as loss and death, understandings of mortality, aspirations in life through ideas of charity, benevolence, kindness and generosity. These are not restricted to religious forms. You do not have to be religious to be concerned with these nor with the negative aspects of these: anger, dislike, hate, division and animosity. These are human traits. We also desire freedom, security, reward and recognition. This is the stuff of human experience from a very young age, even when we can't articulate these terms. Non-religious systems of thought are as concerned with these aspects of human experience and development as are religious ones. We all desire to construct a worldview with which we are comfortable and which guides us whether we are 4 or 40 (or older) even if we can't express it in that way. And our society, in various ways, seeks to encourage us to do so or seeks to impose that on us: from politics to adverts, directed at children as much as adults. It is easier to understand the significance of religious education if we consider it as values education and it overcomes the barrier erected by the division between religious and non-religious. But, at our peril, we ignore ways in which religions have approached the idea of values education. Not because we leave children without an understanding of religion, which in itself would be a lack considering the influence of religion in our world, but because our children would lack an ability to reflect on values and their own worldview, religious or not. This allows us to connect with some of the underlying aims of education with which we might be less familiar when we think in terms of subjects, for example what is called Spiritual, Moral, Social and Cultural (SMSC) development.

Spiritual, Moral, Social and Cultural development

SMSC development is a further initiative that RE, as well as the curriculum and schools as a whole have had a statutory duty to promote since the 1988 Education Reform Act. Whilst there is a general understanding of how moral and social development can be approached, cultural development has been less well understood for schools not in a 'multicultural' environment, and spiritual development has caused confusion and concern. This is telling since, if we have lost any educational idea of how to approach spiritual development outside a faith nurture environment, then either it is a redundant category within a largely secularly understood school environment or it is a significant gap in the educational provision we offer.

Reading in colour: RE as democratic literacy

Philip Pullman in *The Art of Reading in Colour* begins by stating: 'You don't need a belief in God to have a theocracy.' By theocracy Pullman means a form of society that is dictated to by a particular ideology whether religious or not. He continues:

> 'Khomeini's Iran is closer to Stalin's Russia than either would like to believe. The real difference between theocracies and democracies is that the former do not know how to read.' (Pullman, 2004:158)

The point Pullman is making is that theocracies are to be characterised not by their belief in God but by not knowing 'how to read', whereas democracies are defined through knowing how to read.

By 'read' Pullman is referring to the need for citizens in a democratic society to be able to critically enquire and, if necessary, dissent from its government. To enlarge on Pullman's point, the important issue is not whether faith, or religious faith, is involved but whether a society is open to or closed to enquiry, open-mindedness and change. The latter is what makes for a democracy and inclusiveness regardless of religious or non-religious belief. If this is the test then all democratic institutions should be fostering this, but it is particularly applicable to schools and primary schools. To enlarge on Pullman's point, literacy is the basis of culture and education. At its most basic this is literally learning how to read and write. For this to happen we must create a learning environment in which this is valued and in which we instil the confidence in children for them to succeed; this involves parents as well as teachers.

But if we stop there we have surely failed. Literacy is more than being able to read: that is just the beginning. What follows is the capacity to engage with culture and 'reading' of different kinds involving emotional literacy, spirituality, moral reasoning and values. It involves the informed reading of different 'texts' that constitute and represent the values of a society, in literature, art and the urban environment, and which form the way we communicate, what we aspire to and how we live. In short it is about the way we develop those values, abilities and aspirations prized in a democracy, including the ability and willingness to engage in critical debate and work toward common purpose. We could call this citizenship. If religious education does not form a part of this endeavour, the result will be impoverished because religious literacy is essential (and often neglected) for a number of reasons. One is the religious presence both within our country and globally; another in which 'religious' needs to be understood more broadly is the development and ownership of one's own beliefs and values; a third is reflection on those issues and matters that are important for developing our humanity, wellbeing, sense of belonging and identity and the critical ideas and questions that underpin those. If you think beginning to develop these capacities is beyond children in the infant and junior phases of primary education we hope this book will convince you otherwise.

Conclusion

This chapter has, in brief summary, charted the way in which our society has changed over the last 150 years in relation to educational provision and religious education in particular. In the last section it has made a case for the role religious education can play, alongside other subjects, in supporting children's development toward being adults in a society in which they will have a full and sufficient part to play because they can recognise the importance of being 'literate' individuals, be discerning and critical about the value of religion, develop their own emergent worldviews and values and be constructively critical citizens within the social environment they will shape in the future. This is how we and they can contribute to, in QCA (now QCDA) parlance, being 'successful learners, confident individuals and responsible citizens' (QCA, 2006).

2

What is good RE?

Judith Lowndes

Introduction

This chapter discusses current approaches to RE in the primary phase and aims to identify what makes good RE. Drawing on educational principles it will analyse the strengths and scope of the subject and clarify what constitutes good educational provision for religious education and how students and teachers can contribute to this.

The influences on RE

In the previous chapter the importance of RE was discussed. Good RE, therefore, might be the RE that fulfils the role of preparing pupils for life's experiences. That being the premise on which the discussion develops, good RE can be seen in terms of enabling children to engage with and think about, analyse and evaluate issues in human experience that relate to them. This process is informed by recognising how these issues are interpreted by religious people in ways that have meaning for them. Good RE can be seen in terms of approaches in the classroom that enable pupils to access that principle in ways that are most effective and efficient.

To find good RE there is a need to take a critical look at what has influenced and had impact on RE in its current state of development. One major area of influence is government legislation; another is the expertise of the writers and researchers who, in discussions with teachers and pupils, have developed approaches to the teaching of RE over the last few decades.

Government legislation has increasingly centralised guidance for education, including religious education, in terms of statutory and non-statutory requirements. It is interesting to see to what extent the guidance has itself been influenced by the accumulated wisdom of the researchers and writers in RE.

The introduction of the National Curriculum in 1988 provided a more prescriptive approach to the curriculum than previously experienced but it did not include religious education. The 1988 Education Reform Act established the requirement that every local authority should produce its own agreed syllabus to inform schools within the authority about what should be taught in RE. Model syllabuses produced by the Schools Curriculum and Assessment Authority (SCAA) in 1994 and the later Non-Statutory Framework for RE produced by SCAA's successor, the Qualifications and Curriculum Authority (QCA) in 2005, and now the Qualifications and Curriculum Development Agency (QCDA) in 2009, have provided guidance about what should be covered in the RE curriculum. These documents have impacted on the writing of locally agreed syllabuses for religious education that form the basis for RE curriculum planning in schools. As a result, whilst there are differences in the ways in which local authorities have interpreted or reflected the guidance, there has been a general trend towards reflecting the two dimensions of RE identified in the SCAA Model Syllabuses and the later QCA Non-Statutory Framework for RE. These are usually expressed in locally agreed syllabuses, although not all, as 'Learning about religion' and 'Learning from religion'.

The source of the terminology for these two dimensions can be traced back to the collaborative work of Michael Grimmitt and Garth Read at the RE Centre, Westhill College, Birmingham. In the project they developed between 1975 and 1977 an emphasis emerged: 'It was to emphasise and express the interactional nature of the relationship between studying content and responding to it in a reflective manner' (Grimmitt, 2000:34).

Both Grimmitt and Read went on to develop these initial dimensions in later publications. Read says that the approach is to 'help children mature in relation to their own patterns of belief and behaviour through exploring religious beliefs and practices and related human experiences' (Read *et al*, 1992:2). Grimmitt (1987:141) writes:

> 'If religions are studied in such a way as to juxtapose the "content" of religious life-worlds of adherents with the "content" of the pupils' life-worlds, pupils become informed about religious beliefs and values and are able to use them as instruments for the critical evaluation of their own beliefs and values.'

Grimmitt identifies the importance of balance and a relationship between the two dimensions for effective RE and developed a model through which that would be effectively realised. Out of context the two dimensions can be less effective. Of his model he says:

> 'Its strength can be considerably diminished when some of its features are transplanted within a curriculum structure which, in other respects, reflects a rationale for RE which is alien to its intention (as, for example, in the SCAA 1994, Model Syllabuses for Religious Education).' (Grimmitt, 2000:37)

The SCAA Model Syllabuses used the two dimensions 'Learning about religion' and 'Learning from religion' as two separate attainment targets. No model or methodology was provided to draw together the two dimensions, although the intention for teachers to make links between the two was there. As a result they became adopted in agreed syllabuses as they stood, as two separate attainment targets. This original pattern was maintained with the production of the National Non-Statutory Framework for RE (QCA, 2005). The two separate attainment targets were established.

Learning about religion and Learning from religion. What do they mean?

The following descriptions provide a summary of the ways in which the two dimensions are generally described in agreed syllabuses and by teachers.

Learning about religion requires pupils to engage with religious beliefs, teachings, sources and practices, and syllabuses generally provide guidance to schools about what material should be selected from the major world faiths for each of the key stages. It focuses attention on acquisition of knowledge. The roots of this area of learning are found in the phenomenological approach of Ninian Smart, which requires an objective view of the beliefs and practices in religious traditions, as mentioned in Chapter 1.

Learning from religion is generally interpreted in agreed syllabuses to include pupils' own responses to some of the issues that are explored within religious practice and belief and seeks to look for and recognise parallels in their own experience. It encourages pupils to consider what can be learnt from religious interpretations of life's experiences, thereby contributing to children's own spiritual development and encouraging empathy and understanding about the religious beliefs and practices of others.

Each dimension will be discussed in turn. Although each dimension is acknowledged as playing a role in contributing to good RE, the discussion seeks to identify where problems can arise in their interpretation and translation into classroom practice, resulting in RE that might not be so good.

Learning about religion

On the face of it, 'Learning about religion' appears to create little controversy. Clearly there should be a body of knowledge about religion for pupils to investigate. Schools generally provide pupils with a range of religious beliefs and practices to investigate across the primary phase. When this is taught in an engaging way and within a worthwhile structure of learning, it contributes effectively to good RE. Problems can arise when there might be a lack of coherence in the material with which pupils engage. If they superficially dip into a variety of features of religion from a number of faiths, pupils become muddled about what is of particular significance to different faith communities. Agreed syllabuses generally provide guidance about recommended material for each key stage to try to overcome this problem.

There may be pressure from parents or the pupils themselves about which religions and what aspects of religion are explored within a school. We have heard of cases where representations from Muslim parents and pupils have prevented schools from exploring Judaism as part of the RE curriculum, and where Christian parents have requested that a study of Islam be removed from the RE curriculum. There have been other instances where teachers have denied pupils opportunities to explore the imagery of Mary because it is 'too Catholic' or Hindu deities because they are 'too weird'.

This presents an interesting issue that emerges in the Learning about religion dimension, but also in the Learning from religion area. It appears that some parents (and some teachers) make certain value judgements about the material that they want introduced to children. It could be rooted in the 'nurturing respect' philosophy that is prevalent in RE. Indeed, perusal of many RE syllabuses and guidelines and school RE policies identifies respect for the religious beliefs and values of others as one of the important aims of RE. If, in some parents' or teachers' views, a religion or aspect of a religion about which they don't approve is identified on the school curriculum, it appears that they believe that it should be rooted out, because it is not worthy of respect and should not be included because the aim of nurturing respect would not be realised.

If we are honest, there are numerous aspects of religious practice and belief, some obscure and some more obvious, from a number of different religions that many would feel are not worthy of their respect. While many might respect the right for people to hold different beliefs and carry out different practices, it would be a tall order to ask that pupils respect the actual beliefs and practices of others, some of which they may consider to be bizarre, unkind or oppressive. It is worth, here, looking back to what was explored in Chapter 1 and the start of this chapter in relation to why RE is important. If good RE prepares pupils for adult life, pupils should be prepared to engage with religions and aspects of religious belief and practice, warts and all, and have the skills to investigate the material, interrogate it and make a critical analysis in order to be able to make a personal and informed judgement about how they will respond to it. To present a whitewashed, edited and squeaky clean impression of the religions studied might be very well-meaning, but it is not honest, does not represent reality and inhibits children's opportunities to exercise their critical skills and a developing ability to be discerning.

Learning from religion

For many, the title 'Learning from religion' is viewed as entirely appropriate. A project in alignment with this approach was Religion in the Service of the Child, launched by John Hull in September 1989. This resulted in a publication that provided a worthwhile structure for teachers to follow. The contributors never claimed that it would provide a coherent approach to RE but its mention in this instance is to illustrate how Learning from religion can be interpreted. The materials from the project were published under the title *A Gift to the Child: Religious education in the primary school* (Grimmitt et al, 1991) and provided a particular methodology that focused pupils' initial attention on religious items, images or sounds that children should engage with and learn from. Members of the project referred to these examples of religious material as 'numena'. John Hull explains that a numen came to mean 'a religious element charged with the sacred beauty of faith and thus offering to the child something of the numinous' (Hull, 2000:115) The view of members of the project was that the 'numen' is a gift to a child and that engaging with it would, in some way, develop their own spiritual insight and growth; that children would learn from religion. When the stimuli are removed from the context of the religious community into an educational context, one needs to ask what their purpose is within the new context. If it is for their curiosity value and the questions that might be raised about their significance to religious adherents, it would seem educationally sound. If, however, the numena are expected to stimulate similar responses to those of adherents it appears that there might be an underlying nurturing element. We need to ask whether it is intended that children's lives will be improved as a result of their encounter with that which is associated with the 'numinous'.

Many teachers can feel uncomfortable with the assumption that an item, image or sound from a particular faith is imbued with some inherent spirituality or holiness and is worthy of attention because of the way it can benefit a child, like a sort of altruistic blessing, regardless of the faith or belief stance of the children involved. It can be argued that each religious tradition attributes the numena with associated beliefs and feelings. Taken out of the religious context and put in an educational one, they no longer have those attributes. The numena are, however, very significant to members of the faith from which they come and so are worthy of investigation by pupils. The pupils learn about the significance the numena have for adherents. But there has to be a distinction made as to whether this is meant to have a spiritually nurturing function or whether this is simply enriching pupils' understanding of the worldviews of others. Learning from religion would have very different meanings according to which interpretation is being employed. The approach of *A Gift to the Child* epitomises what Learning from religion, rightly or wrongly, appears to mean for some people.

So, the title 'Learning from religion' can result in contrasting pedagogical interpretations. It can be interpreted as implying that religious beliefs and practices embody accumulated wisdom that is inherently good and that children should learn from that. It implies a sense of nurture. In contrast, little mention is made in guidance or syllabuses that pupils might learn from religion in terms of investigating areas of conflict or impasse. Material that is controversial or disapproved of is often omitted because it is not considered to be suitable material for children to learn from. It could be claimed that the inference that religions have only positive attributes to teach people inhibits a critical, analytical approach and can prevent pupils from engaging in an open enquiry into a realistic view of religious phenomena.

To avoid any misconceptions among teachers some agreed syllabuses have not embraced the title 'Learning from religion' and have selected something that is more grounded in common human experience. A 1998 Hampshire, Portsmouth and Southampton agreed syllabus, 'Vision and Insight', for example, identified two attainment targets: exploring and responding to human experience, and investigating the religious traditions. The Brent Agreed Syllabus, 'Living with Beliefs' does not specifically identify attainment targets, but it states: 'The aim of religious education is to learn about and from spiritual insights, beliefs and religious practices and to explore fundamental questions of human life' (Brent Council, 2002).

The discussion about the different interpretations of Learning about religion and Learning from religion highlights the conflict of approaches that has been inherent in the field of religious education for many years. There are religious educators and members of faith communities whose perception is that religion is a positive force in the world and that the accumulated wisdom that religion, through the inspiration of a divine being or as a force for good can bring to humankind can be spiritually inspiring and improving. This school of thought favours the nurture approach to RE where material is edited or carefully selected before it is introduced to pupils in a way that is intended to lead them towards a position of respect. These religious educationalists favour the nurture of particular values. There are others, to whom we make reference later in the chapter, whose approach is more objective and who favour a more intellectual, analytical and critical approach to the study of RE. They enquire into a variety of different values and different expressions of religion without regard to whether religion is to be positively valued or not. You, the reader, might like to reflect in which camp you currently find your allegiance and which approach you consider as contributing most effectively to promote good RE.

The two dimensions have been investigated, but having two separate dimensions rather than one can cause tensions. In the absence of a framework or guidance on how to draw together the two dimensions in children's learning, teachers can experience difficulties with planning, delivering and assessing in RE lessons. The findings of Ofsted inspections of RE indicated this in its 2007 report on RE provision nationally (Ofsted, 2007).

Ensuring an effective balance between the two dimensions can be hard. Teachers may be seduced into emphasising the acquisition of knowledge for a variety of reasons. They may feel that the purpose of RE is to convey information about different religious traditions in our multi-faith society and concentrate on those areas as a result. They may be concerned about assessment, and the straightforward route is to assess what pupils can recall about the information conveyed. They may view the Learning from religion dimension with some anxiety. It provides no clear body of knowledge to convey, and class discussions and enquiries can expose controversial or personal issues that some teachers may feel are best avoided in the classroom situation. When there is a focus on Learning about religion, pupils are provided with fewer opportunities or avenues to relate to the material and the result can be that it has no significance for them in relation to their personal experiences. John Rudge has commented on this as follows:

'How can we avoid allowing our teaching to fall into mere factualism, the process by which religious education degenerates into the transmission of information about religions, because it is the easiest thing to do, it does not require us to think about why we are giving out this information, and it avoids controversy? It is the basis of a curriculum for no one, with no educational purpose, going nowhere.' (Rudge, 2000:108)

Alternatively, it might be the case that a particular emphasis can be placed on the Learning from religion dimension. In these situations teachers may feel confident and be highly skilled in enabling pupils to reflect on and discuss their own responses to life experiences and any issues that those explorations throw up. However, for a variety of reasons, perhaps a lack of resources, or insufficient subject knowledge or even a lack of conviction about the relevance of some of the material, there may be few opportunities provided for pupils to engage with examples of religious beliefs and practices as phenomena in their own right. If this imbalance occurred there would be a lack of reference points for pupils to consider why people's religious beliefs lead them to respond to life's experiences in different ways, and the RE provided would fail to challenge or extend pupils' critical thinking as a result. Such a criticism was raised in relation to the 'experiential learning' model developed by David Hay and exemplified in *New Methods in RE Teaching* (Hammond *et al*, 1990) Michael Grimmitt writes:

> 'While the weakness is not insurmountable, it does confirm the project's tendency to give too little importance to the place of learning about explicit religious traditions in RE and to neglect the structuring power of religious content in determining the RE curriculum.' (Grimmitt, 2000:34)

Good RE, therefore, can be seen as RE that provides an effective balance between the two dimensions identified. Teachers of RE must, by law, make use of the guidance provided in a locally agreed syllabus. To provide good RE the syllabus should ensure that a useful integration of the two dimensions is achieved. Good RE should explore important issues and ideas that have significance within religious traditions and human experience and enable pupils to respond to those in relation to their own experiences in life informed by ways in which they rationalise and make sense of those experiences.

Questions emerge as a result of the issues discussed so far:

- Is respect for the religious beliefs and values of others a realistic or useful aim for good RE?

- Is the model of two attainment targets a useful one?

- Are the two attainment targets appropriate to provide pupils with a broad and balanced religious education?

- Is the terminology used for the two attainment targets helpful to teachers?

- What educational principles should be in place to support good RE?

- How would you approach RE in an educational way?

The great and the good in RE

To find more information about what constitutes good RE the focus now turns to the great and the good in the discipline – the writers and researchers who have attempted to provide distinctive and informed approaches to the subject. Their accumulated wisdom has impacted on and continues to impact on teaching and learning of religious education in schools to varying degrees but, overall, with a lack of significant innovation in classroom practice. Some common threads can be detected and each approach places a different emphasis and in many cases refines and clarifies what is in the accumulated pot of expertise.

It is not the intention to provide a detailed analysis of the historical developments of RE over the last 20 years, but a brief reference to some of the main pedagogies developed will illustrate some of the background to current practice in RE and enable us to identify some contributing factors to good RE. For a comprehensive account of the development of pedagogy in religious education since the 1960s readers may wish to refer to Michael Grimmitt's *Pedagogies in Religious Education* (Grimmitt, 2000). A number of references are made to material included in Grimmitt's volume in the analysis given below.

The two dimensions of religious education, already identified, have their origins in the 1960s and 1970s. The way that children should engage with the relationship between the two dimensions has taxed and challenged religious educators for a number of years. Grimmitt (2000) writes:

> 'With hindsight it is now possible to see that the problem of attempting to reconcile the phenomenological and experiential approaches within an integrated pedagogical model of RE has proved to be the stimulus for the development of nearly all the other pedagogies of RE for the past twenty years.' (p. 26)

Grimmitt's approach to the subject in the early 1970s recognised the importance of pupils building 'conceptual bridges between their own experience and what they recognise to be the central concepts of religion' (Grimmitt, 1973:49)

Readers, make note of the reference to concepts here. There has been a developing interest in the importance of concepts within RE and we identify a focus on concepts to be a highly significant factor in promoting good RE in the second section of this book.

The Westhill Project of the early 1980s also makes reference to the importance of concepts in the teaching of religious education. The project entitled 'Westhill Project RE 5–16' was developed by Garth Reid, John Rudge and Roger Howarth and later Geoff Teece. The project culminated in a particular methodology for RE exemplified in a number of publications that have been widely used by schools. The publications refer to concepts that are identified in two categories: those concepts relating to shared human experiences and those relating to traditional belief systems. These concepts were built into the field of enquiry that was selected as appropriate for different age groups of pupils.

The Warwick Religious Education Project led by Robert Jackson and Eleanor Nesbitt also emerged in the 1980s. The main thrust of the research was the focus on ethnography and religious education, and publications for the classroom were later produced as a result of this project. We find reference, once again, to the significance of identifying concepts to support learning. In the materials produced for key stage 1, pupils engage with actions, objects and technical terms through the story books about children from different ethnic and religious backgrounds. These are grouped together as 'key ideas'. Jackson explains: 'These general concepts suggest areas where bridges can be made from pupils' experience of life to the experience of the children introduced in the story' (Jackson, 2000:138).

The Stapleford Project was set up and led by Trevor Cooling in 1986. Whilst dealing exclusively with Christian material, its main focus was on providing an approach to teaching about Christianity through investigating concepts. Informed by the work of Bruner (1977) and Donaldson (1978), the project developed a concept-led approach:

'Going to the heart of a subject, rather than continually scratching at the surface, was the way to promote excellence in learning. Drawing on this insight, the Project identified the importance of identifying the key concepts that are central to religious education, rather than planning a curriculum solely around the information that was to be learnt.' (Cooling, 2000:156)

Attention now turns from concepts in RE to the ways in which the concepts are expressed within religions. When religious beliefs and practices are explored, good RE avoids stereotypes. The research and published work of the project team with Robert Jackson at Warwick University illustrates the importance of taking account of the inner plurality of beliefs and practices within religions after project members carried out a critique of ways in which religions had previously been portrayed in religious education. Investigations about the way certain concepts or key ideas are contextualised within the lives of real people and interpreted by them, provides pupils with an accurate picture of a religious reality and a potential point of resonance. Exploring an anomalous doctrine and a synthesis or simplification of the variety of practices that exist would not provide a true reflection of what actually happens and what is of importance to large numbers of religious adherents.

Andrew Wright, based at King's College, London, in the Spiritual Education Project, has developed a pedagogy that also recognises the importance of demonstrating diversity within religion, with a particular focus on Christianity. His project takes a further step by suggesting that his approach enables pupils and students to critically engage with religious material by recognising the often conflicting or contradictory nature of religious beliefs. He writes:

'To do justice to the horizon of religion a qualitative pluralism is necessary, one which reflects the genuine diversity of religious and secular perspectives on religion, and accepts the ambiguous, controversial and conflicting nature of theological truth claims.' (Wright, 2000:177)

In a similar vein, Jackson and the project team at Warwick recognised the importance of enabling pupils to develop a reflective, critical approach within RE by stating that: 'There needs to be an approach to teaching that encourages reflection and constructive criticism' (Jackson, 2000:135). This is explained through what they term as 'reflexivity', whereby learners are encouraged to reassess their understanding of their own way of life, make a constructive critique of the religious material explored and interpret the material as a result, thereby developing a running critique throughout the process.

Religion can present positive values but it also presents controversy and conflict, ambiguity and contradictions, as discussed in Chapter 1. Good RE should enable pupils to engage with the issues that arise out of religion, both positive and negative, and provide opportunities to interrogate those issues and interpret them in relation to their own developing worldviews. Some teachers might express anxiety about pupils uncovering any negative aspects to religion because they feel that their role is to present religion as a positive force in the world. As a result they could eliminate any possibilities for critical debate or discussion in the class. Those teachers are selling their pupils short. Children should be encouraged to develop skills in critical analysis and to be discerning and make informed, well-considered judgements about what they encounter about religion. Without this skill they are unprepared for their role as effective citizens within the worldwide community.

So far the main discussion has highlighted religious material and how various approaches have sought to enable pupils to access it and make sense of it in relation to their own life experiences. We now turn to an approach that is fundamentally concerned with the spiritual development and experiences of the child as a way of accessing and making sense of religious material. David Hay, to whom we referred earlier, led the Religious Experience and Education Project: Experiential learning in religious education. The project stemmed from an interpretation of the Darwinian thesis that religious or spiritual experience was an innate part of being human; this was advanced by Alister Hardy. This stimulated the focus of research by Hay, Nye, Morisy and Murphy (Hay, 1979, 1982; Hay and Morisy, 1978, 1985; Hay *et al,* 1996) and led to an influential publication involving research with children (Hay with Nye, 1998). The developing pedagogy from the project and the resulting materials for schools focused on awakening sensitivities to religious and spiritual experiences and thereby enabling pupils to relate to and reflect on the spiritual and religious experiences of others. In Hay's words, this was 'assisting students to have empathy with the personal world of believers' (Hay, 2000:73).

The project team suggests that the most significant feature of being religious is the experiential dimension. Strategies that provide opportunities for experiential learning were devised aiming to awaken pupils' awareness of the religious experiences of believers. The approach has been well received by teachers and pupils because it established the importance of encouraging pupils to be reflective and search their inner selves and reasons for their feelings, beliefs and responses in life. Good RE ensures that pupils are provided with opportunities to fully engage with their thoughts and ideas and their inner selves, to be reflective, to question their assumptions and consider points of resonance with others. However, whilst drawing on religious material and practices the strategies were not designed to represent religions as such but draw on religious material of a spiritual kind to develop pupils spiritually. As with the Learning about and Learning from discussion above, there is a significant difference in the purpose of RE if its principal aim is promoting the spiritual development of pupils by drawing selectively on enriching religious practices and writings for that purpose, as opposed to the study of religions in a more critically informed fashion.

Hay's approach typifies a problem that RE has failed to resolve in its development since becoming informed by the study of religions in the 1970s. How do we make the study of religions meaningful to pupils when they might not, themselves, be religious or think of religion as important in their lives? Previously, RE had been confessional in that it was the nurture of children into the Christian faith. Since that idea of nurture, appropriately, disappeared it has been difficult to resolve the tension between RE having a descriptive function (Learning about religion) and a quasi-nurturing function (Learning from religion). Whilst Hay's approach is clearly in the latter category, as a way of making the subject meaningful, it does not provide the development of those skills of enquiry into religion that would enable pupils to make their own judgements about it. Since Learning about religion does not fulfil this developmental function either, a key focus for providing good RE is to determine how we can solve this problem.

Also concerned with children's experiences and the way children learn in religious education was the Children and Worldviews Project that began in 1993, led by Clive and Jane Erricker, the former also being a joint author of this book. The project developed because of the conviction that RE at the time was (and still is) generally content-driven and over-concerned with acquisition of knowledge about religious beliefs and practices. The project team believed that there was insufficient emphasis given to the experiences of children themselves and the way children make sense of that experience (Erricker and Erricker, 2000; 2000a). Their research, which is discussed at the beginning of Chapter 4 of this book, indicated that effective learning takes place when children are encouraged to be reflective about and articulate responses to their experiences in life, when they are enabled to share their 'narratives' in an environment that is respectful, safe and free from criticism or ridicule. Good RE happens when it is child-centred and child-driven and when it deals with concepts that are of interest to children and that resonate with their lives. However, this approach was resistant to the value of religious education and proposed a form of values education in its place. Grimmitt made the following criticism:

'The fact that this theory of human learning challenges contemporary orthodoxy, both religious and educational, is no reason for drawing back from applying it to these two significant areas of human experience and endeavour. But this is what the project does.' (Grimmitt, 2000:46)

The approach to religious education in Part 2 of this book is a response to Grimmitt's comment and an attempt to overcome the difficulty of making RE meaningful to pupils but also focusing on religions.

Conclusion

In this chapter we have discussed the parameters of the subject as it currently stands within the legislation and the guidance provided through government agencies. We have analysed the pedagogies that have emerged in the late 20th and early 21st centuries to identify what has contributed to good RE. If a recipe were to be created for some of the vital ingredients it would include the following:

■ a focus on significant concepts;

■ exploration of religious material;

■ use of religious material that reflects diversity;

■ use of religious material that may raise contentious issues;

■ reflection and expression of pupils' own experiences in life;

■ strategies that provide experiential learning;

■ an approach that is child-centred and enables pupils to express their feelings and responses and to tell their stories within a secure environment;

■ an effective balance between the two dimensions of human experience and religious experience;

■ encouragement for pupils to take a critical view of what they encounter in RE lessons.

This may seem like a tall order, but read on. This book suggests how you can achieve good RE in your primary classrooms with the above elements in mind.

3

How do we create effective learning?

Elaine Bellchambers

Introduction

This chapter explores how we create effective learning. In places it is contentious, given the nature of the material and the political element of education. There is an endeavour to link current educational initiatives with the teaching of religious education within the context of the QCA's (now QCDA) *A Big Picture*. It is written in the spirit of enquiry and will provide discussion opportunities about what constitutes effective learning. It addresses our ideas of knowledge and belief, the value of constructivism and social constructivism within the democratic classroom, and the importance of attending to diversity and inclusion and critical and creative thinking.

Good education

The United Nations Convention on the Rights of the Child, Article 29, states that Parties agree that education of the child shall be directed to:

(a) the development of the child's personality, talents and mental and physical abilities to their fullest potential;

(b) the development of respect for human rights and fundamental freedoms, and for the principles enshrined in the Charter of the United Nations;

(c) the development of respect for child's parents, his or her cultural identity, language and values, for the national values of the country in which the child is living, the country from which he or she may originate, and for civilizations different from his or her own;

(d) the preparation of the child for responsible life in a free society, in the spirit of understanding, peace, tolerance, equality of sexes, and friendship among all peoples, ethnic, national and religious groups and persons of indigenous origin;

(e) the development of respect for the natural environment. (UNICEF, 1990:9)

The Qualifications and Curriculum Authority (QCA), now the Qualifications and Development Agency (QCDA) also states that: 'Good quality religious education can transform pupils' curriculum assessment of themselves and others, and their understanding of the wider position of the world in which we live' (QCA, 2004:3).

How can this good quality be achieved? First let us consider what learning entails:

■ A change in behaviour as a result of experience or practice.

■ The acquisition of knowledge.

■ Knowledge gained through study.

■ To gain knowledge of, or skill in, something through study, teaching, instruction or experience.

■ The process by which behaviour is changed, shaped or controlled.

■ The individual process of constructing understanding based on experience from a wide range of sources. (Pritchard, 2005:2)

Alan Pritchard cites these definitions in his book, but they need closer inspection. What is this concept of knowledge? To use another term, knowledge is referred to as 'epistemology', a way of knowing. There are various schemas for types of knowledge depending upon who you read, but briefly they fall into the following categories:

■ logical;

■ semantic;

■ systemic;

■ empirical.

Logical ways of knowing constitute an understanding of the relationship of ideas to one another. The rules or laws of logic permit claims to knowledge that are further statements of ideas consistent with the rules and ideas already accepted.

Semantic knowledge is the result of learning the meaning of words. Knowledge of words is knowledge of definitions. Such definitions are set in dictionaries.

Systemic knowledge is gained, for example, through mathematics and geometry, which is the result of learning a system of words or symbols and knowing how they relate to one another and the rules operating in that system resulting in claims that are consistent with those definitions and rules.

Empirical knowledge comes through our senses, through our observation and somatic knowing. Somatic knowledge is knowledge known by the body, through physical sensation: when we are touched, we 'know' we are being touched, even with our eyes closed.

Belief and its relationship to knowledge

These categories of knowledge present problems to us when we try to discuss belief. Belief does not imply knowledge. Claiming to know that something is true based on belief does not constitute knowledge from a scientific perspective. Beliefs are about ways in which we try to make sense of things and events such that these fit within a specific worldview. But according to scientific criteria, knowledge is based on empirical evidence derived from scientific investigation. In effect scientific method has narrowed down and refined our ways of knowing. And yet we still need to investigate ways in which others claim to know and how belief is entwined in that system of knowing. For example, semantic knowledge is language-based and language is a social construct, variable according to time and cultures. So any writings or oral traditions of a society will reflect the values and beliefs contained within it. Empirical knowledge in some cultures is valued more than in others. Nevertheless, in all cultures, different ways of knowing persist to a greater and lesser degree and belief is prevalent as both a supplement to these or arises predicated on these different 'ways of knowing'. It follows that distinguishing between knowledge and belief is not as simple as one might first assume. Whilst it is correct to say that we can evaluate belief logically and on the basis of empirical evidence we cannot entirely eradicate belief. In other words, we are unable to simply replace belief with forms of knowledge that make belief redundant. This becomes most obvious once we consider the difference between what we can 'know' empirically and what remains to be known or otherwise dismissed. For example, the idea of salvation in Christianity can have no empirical foundation and yet for some it is 'true', which is the same as saying it is believed. And we are certainly aware that people live according to and die for such beliefs. Such beliefs are related to and provide a means to the interpretation of human experiences. As such, we cannot consider education complete unless we take account of these or otherwise dismiss them as not conducive to 'knowledge'. To do the latter would remove belief from the project of education, presumably on the basis that it has no verifiable empirical foundation, but that would certainly result in an impoverishment of our understanding of humanity. It is also true that we sustain a belief in those who provide us with empirical knowledge as an act of faith. Also, at a mundane level, we all have beliefs: the very fact that as a teacher you plan the week in the classroom is based upon the belief that you will be alive still to deliver the lessons. Beliefs are held from a variety of experiences: upbringing, personal experience, other people's experience, reflection on one's life and the teachings of people with greater knowledge than yourself.

An example of the creation of belief might go along these lines. Agnes (a fictional character) is 81. Her husband died a couple of years ago. His chair remains in the sitting room by the fire. One night last week Agnes saw him sitting opposite her, smiling. The effect this has had on her has inspired her and therefore she believes in the existence of God and, equally, she is convinced that there is life after death. Would this type of experience provide evidence that there is a God? For those who experienced it, yes very likely, and they would call it a religious or spiritual experience. But is their experience enough evidence for others to believe? Probably not, for all sorts of reasons, the obvious one being society's preference for particular types of evidence. Walker (2003:6) says that as a culture we rely heavily on scientific evidence. Science works on a principle of verifiability and falsifiability. This means that if there can be a way found to show that it is true, it is only scientifically evidenced as such if it is verified according to scientific criteria. Religious experiences cannot be verified in this way. So there is no way of evidencing the validity of a religious experience. However, you cannot scientifically evidence the existence of love, using the method given above, yet we often claim to have experienced it. So perhaps the experience is sufficient to establish the importance of belief, even though it cannot constitute scientific knowledge. In summary, whilst of course scientific knowledge is necessary that does not mean that it is necessarily sufficient.

Religious experiences are often criticised because they are too personal, too subjective for critical examination. One cannot get inside the head of another person. We may all agree on a colour being red, yellow or blue, but I cannot know *how* you experience those colours, and vice versa. So dealing with belief in the RE classroom has to be more than just giving information. Pupils need an opportunity to explore the process of how beliefs develop in order to appreciate their power and understand their significance.

Constructivism as a means to knowledge acquisition

Knowledge can be understood differently from the way we have described it above. A methodology that supports a different type of knowledge acquisition is constructivism. Constructivism is a philosophical approach according to which all knowledge is 'constructed' in as much as it is reliant upon convention, human perception and social experience. Knowledge and understanding are therefore constructed by the individual. Learning takes place when pupils revisit current knowledge and adjust, adapt or revise it in order to incorporate new ideas. They can then engage in dialogue, share and reflect on the insights of others. The teacher's role is to 'assist learners in assimilating new information to existing knowledge and to enable them to make appropriate modifications'. (Grainger and Wray, 2006:53)

The constructivist approach is predicated on the belief that child development is a cumulative building of skill and capacity. If the ability to understand, synthesise, apply and critique are valued, then these will not occur in an unmediated way: firsthand experience and ability-related opportunities are vital. The teacher needs to engage pupils in talk, and support the development of understanding through what is commonly called 'scaffolding'. To remind ourselves of the process of scaffolding we need to re-visit Vygotsky (1978) and his work on the zone of proximal development

(ZPD) Jacques puts this well: 'it is the gap between actual development and potential development to be bridged by appropriate intervention' (Jacques and Hyland, 2004:69). In other words, this is a partially acquired skill or concept that can be further developed with the assistance of a more skilled adult or peer. Scaffolding is the process of support given at the appropriate time and level to meet the needs of the individual child. It may take the form of discussion, a variety of tasks, a range of resources or by providing a procedure list.

It is crucial therefore that all those engaged in the process of scaffolding learning recognise that the starting point is the conceptual understanding of the child and how that is built upon. It is not an overlaying of information. The idea is that individual experience and the pupil's cultural knowledge become the central focus of attention in a constructivist model. We must acknowledge who these children are and, as Bigger and Brown (1999) state:

'motivate responsible [children and] young adults with a thirst for understanding, a curiosity about life, a concern to contribute to the communities in which they find themselves and to build relationships with other people'. (p. 3)

The *Excellence and Enjoyment* document (DfES, 2003) supports this notion, stating that:

'primary education is about children experiencing the joy of discovery, solving problems, being creative... developing their self confidence as learners and maturing socially and emotionally'. (p. 4)

Put another way by Freire (1993):

'knowledge emerges only through invention and re-invention, through restless, impatient, continuing, hopeful inquiry human beings pursue in the world, with the world and each other'. (p. 53)

Learning does not take place in a vacuum: it is contextualised and this may be viewed in terms of culture, beliefs, practices, surroundings and even the time of day. Contexts for learning are only relevant if they are meaningful to the child. Pupils need to be offered problems/material relating to their experiences in the world. These contexts therefore require considerable thought as to the child's experience and preferred mode of learning and emotional growth. Vygotsky's social constructivist approach to teaching and learning provides pupils with an individual interactive and engaging route to learning that offers the opportunity to relate their learning to their experiences. In social constructivism knowledge is seen in relation to individuals and the social and cultural setting in which they find themselves (see Pritchard, 2005:6).

Pritchard (2005:111) identifies the elements of social constructivism as follows:

- Children learn through being active.

- Learning is a socially mediated activity.

- Emphasis is placed upon the role of the teachers or 'more knowledgeable other' as a 'scaffolder'.

- The teacher is a facilitator who provides the challenges that the child needs for achieving more.

- Development is fostered by collaboration (in the zone of proximal development) and is not age-related.

- Development is an internalisation of social experience, children can be taught concepts that are just beyond their level of development with appropriate support. What a child can do with an adult today, they can do alone tomorrow.

Democratic classrooms

How can teachers implement this teaching and learning approach? Obviously the teacher is crucial: the characteristics of a good religious education teacher will be explored in the following chapter. The concern here is the learning environment that facilitates enquiry and the teaching and learning initiatives currently within the education system. What we have to avoid is the form of schooling described below:

> 'Schooling creates and reinforces meanings related to personal identity and control over students' futures. Critically all humans have potential and abilities that are too often thwarted by undemocratic conditions under which they live.' (Gale and Densmore, 2000:154)

A number of recent government initiatives – *Excellence and Enjoyment* (DfES, 2003), *Every Child Matters* (DfES, 2004) and *The Children's Plan* (DCSF, 2007) – acknowledge that teaching is not simply a matter of imparting factual information. Rather it is a tool with which to provide children with skills to take ownership of their learning:

> 'Teaching and learning is most effective where teachers are enthusiastic and knowledgeable and have the confidence to stand back and encourage pupils to become independent learners.' (DCSF, 2007:63)

How does the teacher provide democratic conditions for learning and stand back and encourage the independent learner? There has to be some risk in this, some relinquishing of teacher control and power. The nature of the learning environment depends upon the nature and characteristics of the teacher, and a positive learning environment is what needs to be created. Classrooms need to be seen as communities of enquiry that offer both the teacher and pupil opportunities for partnership. There need be no loss of control on the teacher's part, but expectations may need revision.

In a learning environment that offers enquiry, Fisher (1990) suggests the teacher has control over the stimulus and therefore the content of enquiry; she or he decides the amount of time for thinking and reflection. During this time for reflection the pupils are asked to contemplate the stimulus for learning in order to identify features they find interesting, puzzling or perhaps disturbing. It is very much what the pupils find interesting, not what the teacher does. The teacher needs to choose the stimulus with great care to ensure curriculum coverage, but run with the outcome of the pupil's comments. The pupils then offer their ideas in the form of questions. The questions are then shared and connections between them sought. The pupils take turns in sharing their ideas, experience, arguments or examples in order to construct an answer to the questions. They are then able to develop each other's ideas by adding to them or critiquing them.

For this kind of learning opportunity to happen pupils need to feel comfortable and safe in the lesson. Religious education frequently deals with sensitive issues, often to do with identity, prejudice and vulnerability. For pupils to feel able to contribute they must feel they can do so with no fear of bias or humiliation.

Giddens (1994:74) identifies three dispositions that characterise democratic classrooms:

1.	active trust;

2.	mutuality;

3.	negotiated authority.

He asserts that these categories are underpinned by 'getting to know and getting along with the other' (Giddens, 1994:75). This role involves the appreciation of the other on the basis of who they are, not their role: 'the relationship depends on who the other "is" as a person, rather than on a specific social role or what the individual does in life' (Giddens, 1994:75). The implication of this for teachers is that in democratic classrooms teachers are respected for their willingness to take risks, and 'open up' to their pupils, to offer to give the pupils something of their self. 'Giving of self, sharing identity, necessarily requires some familiarity with that identity. Teachers need to know who they are and what they believe' (Giddens, 1994:75).

You will appreciate this is not a simple task, either for teachers or pupils. Pupils need to feel that their own culture is respected in school and be encouraged and supported to acknowledge their culture in order to succeed. Teachers are required to link what goes on in the classroom with home and wider communities. They need to have established good, appropriate relationships, value the pupil as a human being rather than purely on an academic level and respect the pupil's ideas and expressions of belief. Respect is crucial for trust and mutuality. It is much more than tolerance. Tolerance may carry with it a value judgement. Where beliefs and values create tensions negotiation is required.

Valuing identity, diversity and difference

Suffolk County's *Interfaith Handbook* (SIFRE, 2003:6) reminds us that pupils who arrive at school with English as an additional language may provoke thoughts about how limited they are. What has to be remembered is that within their own cultural setting they will have made considerable progress in their language, their first language. They will have developed conceptually within the cultural context of the home and community and will know stories, songs and rhymes, and they will bring with them a learning style based on their own cultural experiences.

Accommodating this is no easy task for the teacher who lacks the experience of dealing with such pupils and is further hampered by very limited funding, but inclusion is a significant issue in a community of enquiry. This applies not just to EAL pupils, but those with a range of disabilities. Such pupils should be able to access the mainstream curriculum successfully and should feel, behave and be treated as full class members, as UNESCO identifies:

'Regular schools with this inclusive orientation are the most effective means of combating discriminatory attitudes, creating welcoming communities, building an inclusive society and achieving education for all: moreover, they provide an effective education to the majority of children and improve the efficiency and ultimately the cost-effectiveness of the entire education system.' (UNESCO, 1994:ix)

Topping and Maloney (2005) identify that concern is often expressed about pupils with emotional and behaviour difficulties, possibly because of the perception that these pupils may damage the education of their peers and cause high stress levels for the teacher. They go onto say that:

'Many more boys than girls are perceived as having special educational needs. Also, teachers tend to perceive learning difficulties more readily in children of South Asian origin and behaviour difficulties more readily in male children of African-Caribbean origin. … It becomes apparent as a result, that teachers' own bias and prejudices need acknowledging and need to be examined if active trust and mutuality is ever to stand a chance. Equally teachers need support in gaining the necessary subject knowledge and skills to manage sensitive issues that may occur in such situations.' (p. 6)

The NACCCE report (1999), commenting on diversity, says:

'Diversity should be seen and celebrated as being valuable and enriching to the school environment: not as a problem but a strength or asset. Children need to be comfortable and empowered in their own cultures.' (p. 119)

Linked to this and the learning environment is the government's *Community Cohesion: a draft guide for schools and consultation response* (DfES, 2007). It states:

'We passionately believe that it is the duty of all schools to address issues of how we live together and dealing with difference. However controversial and difficult they might sometimes seem.' (p. 1)

In the classroom, teachers must facilitate the intentions held within this statement. In this document the government identifies the following as the characteristics of a school promoting community cohesion:

- valuing diversity;

- similar life opportunities for all;

- strong and positive relationships being developed between people from different backgrounds and circumstances in the workplace, schools and neighbourhoods.

Starting with valuing diversity and developing strong, positive relationships, and bearing in mind the Convention on the Rights of the Child, what does diversity actually mean? The *Collins Concise Dictionary* has 'diversity' meaning the state or quality of being different or varied, a point of difference. So what does 'difference' mean? It is identified as the state or quality of being unlike. Where are the differences likely to be found? This requires us to explore aspects of identity. Identity is about belonging, about the beliefs, interests, feelings and habits you have in common with some people and that differentiate you from other people. It provides you with your sense of self and, most crucially, involves social relationships. You might consider the following questions from SIFRE (2003a: Sheet 1) with regard to the way in which you define yourself:

- How important is what you look like to the way you define yourself and how others define you?

- How important is the language and way you speak as a defining characteristic?

- How important are your achievements (academic, sporting…) in defining you?

- How important is what you eat or drink (meat, rice, sweets) in defining you?

- How important is your name?

- How important is your gender (the way in which you express your male/femaleness) in defining you?

- How important is what you believe (about life, morality, God) in defining you?

A discussion with a friend or colleague about answers to these questions quickly establishes difference. Even those with whom we share a community are different from us. Some of these questions raise controversial and more complex issues. For example, what is meant by sex, sexuality and gender? Sex is either male or female. Gender on the other hand is the manner in which you express your male/femaleness. Sexuality is whether you are heterosexual, bisexual, gay, lesbian, and so forth. As the government is asking schools to value diversity and foster strong, positive relationships, how does it view these issue and is it supportive of schools in valuing difference and diversity in these respects?

The preamble in the Convention on the Rights of the Child (UNICEF, 1990) states:

> 'Convinced that the family, as the fundamental group of society and the natural environment for the growth and well being of all its members and particularly children, should be afforded the necessary protection and assistance so that it can fully assume its responsibilities within the community.' (p. 3)

This would suggest that the social and economic structure of our society might be conceived as based on a concept of the family consisting of a heterosexual couple and children. Family units that stand outside this are generally perceived as 'other' and whilst equality of rights is spoken of, the reality is often somewhat different. People have the right to and choose to express their gender/sexuality in whatever manner they decide; it is fundamental and crucial to their sense of self. Perceived difference from the norm means they are routinely viewed as threats or jokes, to be feared, even hated, and truths about them can be distorted. This brings a violent disintegration of these people's (pupils') sense of self, value and identity. How, then, are schools to support individuals, families and groups that differ in this way as an aspect of promoting and valuing diversity and difference? There appears to be a tension between what is required of schools and the values promoted generally in society. How do we prepare our pupils to cope with these tensions as they grow older?

Life opportunities

Let us turn now to the statement of similar life opportunities as required in the guidance on the duty to promote community cohesion (DCFS, 2007). What is the relationship between similar life opportunities and equality? Are they commensurate with or in tension with one another? According to the *Collins Concise Dictionary,* 'similar' equates to showing resemblance in qualities, characteristics or appearance. 'Equality' means identical qualities, characteristics and rights. All institutions have an equal opportunity policy, but how does this accommodate the promotion of community cohesion that values diversity and difference?

To consider the impact of these issues on effective learning we need first to go beyond the classroom situation and consider the larger capitalist socio-economic context that influences them. Capitalism is an economic system centred upon desire,

desire to make a profit and desire to consume. Jung Mo Sung in his book *Desire, Market and Religion* (2007) explains that growing income concentration and increasing social exclusion are the effects of technical progress. This arises due to the difference in the average labour productivity between technologically advanced countries and the less advanced others. The resultant income generation is the only way for an elite group to obtain the necessary income to have access to an opulent way of life. The wider the gap created in this way the greater the social inequality and exclusion. He goes on to comment that our society has a huge social inequality problem, due in part to a fudging of the difference between the need to have and the desire to have. Basic needs are required to survive and live. Beyond this is the need to be recognised as a person and a significant person. This is the social need and psychological desire exploited by marketing and consumerism. Sung quotes Hayek on this issue: 'the new things will often become available to the greater part of the people only because for some time they have been the luxuries of a few' (cited in Sung, 2007:36). Hayek goes on to explain this further:

> 'I desire an object, not for the object itself but because other people desire it. Thus the object desired by many is scarce in relation to the people who desire it. This creates rivalry, which today is called competition, a motivator for progress. There will always be unsatisfied people in the dynamics of desire... It is an endless race for more consumption.'

How can the school suggest that all be valued equally when the economics of our society imply otherwise, when the experience of some pupils in our classrooms is very definitely those of the more or less excluded? The tension between what the school is asked to promote and what society promotes is apparent. With such a dilemma, what sort of teaching and learning needs to happen to support difference, diversity, equality and life opportunity? Again, it's back to the learning environment and developing pupils' skills in thinking and questioning. Teachers need to provide a learning environment that provides them with an opportunity and the skills to problem solve and ask the pertinent questions. It is through the ability to think critically and problem solve that our pupils can begin to understand the world around them. The questions raised here need to be considered by the staff.

Critical and creative thinking

> 'A teacher committed to teaching for critical thinking must think beyond subject matter teaching to ends and objectives that transcend subject matter classification. She realises that understanding a situation fully usually requires a synthesis of knowledge and insight from several subjects. She also sees that in-depth understanding of one subject requires an understanding of others.' (Paul, 1993:11)

One cannot ask questions in religious education without asking and answering related questions in psychology or sociology for example. Given some of the tensions between what is required in the classroom and the world outside the classroom, critical thinking is a must if pupils are to develop their own opinions and understand why they hold their views and how and why they differ from those of others. This requires a form of enculturation. Perkins comments that critical thinking is more than the teaching of skills and strategies. Rather it is about creating a culture that 'enculturates students into good practices' (Perkins, 1994:98).

Along with interpretation and evaluation of material sources, ideas, observations and communication, critical thinking demands the ability to think about assumptions, to ask relevant questions and tease out the implications; in other words, to be able to think a concept or issue right through. For Fisher (2001) the critical thinker is a person who believes that there are many situations in which applying a reasoned approach is the best way to decide an issue. He is careful to say that this does not imply only one way of thinking, 'rather it encourages a suitable practice that can increase our thinking capacity' (Fisher, 2001:14). John Dewey, the father of modern critical thinking, called it 'reflective thinking' and defined it this way: 'Active, persistent, and careful consideration of a belief or supposed form of knowledge in the light of the grounds which support it and the further conclusions to which it tends' (Dewey, 1909:117). For Dewey the active aspect is crucial to reflective thinking. It is a process in which you think things through for yourself, you decide the questions you wish to ask and find the relevant information, rather than be spoon-fed and passively accepting information. It is not about snap decisions or judgements: it is about stopping to think.

Carl Haywood, in an address to an educational conference in the north of England in 1997, suggested that teachers who facilitate thinking for pupils adopt the following procedure:

1. Ask process orientated questions.

2. Challenge responses, whether correct or incorrect.

3. Require justification of answers.

4. Promote transfer and generalisation of principles.

5. Emphasise order, structure and predictability.

6. Model the joy of learning for its own sake and its own reward. (Haywood, cited in Gale and Densmore, 2000:26)

The QCA's *A Big Picture* (QCA, 2006) and the requirements of the new creative primary curriculum (Rose, 2009) demand critical thinking techniques. The NACCCE Report (NACCCE, 1999) *All Our Futures: Creativity, culture and education* also says that there are a number of distinctive systems and approaches to creative thinking, including problem solving. It identifies the following as the best known:

- The work of Edward de Bono in promoting 'lateral thinking' and his techniques of group creativity through the 'Six Hats' method.

- The Synectics method which promotes the use of metaphor and analogy.

- Accelerated Learning which uses techniques of association and visualisation to improve memory and make creative connections.

- Thinking Skills which promotes a number of techniques, particularly in raising attainment in mathematics and science.

- Mind Mapping, a technique developed by Tony Buzan for recording information and seeing patterns in ideas. (NACCCE, 1999:122)

The report goes on to say these systems have considerable potential in education to enable teachers and pupils to tap into their own process of creative thinking.

Fisher and Williams (2004) suggest that creating is to generate something, to bring something into being. They state that: 'Creativity, like evolution and education is founded on experimentation, variations that sometimes succeed, sometimes fail. Creativity therefore requires courage to take risks, the risk to be different' (p. 8). It is helpful to identify the differences between creative and critical thinking; they are shown in Table 3.1.

Table 3.1 The differences between creative and critical thinking (Fisher and Williams, 2004:10)

Creative thinking	Critical thinking
synthesis	analysis
divergent	convergent
lateral	vertical
possibility	probability
imagination	judgement
hypothesis forming	hypothesis testing
subjective	objective
an answer	the answer
right brain	left brain
open ended	closed
associated	linear
speculating	reasoning
intuitive	logical
yes and…	yes but…

An issue that springs to mind looking at this list is that of the divergent and convergent thinker. Divergent thinking is the ability to generate a range of answers to a given problem. Often the school environment penalises the divergent thinkers. We reward the right answers and penalise those we deem to be wrong. This will surely make pupils very reluctant to attempt creative solutions if the chances of error are greater. School rules, regulations and organisation fit the convergent thinkers comfortably and hence teachers may well prefer this way of thinking to that of a divergent thinker.

Additionally, creative thinking requires intuitive thinking. This is knowledge or perception not gained through just logical reasoning; rather it is instinctive. The use of the imagination is an ability to produce mental images of what is not present or what has not been experienced. How is the teacher who is embedded in a culture of assessment able to judge such activity? The NACCCE report acknowledges that assessing creative thinking is more difficult than testing factual knowledge. It recommends that pupils have time to experiment, to make mistakes and to test various approaches without fear of failure. It says:

> 'Immediate assessment can overlook aspects of creative development which only become visible in the longer term. There are also the issues of comparability. How should young people's creative work be compared between schools or regions?' (NACCCE, 1999:128)

To enable effective learning for all, we need to balance the creative with the critical. The focus of education must be on creating pupils who are able to think and do new things, not just mimic what has gone before, but to be able to rise to the challenges of the 21st century. Creativity offers individuals the fun of play, self-expression and achievement as well as the skill to manage conflict. It often takes imagination to understand others and creativity to resolve conflict.

For Fisher and Williams, the key features to creativity are motivation, inspiration, gestation and collaboration. Motivation when engaging with an activity looks like 'wanting to' (Fisher and Williams, 2004:4). It recognises that the problem, belief, concept or issue is worth further investigation, it is intrinsically worth it. Inspiration is linked to curiosity: we all thrive on having people who inspire us and this provides a stimulus for our own creativity. Being creative, say Fisher and Williams (2004), takes time: there needs to be a period of gestation where thoughts and reflections can happen and new ideas take shape. Through working collaboratively we become more creative: 'creative success depends on having a fertile ground where new ideas and activities can take root, an environment in which ideas can be created, tossed around, shared and tried out' (Fisher and Williams, 2004:16)

How does creativity contribute to religious education? Broadbent (2004) states that 'religions are dynamic and life changing, they are about revelation and inspiration' (p. 150). Equally, they may be authoritarian and quite destructive. She goes on to suggest that architecture as an expression of belief offers a connection between religion and creativity and that new ways of living and philosophies are the results of revelations and creative responses to these:

'Architecture both reflects and inspires distinctive beliefs and forms of worship [through] which painting and even religious music explain and express the artists and composers inner commitment in various forms.' (Broadbent, 2004:157)

The contribution of religious education

The multi-dimensional aspects of religion need to be reflected in the classroom. Here we consider imagery as one aspect of that. The world is full of visual images: signs, posters, advertisements, newspapers, magazines and films are seen on a daily basis. Children learn quickly to 'read' information or interpret the image presented. They begin to unpack the meaning behind the image. Advertisements are a prime example of visual imagery that conveys meaning. By using such and such the user will acquire the life style, looks, the status, be envied and so on. They rely upon you being able to picture yourself in the given situation. Critical thinking applied to such imagery questions the assumptions, it asks the pertinent questions and it identifies the implications. All these are vital skills in beginning to understand how the process of belief begins, what it means to be human, social persuasion and the society to which we belong.

Imagery is easily remembered. It provides a focus, motivates thoughts, stimulates or inspires a reaction. It may encourage empathy, feelings and emotions and also encourage research and enquiry. If we apply Fisher and Williams' key features of creativity to visual imagery, it may look like this, using as an example Caravaggio's (1571–1610) painting 'The Taking of Christ' (1602), which deals with the betrayal of Jesus by Judas. It can be found at http://www.nga.gov/exhibitions/caravbr-2.htm.

Below is a sequence of ways in which pupils can be asked to respond to this stimulus:

Motivation: I want to know what is going on, what looks interesting. Why is the figure being jostled in this manner and by whom?

Inspiration: I'm curious; do I like/dislike this image? Is it creating feeling or emotions I can relate to? Why are the hands held in such a position?

Gestation: I need to think about and reflect upon this image. How does it fit with the things I have been learning? What new insights does it offer on a personal level about this event?

Collaboration: How do other people feel about it? Do they share my views and questions? What are their questions? What insights, points of view can I gain from their ideas?

When using paintings as a stimulus the teacher does need to be aware that paintings may be 'read' at two levels. First, there is evidence of the painter's skill, technique and colour choices. Second, there is the evidence contained within the picture regarding the incident, evidence that has already had an interpretation added.

The handling of artefacts also stimulates interest and discussion. It is a good counter-balance to a more didactic learning approach, offering opportunities for critical and creative enquiry, sensory exploration, reflection and intuitive approaches. Through both creative and critical questioning and thinking pupils can gain glimpses into the nature of faiths and so begin the development of understanding belief, ritual and doctrine. Howard (1995:3) recommends, when using religious artefacts, to consider the following questions:

- Does the planned lesson explore the symbols on or in the artefact?

- Does the lesson explain the meaning of the artefact?

- Does it explore the way in which the artefact is used by believers?

- Does it encourage an understanding of the way in which the artefact is regarded within the faith and hence the respect for it?

For example, the festival of light within the Jewish tradition is Hanukkah. The artefact that is associated with this festival is a Hanukiyah, an eight-branched candlestick. Pupils are invited to engage with the artefact by asking questions about what it is. Is there a story about it? How might it be used? The Hanukiyah is a reminder to the Jewish people of the miracle of the oil for the temple lamp. The lamp was the sign of God's presence in this sacred place. The Syrians had let it go out, and when the Jews returned, they could only find enough oil to keep the lamp lit for one night. The miracle was that the lamp kept burning for eight days and nights, until a fresh supply of oil could be made. So the Hanukiyah is a powerful symbol, a reminder of God's presence and intervention in their history. Jews believe that God helped the small army of Judas Maccabeus to victory over the Syrian Greek king, Antiochus IV.

Baldock (1990) comments that the signs 'function is to communicate information… it is one tangible reality expressing another, equally tangible' (p. 9). For example, the signs on public conveniences are themselves tangible and express another tangible object. Road signs express the tangible. There is a difference between a sign and a symbol/artefact:

'The symbol or artefact may itself be tangible and a recognisable object or concept (for example a cross or image of a Hindu god) but there is frequently no obvious or visible relationship between the symbol or artefact and what it expresses.' (Baldock, 1990:9)

It will always remain a mystery and we may only begin to understand when we go beyond the outer tangible appearance of the symbol or artefact we encounter. Baldock is saying here that if no attempt is made to engage with the artefact in any way other than looking and describing it, then what it tries to express will be missed.

Therefore when using artefacts in the classroom, it has to be more than descriptive. This reminds us of the importance of engaging with symbolism within religious education and the need for pupils to develop the skills that this entails. The creative and critical thinking involved is the basis of religious literacy and a larger social and cultural literacy essential for their development.

Conclusion

Effective learning depends on a range of teaching and learning opportunities to provide pupils with a variety of ways of enquiring into knowledge that challenges, stimulates and engages. Carefully and sensitively thought through, a community of enquiry offers pupils confirmation of their intrinsic value as human beings who have experience and insight to bring to the learning process. There needs to be partnership in learning. Appropriately conducted this will have considerable impact on community cohesion and pupils' understandings of diversity and difference, providing opportunities to understand and negotiate differences. However, there will always be tension between what goes on within school and the outside world with values that appear, in some cases, quite different to those promoted within schools. The skills to critically question and think creatively, identifying assumptions and misconceptions, will provide our young people with a chance of developing their fullest potential and respecting human rights and fundamental freedoms.

Conceptual enquiry as an approach to RE and the primary curriculum

4

Why conceptual enquiry?
An introduction to the methodology

Clive Erricker

Introduction

This second part of the book will introduce a constructivist conceptual enquiry approach to religious education using a generic methodology that seeks to move the subject forward by giving specific direction to learning and thus making it more effective and purposeful. This chapter begins by introducing the research from which the methodology was derived and focuses in particular on the idea of what can be called personal or spiritual development that underpins it. It then relates the findings of that research to a conceptual enquiry methodology to show how religious education can be a vehicle for explicitly promoting the formation of young people's identities and enhancing their religious literacy. This approach builds upon and develops the characteristics of good RE identified in Chapter 2 and of effective learning identified in Chapter 3.

The research of the Children and Worldviews Project

Effective learning involves children 'speaking their minds' but in an informed way. For this to happen we must draw on their experience and provide material or narratives beyond their experience for them to consider and respond to. In this section of the chapter we shall present some research conducted by the Children and Worldviews Project (see Erricker *et al*, 1997) that shows what children are capable of by drawing on their own experience and seeking to make sense of it. We shall then consider how this affects the way in which we present children with further material that can enlarge their perspectives, enrich their reflections and progress their learning in religious education and, hopefully, beyond.

Children's voices

This research took place with 6–10-year old children, beginning with my own daughter, between 1992 and 1997. It provides a thread of conversations around the concept of loss and shows how children relate their narratives to that concept.

Polly's story

When she was 7 years old my daughter Polly engaged me in an enlightening conversation. Unannounced, as we drove past a local cemetery, she asked me whether her dead grandfather had 'one of those'. She was referring to a headstone. I replied that he did not. She asked why. I replied, with some trepidation, that he had said, in his will, that he did not want one. She asked why and what was a will? I explained about a will containing your final wishes. She then asked what happened to him. With greater trepidation still I explained he wanted to be cremated. She asked, what does cremation mean? I explained it meant you wanted your body to be burned. This moved on to a larger conversation in which she, seeking to make sense of what exactly happened to him, moved into a more philosophical speculation, which I later recorded:

P: Do you remember that question you asked?
Q: What question did I ask?
P: Which part of you is you?
Q: What did you say?
P: Ok, I'll tell you… Your Being.
Q: What does that mean?
P: It means that is the part of you that is you.
Q: You explained to me, when the body dies what happens to the being, didn't you?
P: Well, you don't really die. The smoke goes up and there are lots of ashes going up like paper… As the smoke goes along it crumbles and eventually there is just a little bit that's left.
Q: And that's how small your being is?
P: Well we're not quite sure how big it is.

It is necessary to note that Polly never knew her grandfather: he died two weeks after she was born. We had a photograph of him holding her in his arms just after she was born and just before he died. Also, in the family, we had conversations about him from time to time, and her elder sister and brother were able to talk from experience of knowing him. Polly could not.

At a later date she asked me to take her to the crematorium. I agreed we would go on a Saturday morning. The day before, she wrote a letter to him, emptied the grate in our wood-burning stove and put in her letter and set fire to it. The ashes in the tray beneath she emptied into a carrier bag and we took this with us. At the crematorium, on a rainy morning, she noticed plaques to those who had been cremated. I explained that her grandfather did not wish for one of those. Nevertheless, we had to see them all before she was convinced. She found a spot, down by a pond, where she decided to empty the ashes of her letter. Then she said, 'Ok, let's go home'. And we did.

The point of this story is that she had to find out for herself. She asked the questions and she decided on the answers. The reason for all this was a question in her own mind of which I was unaware. She settled it in her own way. I could not provide the answer. That is how children learn, we later discovered.

Polly having alerted us to this, we conducted research with other children to see if this was generalisable. What we took from the experience with Polly was:

- her use of enabling metaphor and conceptual construction;

- the importance of events in her life-experience;

- her need to construct meaning and resolve issues.

Following this we interviewed children in schools to find out whether this depth of conversation and characteristics of response were replicated. Below is a strand of this research that relates closely to the concept involved in conversations with my daughter: that of loss.

In one school with a group of four 7-year old children we used the poem 'Looking for Dad', from Brian Patten's collection *Gargling With Jelly* (Patten, 1985) as a stimulus. The poem is about a young boy whose parents keep yelling at him to tidy up his room. But later in the poem the parents are yelling at each other, not him. Then dad disappears. The boy searches for him everywhere then tidies up his room in the hope that dad will return. The poem ends with the boy, 19 days later, sitting and waiting for his dad to return and admire his very tidy room.

The children responded in various ways in discussion with each other as to what the poem was about. We used the question: Where do you think dad has gone? In this discussion one child suggested dad had gone to heaven and another child responded to that by telling her own story about her Nan.

Victoria's Story

I think that in heaven you can ride a white pony and have marshmallows. Before my Nan died she told me lots of things because she knew she was going to die and she told me about all the things she was going to do and she said she was going to send me a postcard. Before she went she gave me a piece of paper and stuck a photograph on it. I've still got it.

She said she would be happy and she wanted me to be happy when she died. On that day she got a picture of her and all the family, stuck it on a postcard and wrote on the back, 'I'll see you in your heart.' Now she's always with me. Now I talk to her all the time. I talk to her when I'm lonely. When I've argued with my friends I go and sit on the wall and think about her and talk to her. When I get fed up I sit there and talk to her about my friends. She tells me that she is riding on things. She says she's having a really nice time. She says she's going to ring me up. She says things in my head, she rings up my brain and talks to me.

The construction of Victoria's response reveals similar features to Polly's:

- the conceptual connection being made;

- the use of figurative language (metaphor);

- it involves a narrative progression that maintains the relationship;

- it is based on personal experience and seeking to make sense of that experience.

Our next strategy was to see what the response was when you took one child's story to other children to use as a stimulus. Thus, on one occasion Victoria's story was read to 60 10-year old children during a 20-minute period within which they were asked to respond. They did so by speaking into a tape recorder and subsequently by writing what their response was on paper, with a decision being made as to whether they wished to speak further about their response (either alone or in pairs). Forty-seven children indicated they wished to do this. Amongst these responses were those directed to Victoria asking for more information and those relating their own experiences in response. Two of these were from boys whose parents had split up. One lived with his dad, the other with his mum. They had written on a sheet of paper handed out to each child:

'I remember when my mum and dad split up, I was very upset because my mum throw a shoe at my dad and take a chunk of skin out of dads face. I still cry when my [me] and mum met [meet] mum gets very upset so she always takes me out a lot to stop he [her] cry and get her mid of [mind off] this. Please read this.'

'My mum and dad split up 4 years ago. I feel angry partly with myself but mostly with my dad because he caused the argument here is a picture of what he done to my sister.' *(Picture of a man standing behind a girl. The man is holding a knife labelled 'stabber' and the girl is labelled 'sister' and saying 'help'.)*

At their request we interviewed these two boys together. They were friends, aware of each other's circumstances. The interview lasted one and a half hours, moving to four different locations during the school in this time. Below I summarise some important points in this conversation.

Lee and Glen

Our conversation revolved around the difficulties of dealing without one of your parents and the problems that can cause. They mentioned the feelings that come especially at Christmas, when the family is split up and you can't celebrate properly by having both parents together. Then they described these circumstances in the following way:

L: It's like a key that almost fits the lock but doesn't turn.

Q: What would happen if you could turn the key?

G: You'd see your family back together again.

L: It would open the door.

Q: … and that key, can you find a way of turning it or do you think it just will never turn?

L: It will never turn.

G: It will never turn for me either.

Q: It will never turn for you?

G: No, I don't think, even if I do get another person it probably won't be like my mum.

L: No, nothing's like your mum at all.

Q: Would it help to have somebody in school who wasn't a teacher who you could express yourself to?

G: What, like you, or somebody like you?

Q: Yeh.

G: Yeh.

L: Yeh.

Q: Yeh?

G: Even for people who are still like together, but they have an argument in the night and that can upset somebody enough to bring them into tears in school in the morning still, and that needs speaking about, like Zoe, what happened, she split up and the teachers couldn't stop it where she didn't know, they didn't know what to do. Like they couldn't stop it and they couldn't say, 'we'll discuss it', but like they wouldn't know what to do.

L: Like cos they're not involved.

G: And they're not qualified to do it are they?

L: No, you have to be somebody that knows what it feels like, like in, you don't have to have been through it, but you have to *know* what it's like.

Q: Can you sense that in people then?

L: Yeh.

G: You can sense if people like have been through that experience cos they're normally upset quite a lot and they're in a lot of stress and they take it out…

L: If people enjoy, enjoy listening, to things like this, then that's a good sign and if they enjoy talking about it with you then that's good as well.

Lee and Glen's conversation reflects similar features in their responses to those of both Polly and Victoria.

Summary

This section has given research examples of children's narratives in order to determine what might be considered educationally necessary but not necessarily sufficient to address what can be understood as children's spirituality and their 'spiritual development' or, put more broadly, their identity formation and development of their worldviews. They are:

- conceptual connection;

- use of figurative language (simile and metaphor);

- narrative progression;

- based on experience and making sense of experience;

- a questioning process;

- a process of enquiry;

- acknowledgement and affirmation of subjectivity and interpretation;

- the process involving children in talking with one another, not just being taught by an adult.

How does the above relate to creating effective learning in religious education?

Religious education needs to be about how we make sense of the world and our place in it. It is about the construction of meaning arising from experience; thus it is about narrative and how our narratives relate to those of others. Underpinning this is the conceptual thread that ties narratives together. In the above, that thread was the concept of loss, which made it possible for children to respond to one another regardless of age or differing circumstances. And when this happens children show the ability to communicate above their usual 'ability levels' because there is a need to express themselves and be heard. They also listen carefully as they want to hear what is being said by others and respond accordingly. In knowing this it helps us to reconsider our role as teachers. 'Teacher' is an inadequate term for our role. It suggests we teach something when, in fact, our participation is in facilitating learning, which involves a variety of roles and skills. We need to be able to:

- stimulate pupils with narrative texts (oral, visual and written) that promote responses to issues they raise or raise issues for them to respond to;

- respond to their questions and observations with replies that stimulate their thinking further;

- ask our own thought-provoking questions;

- require pupils to develop skills through activities and tasks that are challenging and require different skills;

- use different learning modes that encourage cooperation, interaction, creativity, critical thinking and debate;

- encourage deep thinking to progress learning.

In doing all this we need to bear in mind that we are seeking to help pupils develop personally and spiritually. Religious education has both intrinsic and extrinsic educational aims, for example the understanding of religions and the narratives of others and the development of pupils' capacities and skills. We need to keep in mind how these can be provided for at one and the same time. The section below will address how this can be accomplished by explicitly providing a conceptual thread to pupils' learning, but first it addresses the current educational climate and recent changes to curriculum guidance and the significance of pedagogy, the theory and practice of teaching and learning.

Pedagogy and curriculum in religious education

Much has changed in the approach the Qualifications and Curriculum Authority (QCA) has taken and is now taking, as the Qualifications and Curriculum Development Agency (QCDA), to the idea of curriculum. The most significant shift is the emphasis now placed on the overall development of the learner as an individual rather than the acquisition of knowledge and understanding within discrete and separate subjects. The QCA's *A Big Picture of the Curriculum* identifies three aims: successful learners, confident individuals and responsible citizens (QCA, 2006). In the Rose review of the primary curriculum (Rose, 2009) it is proposed that these aims should be applied to the primary as well as the secondary curriculum. Also, there is, in the same review, an emphasis on learning and teaching being conceptually based and emphasising processes and skills. These twin changes recognise the significance of pedagogy and introducing a more person-centred approach to learning that provides links between learning in subjects through areas of learning and cross-curricular studies. The intended result is a more creative primary curriculum with greater emphasis on personal development. Although RE is a discrete, separate area of learning it needs to be able to make a significant contribution to the aims and design of this new primary curriculum and demonstrate its value to pupils' personal development. Proposals for updated non-statutory guidance on RE emphasise the need to address changing patterns of religion and belief and allow for a wider range of religious and non-religious worldviews (QCDA, 2009).

The need to shift emphasis towards the overall development of the learner is further reinforced by a number of threads running through Ofsted's most recent report on RE, *Making Sense of Religion* (Ofsted, 2007). While the report broadly supports the notion of a national basis for RE, and even goes as far as recommending a review of the current guidance, it highlights the need to go further in the pursuance of a more effective basis for defining progression in the development of the learner in RE. The report's critique of two attainment targets for RE, as found in the non-statutory national framework (QCA, 2004), focuses primarily on practical problems in their use in planning and assessment. This is significant because although the non-statutory framework for RE has no legal standing in relation to the production of locally agreed syllabi, it has, nevertheless, had considerable influence on the way locally agreed syllabi for RE have been constructed and developed. However, the Ofsted report also implies that there are more fundamental issues related to the definition of progression, which means the two-target structure (Learning about and Learning from religion) does not provide a secure pedagogical basis for the subject. The report points out that while the two attainment targets have helped remind us that RE is concerned with the development of the whole learner through its reference to 'learning from', it has proved problematic as a way of constructing an effective pedagogy and definition of progression because, in practice, teachers have focused more on 'learning about' religion. This relates to the critical assessment of the value of these attainment targets in Chapter 2 of this book.

This return to the significance of pedagogy requires us in religious education to clarify our own practice: be clear about what we mean by pedagogy, the relationship between theory and practice, and the similarities or distinctions between RE and other subjects in these respects. In the section below I shall draw on Michael Grimmitt's understanding of a constructivist pedagogy and show how a conceptual enquiry-led approach can be developed from it. This develops the discussion of constructivism in addressing effective learning that was presented in Chapter 3.

Constructivism

Michael Grimmitt explains that:

> 'Constructivism is a theory… about knowledge and learning… At root it identifies knowledge as a human construct which is a consequence of the way in which individuals and communities order their experience. As such, what is conceived of as "knowledge" does not and cannot reflect some "objective", ontological reality because that is unknowable. Human knowledge, as a consequence, reflects the way in which individuals and communities order and organise their experience of the world, using concepts which fit the situations they encounter. A characteristic

of human knowledge… is that it is subject to multiple interpretations or "constructs" and is controversial or problematic by nature.' (Grimmitt, 2000:208)

In outlining his understanding of pedagogy, Grimmitt (2000:16–17) states:

'A pedagogy is: a theory of teaching and learning encompassing aims, curriculum content and methodology… or a science of teaching and learning embodying both curriculum and methodology… to relate the process of teaching to that of learning on the part of the child.'

He translates this into religious education by considering how religion and education can be brought into a relationship that will reflect how and why pupils will benefit from the study of religion in terms of what aim, curriculum content and methodology (ies) would enable appropriate learning outcomes to fulfil the aim. He puts it another way by asking what kinds of interaction are required. Importantly he speaks of assimilating and accommodating the content as understood within its faith context and then recontextualising it within the pupils' own self-understanding (see Grimmitt, 2000:18).

Grimmitt then asks three questions that act as a test of the sufficiency of a pedagogy:

'1. What kind or kinds of interaction between the pupils and religious content does the model seek to promote?
2. What pedagogical procedures or strategies does the model deploy in order to achieve the kind or kinds of interaction identified above?
3. What pedagogical principles inform the model's pedagogical procedures and strategies, including its approach to the choice of curriculum content?' (Grimmitt, 2000:26)

With the findings of the Ofsted report in mind, we can add a fourth question:

4. Does the pedagogy translate effectively into a learning process that is accessible to teachers and offers a clear definition of progression that can ensure effective planning, teaching, learning and assessment?

To achieve the above I suggest that a pedagogy must base itself on certain specific criteria, which underpin constructivism, as follows.

Enquiry

Enquiry involves pupils actually carrying out an enquiry supported by their teacher. Enquiry is a process involving an open-ended key evaluative question that the pupils seek to answer. This might be best understood in the way John Dewey described it:

[Dewey] 'focused a great deal of attention upon inquiry as a way of making sense of, and giving meaning to… our world and existence, rather than validating certain objects of knowledge… he envisaged a global society in which young learners actively experience inquiring through their education. Lessons which adopt a Deweyan perspective are not focused upon the learning or memorization of facts by which pupils can be certain. Rather they are characterised by the children questioning and trying to become better investigators as "persons" rather than as "learners"'. (Webster, 2009)

Conceptuality

Conceptuality involves focusing the enquiry on one key concept throughout the enquiry process. This ensures the thread of the enquiry is maintained. The key evaluative question will be based on the key concept the pupils are enquiring into. Thus, the outcome of an effective enquiry will be a more complete and complex understanding of interpretations of that concept, the value placed on that concept by others and pupils' own evaluations of that concept and its usefulness.

Integrity

Integrity involves ensuring that the key aspects of the pedagogy are intimately and explicitly related to each other. This is discussed in more detail below, but in summary the levels of attainment must clearly reflect the intended learning outcomes of the process of conceptual enquiry and pupils need to be clear as to what those outcomes involve as they carry out the enquiry. In turn the purpose of the subject, the attainment target and the procedure given for their operation in the classroom must be consistent with one another. Here this consistency is dependent on the methodology employed.

The Living Difference project: an exercise in pedagogical design

Purpose statement

Pedagogy must start by identifying the educational importance and value of a subject in the larger context of educational design. In other words, for religious education, it must establish both its intrinsic credentials and its extrinsic usefulness. The purpose of RE, as identified in *Living Difference: The agreed syllabus for Hampshire, Portsmouth and Southampton*, offers the following, which acts as the basis for the conceptual enquiry methodology that follows:

- To support pupils in developing their own coherent patterns of values and principles.

- To support their spiritual, moral, social and cultural development.

- To encourage them to interpret and respond to a variety of concepts, beliefs and practices within religions and their own and others' cultural and life experiences.

- To develop the capacities to interpret, evaluate and respond to differing values and beliefs… through extending their thinking and analytical skills and their creative, imaginative and emotional development.

- To foster mutual understanding between pupils of differing religious and cultural backgrounds. (Hampshire, Portsmouth and Southampton Councils, 2004:7)

The significance of these statements of educational purpose and pedagogical principle lies in the orientation toward the development of pupils' capacities, skills and their overall development as empowered individuals. The focus on religion is contextual rather than essential. Put another way, educational development is not *essentially* dependent upon the subject content, rather the subject is a vehicle used for the larger educational development of the learner. If that were not the case the educational rationale for studying the subject would be wholly dependent on the content of the subject rather than an open-ended enquiry into the place and value of religion in the modern world.

Attainment target

The attainment target given in Living Difference is 'Interpreting religion in relation to human experience' (Hampshire, Portsmouth and Southampton Councils, 2004:16). This can be compared with the 'learning about' and 'learning from' attainment targets of the QCA non-statutory framework. This is subtly different to Learning about and Learning from religion in which the primacy is given, in both respects, to religion as the subject of study. First, it is presumed that Learning about religion is the precursor to the development of the learner (content comes first); second is the presumption that this will in some way provide the edification required, in a positive sense, to develop the learner (an implicit assumption that religion is beneficial). The Living Difference approach focuses on *interpreting*, which provides the basis of development. The aim is to progressively address young people's capacity to interpret in relation to their own experience and that of others. The attainment target therefore underpins the pedagogic procedure to be followed.

A methodology for conceptual enquiry

A methodology is a particular procedure or process that puts into practice a particular principle. In this context the methodology for teaching and learning is applied to address the principles identified in the purpose statement and the attainment target: interpreting religion in relation to human experience. The process of enquiry methodology that Living Difference proposes is set out in Figure 4.1. Diagrams, whilst helpful for their clarity, always require commentary to elucidate the underlying process and intention, which is what is provided here.

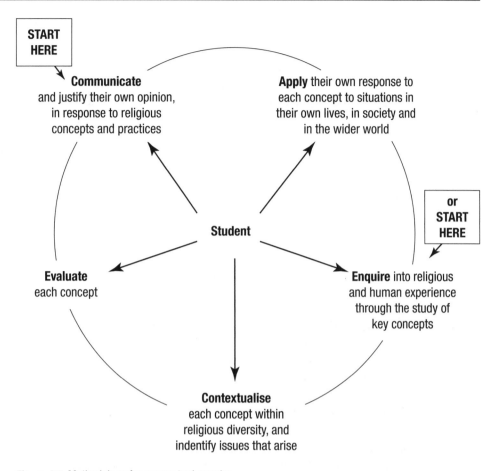

Figure 4.1 Methodology for conceptual enquiry

In Figure 4.1, five elements are present with two possible starting points. There is a need to follow this process systematically and, at the same time, to be aware of the implications of the terms themselves. The aim is to follow the same concept throughout the enquiry.

1. *Communicate* can be one starting point. This is where pupils communicate their own responses to the concept. They are interpreting the concept from their own perspectives. This is a useful starting point if the concept is part of their own experience (such as with concepts like belonging or celebration) as it provides opportunities for pupils to share their experiences and recognise that others have different experiences and respond to a concept in different ways.

2. *Apply* is the element where pupils consider how the concept applies to them and how it applies in different ways in different situations and to different people. This element challenges pupils' perceptions and asks them to consider

interpreting the concept from a different perspective as well as enriching reflection on their own perspective.

3.   *Enquire*. This is where the pupils enquire into the meaning of the concept in a more complex way. They unpack the concept and consider its characteristics, seeking a broader interpretation. For example, if the concept is celebration, what constitutes a celebration and what are the characteristics of a celebration? If the concept is community, what are the characteristics of a community? This is a useful place to start the enquiry if the concept is fairly challenging or if the pupils have no experience of the concept.

4.   *Contextualise* is where the concept is contextualised within the religious material related to it. For example, how Christians celebrate Jesus' birthday or how a Buddhist, Christian or Jewish community functions.

5.   *Evaluate* is where the pupils evaluate the significance of the concept for the religious people investigated (evaluate from within) and also consider, reflect on and articulate their own opinions about that (evaluate from without).

   If we divide the cycle into two halves, within Communicate and Apply pupils are drawing on their own experience of the concept. Within Enquire and Contextualise they engage with specific examples of others' (religious) interpretations of the concept. Within Evaluate they draw both together by demonstrating their understanding of the interpretation of others (Evaluate within) and then re-evaluating the concept in the light of this new awareness (Evaluate without). However, if we start at Enquire, pupils are introduced to the concept directly, engaging with it beyond their experience. Then, when they have evaluated the concept in relation to the interpretation of a religious group or tradition they respond to it from their own perspective through Communicate and Apply. In the examples presented below we show different ways of following this process. In some cases you may wish to incorporate the Communicate and Apply at both the beginning and the end of the cycle in order for pupils to evaluate how their understanding might have changed and developed.

   However, the next step is to take account of Figure 4.2: a hierarchy of concept development. Here the types of concepts are divided into three, and this will affect the way in which you decide where to start the cycle.

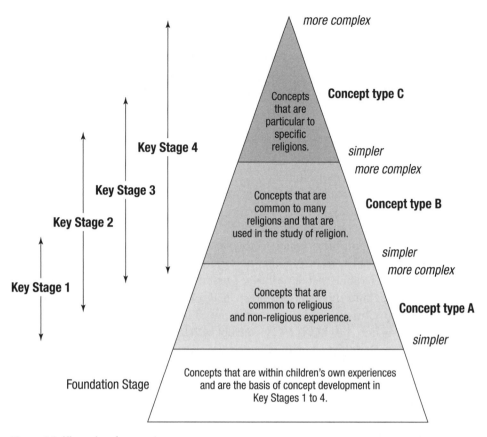

Figure 4.2 Hierarchy of concepts

Types of concepts

We have devised three categories for these. For religious education, conceptual enquiry requires the identification of concepts that have importance for believers in specific traditions (type C concepts), concepts that are important for the study of religion (type B concepts) and, in a broader sense, concepts that are important in the classification of human experience (type A concepts). All three types of concepts contain some that are simpler and others that are more complex; this is particularly true of type A concepts.

Type A concepts focus on concepts that are generic within human experience; therefore, whilst wide-ranging, there has to be a systematic way of relating them to children's development and experience and linking them explicitly to religious practices. Younger children lack the ability to think in a more sophisticated fashion but can respond to terms within their own vocabulary and experience. The concepts used have to be readily accessible to them. Belonging, Celebrating and Special(ness) are the most obvious concepts to introduce with children in foundation stage and year 1. Here they link their own vocabulary, narratives and concerns to those that are most transparent within religious behaviour. As children progress, further concepts of a more complex kind can be introduced that build on these: story and authority, for example, link their own experience and that of religious groups in an accessible way. The most complex of these types of concepts need to be reserved for their upper primary and secondary experience: interpretation, freedom and justice, for example.

Type B concepts are those that are commonly used in the study of religion and which are common to many religions. These are identifiable by their use of figurative language: symbolism, ritual, sacred, myth and worship are obvious examples. These are the basis of religious literacy.

Type C concepts are those that are particular to a specific religion. As such they are the basis of worldview analysis or understanding the way in which a particular tradition makes sense of the world and the way in which different branches of a tradition interpret those concepts to give a distinctive cast to its worldview. Thus, a type C concept has to be one that underpins the beliefs and practices of the religion in question, not one that describes the practice itself. What we are seeking to get at is the 'why' behind the 'what' of practice and behaviour. Thus, resurrection is a key concept in Christianity but prayer is not. Torah is a key concept in Judaism but Passover is not. Tawhid is a key concept in Islam but salaat is not. Dukkha is a key concept in Buddhism but puja is not. Dharma is a key concept in Hinduism but prasad is not. Sewa is a key concept in Sikhism but langar is not. (See Appendix 1 on pages 78–86 for a list of concepts in each category.)

Three examples are provided of these different types of concepts and how they can be engaged with at different stages in pupils' experience in primary education through using the conceptual enquiry cycle presented in Figure 4.1.

Example 1: Remembering

This is based on a cycle of enquiry by Lowndes (2006). It is intended to be taught to younger pupils, for example, year 1.

If we begin with the Communicate and Apply elements, pupils are engaged in an enquiry into and reflection on a concept within their own experience in order to prepare them for enquiring into the same concept within a religious context. Communicate and Apply break this process down into two parts. The first is a process of engagement that seeks to facilitate pupils reflecting on their own experience of the concept and articulating their own views and understandings of it. The second builds on that by presenting pupils with a situation (a context they can readily respond to) within which those views and understandings of the concept need to be applied and commented on. Necessarily this requires discussion, facilitated by the teacher, focused on interaction and the sharing of views and experiences rather than a didactic approach to learning. However, we need to take account of Figure 4.2, the hierarchy of concepts, to refine what this process entails. The focus for learning in conceptual enquiry is defined not by the introduction of specific content but by choosing a concept appropriate to the age and ability of the learners. For example, with the youngest pupils, in year 1 or foundation stage, the concept of remembering would be appropriate as a simpler type A concept (common to religious and non-religious experience).

Communicate a response to the concept of remembering

In Communicate the teacher may provide the stimulus by focusing on who she likes to remember (people and events she has important memories of) such as the birth of her child or the first time she walked or the first card she made for her. She then invites pupils to relate a memory that they have about someone or some event that they remember and draws attention to words they use associated with remembering and encourages them to think about why they remember. She may ask them to draw a picture of the event/person they remember and annotate this with 'I remember this because…'.

Apply their response to remembering to their own and other's lives

In Apply, discussion focuses on what helps us to remember. The teacher may model this again by showing how she does so, for example with pictures and mementos, such as a name tag of her baby in hospital. Pupils share their thoughts on this and bring in items for a 'remembering table' and tell the story behind their object. The teacher may then move on to types of memories – what pupils like to remember and whether some memories are happy and some sad. This may conclude with reflecting on whether we all remember different or the same things and whether we remember at the same or different times. We can then ask whether remembering is helpful to us and, if so, in what ways. Also, with some pupils, they can be encouraged to think about what qualities they associate with the event and person remembered; what they value as a result: kindness, love, joy or being brave, etc.

Enquire into the concept of remembering

In Enquire the enquiry into the concept is broadened and deepened and connections with religion begin to be made to prepare further for the Contextualise element of the cycle. Objects may be introduced from religions that are connected to remembering. These will depend on what you wish to introduce as a context after the Enquire element. For example, a Sikh kirpan can be introduced and students can be asked to speculate on what Sikhs remember when they see a kirpan. Such speculation has to be followed by the story and person it relates to: the founding of the khalsa and the importance of Guru Gobind Singh. Pupils can then make the connections between the object and its significance for Sikhs and what they remember when they wear the kirpan. Pupils can be encouraged to think about why it is still important for some Sikhs to wear the kirpan, as a result. What does it help them remember and why? It may be important to mention that at this time Sikhs were threatened by others so the kirpan was a way of defending themselves if attacked but it also identified them as Sikhs.

Contextualise the concept of remembering in Sikh practice

In Contextualise the Sikh celebration of Baisakhi can be introduced as a way of remembering the founding of the khalsa and remembering the importance of Guru Gobind Singh. Here a Baisakhi celebration can be simulated in which pupils retell and act out the story with the classroom decorated in the manner of a gurdwara at the time of this celebration, with flags, food, decorations and Sikh devotional music. Also, the other signs of being a Sikh that Guru Gobind Sikh introduced when he started the khalsa can be introduced (the five Ks): kangha, the comb; kara, the bracelet; kesh, uncut hair; and kacha, shorts, which made Sikhs readily identifiable. Discuss what each item helps Sikhs to remember and how that is related to the way Sikhs take pride in who they are.

Evaluate the concept of remembering

Evaluate should consist of both an evaluate within question (about the concept in the context) and an evaluate without question (about the concept outside the context). In Evaluate within pupils are asked to respond to the key evaluative question: why is it important for Sikhs to remember the story told during Baisakhi about Guru Gobind Singh? Some possible reasons can be given for pupils to discuss, such as:

■ It brings them together.

■ It is an opportunity for a celebration.

■ They can remember why they wear the five Ks.

■ They can remember the five brave men in the story.

■ It helps them remember what it means to be a Sikh.

These are all positive reasons, but you want the pupils to decide which they think are the most important and why. To help them do this you can give out a Post-It to each pupil on which they write their decision and why they have made that choice. These can then be displayed and discussed. Taking this further, you may ask them whether it is still important to wear the five Ks today to remember what it means to be a Sikh (many Sikhs do not – why is that?)

The evaluate without question could be: is it always important for us to remember or are there some things it is good to forget? This gives pupils the opportunity to say what things they might have forgotten and why. Also, for more able pupils, they have a chance to reflect on things that have faded in their memory over time and why, for example memories of people they have not seen for a long time or events that they would rather forget.

If remembering is taught in year 1, in terms of continuity and progression it would be useful to teach a cycle on the concept of remembrance later, perhaps in year 5.

Rather than start at Communicate it is possible to start at Enquire; this depends on whether you think pupils need to relate the concept to themselves first and whether the concept is immediately accessible to pupils. In this second example, with older, year 5 pupils, we start at the Enquire element using the type B concept of sacred (type B concepts are common to many religions and used in the study of religion).

Example 2: Sacred

Enquire into the concept of 'sacred'

1.   Pupils brainstorm the word 'sacred' in small groups. Feedback and compare ideas.

2.   Pupils in groups discuss and list what they would need to create a sacred place and then compare ideas.

3.   Individually or in pairs pupils design a sacred place (anything/anywhere not necessarily relating to religion) focusing on their discussions.

4.   Pupils produce labels (this provides an ICT link) which explain how particular features make their place sacred.

5.   Discuss key elements that they consider make a place 'sacred'.

Contextualise the concept within religious places of worship

1.   Visit and investigate a Church. Pupils photograph/draw features which they think make a church sacred. They may wish to question a member of the church or the verger or priest/minister.

2.   Pupils produce a guidebook (literacy/ICT link) for a visitor to the church, describing or explaining sacred features and what they consider makes them sacred.

3.   Repeat above activity for a Mosque (or Gurdwara/Hindu Temple/Synagogue, etc) through a virtual tour or a visit.

Evaluate the concept of sacred place within Christianity and Islam (or another religion)

Discuss with pupils:

■   Is it important for believers to feel that a place is sacred? Why/why not?

■   Can a place be sacred on some occasions and not on others?

■   Do all Christians and Muslims feel that the Church and Mosque are sacred?

■   Do you think Muslims and Christians would mind exchanging places of worship? Why/why not?

- Hot seat volunteer pupils in role as a Christian or Muslim who have been offered an alternative place of worship because theirs is being converted into a supermarket. How would they react?

- Is it important for everyone to have a sacred space? (evaluate without). What do pupils think?

Communicate their own understanding of sacred place

Ask pupils to spend some quiet reflective time imagining being in their own sacred place (play quiet music perhaps):

- Would they call it sacred or would they rather use another word? What word would they use as an alternative?

- What is it like, what is around them, who are they with, what can they see, hear, smell, feel?

- Why is it sacred (or otherwise)? How do they feel when they are in there?

- Pupils draw and annotate their sacred/(alternative description) place or create a poem about it.

Apply their own understanding of sacred places to their own and others' lives

- Discuss and compare pupils' personal 'sacred' places. How do pupils feel about each other's sacred places? Can they explain why it is sacred (the place where I was born, a football ground, where the dog was buried, etc)? How do people show a place is sacred?

- Discuss: Is it important to show respect for other's sacred places? Why/why not? How can respect or non-respect be shown? What happens when a lack of respect is shown to another's sacred place?

- Pupils in groups devise short scenarios to illustrate a situation where a lack of respect for a 'sacred' place has been shown and how people can react. Pupils role play their scenarios for discussion.

- As a class pupils discuss why people can show a lack of respect for a 'sacred' place, for example, through malice, ignorance or other reasons.

Example 3: Resurrection

This is based on a cycle of enquiry by Kath Bagley, Hampshire Primary Advanced Skills teacher in RE (Bagley, 2009). It is intended to be taught to the oldest primary school pupils, in year 6.

This year 6 cycle of enquiry on resurrection takes place in the weeks leading up to Easter and builds on units already taught in years 3, 4 and 5; respectively: symbol as shown by the cross, ritual as manifested in use of the paschal candle, and suffering as exemplified in the controversy stories and images of Jesus. By moving on to the concept of Resurrection, the pupils are being introduced to a more specifically Christian concept.

By the end of the unit, by developing skills such as reflection and interpretation, pupils working at level 4 will be able to:

- Explain the concept of resurrection.

- Explain how resurrection is significant within the context of the Easter story and for Christians.

- Evaluate, by explaining interpretations of resurrection and identifying some issues raised.

- Express a personal response to the concept of resurrection.

- Explain how their response to ideas about the concept of resurrection affect them and others.

(The crucial importance of the level descriptors above in the planning and delivery of conceptual enquiry is discussed below.)

The cycle starts with Enquire.

Enquire into the concept of resurrection

In Enquire pupils are introduced to the question: what does resurrection mean? This involves discussion in which misconceptions such as ghosts and hauntings will inevitably be brought up, or children will pose some scientific explanations for resurrection. What do people mean when they use the word (both in a religious and an everyday sense)? It becomes evident that people have different ideas of the concept.

Contextualise the concept of resurrection in the biblical accounts

In Contextualise an account of the discovery of the empty tomb is read as well as resurrection stories such as the incident on the Road to Emmaus. Children try to imagine the thoughts of the various characters involved and share ideas through drama. Images of the resurrection are also examined to stimulate further ideas.

Evaluate the concept of resurrection, from within and without

In Evaluate pupils discuss such statements as:

- If Christians did not believe that the resurrection had happened, they would not be Christians.

- All Christians believe in the resurrection and that there is life after death for believers.

- It would make no difference to Christians if they found out that the resurrection hadn't happened.

Three Christian artefacts are then shared with pupils: the empty cross, the cross of the suffering Christ and the cross of the risen Christ. What might Christians feel about each one?

Pupils work in groups to sort statements according to whether they are ideas a Christian or a non-Christian might have. For example:

- Jesus could have saved himself if he wanted to.

- I believe that Jesus was a good man and a talented teacher, but I don't believe that he rose from the dead.

- Jesus was able to overcome death because he was God's son.

- Jesus rose from the dead because some magic power from the cross helped him.

- Jesus triumphed over death.

Pupils are led to the understanding that resurrection is a key belief for Christians although not all Christians interpret it in the same way, and non-Christians might have differing views – there will be diversity of belief.

Communicate a response to the concept of resurrection

In Communicate pupils explore their own notions of death and whether life goes on in some way. They then paint a picture to symbolise and express their own beliefs and write a 'gallery label' to accompany the painting, explaining their ideas.

Apply their response to the concept of resurrection to their own lives and those of others

In Apply pupils consider some prepared statements about death and the possibility of life after death. With the teacher chairing, they then debate the motion, 'People who believe in an after-life are more likely to behave better in their earthly lives.'

The unit ends with the children writing down ideas about what they have learnt and whether their ideas have changed.

Kath remarks that this enquiry is very successful in that it promotes group discussion (often pupil answering pupil without the teacher mediating). Even initially sceptical children became engaged and increasingly willing to share their ideas about this difficult concept. While many were sceptical, they were accepting of the fact that other people might have different perspectives and respected this in the way they offered their views. The ideas expressed in their paintings were overwhelmingly about some sort of life after death but were extremely varied and often involved very complex ideas, including ambivalence as to whether death was the end or not.

Pupils' remarks in the debate are also surprisingly astute and thoughtful, for example:

'If you believe that life goes on after death, you won't pay as much attention to the present.'

'It would be like living on earth was just the waiting room.'

'You might take more risks if you believe that you are not going to actually die.'

'It will make you better behaved if you know you are going to be judged when you die.'

The three examples above show how progression works according to conceptual enquiry: remembrance to sacred to resurrection. Other concepts can be employed to the same end, as Kath Bagley suggests. The most important aspect of this is to determine how each concept you use will in turn relate to another at a later stage so that pupils are aware of the connections, even though they may use material from different religions. Overall, this is expressed in Figure 4.3, which encapsulates the idea of a spiral curriculum extending across key stages.

Most importantly, we must return to the idea of integrity introduced earlier in this chapter. The cycle is an integrated process of enquiry whereby the enquiry progresses into greater complexity and depends upon using higher level skills of analysis and communication as it moves on, dependent on and reintroducing prior learning in progression from one element to the next and, across cycles at different stages, progressively draws on prior learning. It is not just a structure to be followed.

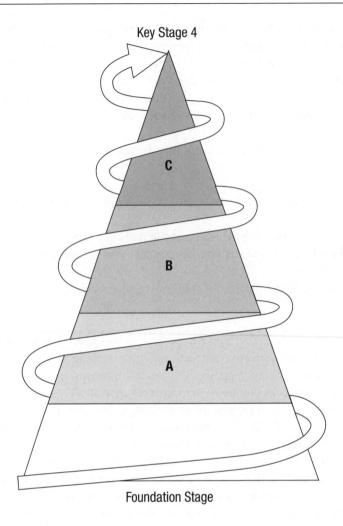

Key Stage 4

C

B

A

Foundation Stage

Figure 4.3 Spiral progression

Levels of attainment

The progressive construction of the five elements of the levels of attainment is integrated with the five progressive elements of the conceptual enquiry methodology (see the levels of attainment in Appendix 2 on pages 86–90). Thus teachers can be clear as to what they are seeking to achieve for their pupils and older pupils can recognise the specific ways in which they need to improve. They can be supported in identifying the distinction between different levels – moving on from identifying and talking about, to simple descriptions, to describing and then explaining. The levels therefore become the intended learning outcomes to direct pupil learning, which gives teachers direction, and of which pupils can, increasingly, gain ownership. In this way the levels cease to be just a test of the pupils' ability and become the basis upon which the enquiry is conducted – a means for the teacher to measure progression and determine how to progress further.

The development of skills

Whilst the methodology operates at the level of a pedagogic strategy the development of skills and thus progression through the levels of attainment will only occur if the tasks set and the techniques for learning incorporated within each element of enquiry create an appropriate learning curve. In outline this can also be illustrated through learning steps that ensure each element builds on the previous one. This necessitates that higher order skills should progressively be acquired as pupils go through each cycle and through the primary curriculum, and that tasks should be given that are fit for this purpose. The level of skill can be identified from Bloom's taxonomy, which ranks skills in a hierarchical fashion (from lowest to highest), as follows: knowledge, comprehension, application, analysis, synthesis, evaluation. In a newer version the corresponding skills, stated as verbs rather than nouns, reads: remembering, understanding, applying, analysing, evaluating, and creating; see Atherton, 2009; http://www.odu.edu/educ/llschult/blooms_taxonomy.htm.

Identity formation and religious literacy

In the primary phase, identity formation and religious literacy are the two overall foci in addressing pupils' development and progression in their learning. In upper primary they will also be starting to address the interpretation of worldviews, but this and worldview analysis are of particular significance in the secondary phase. Here we need to recognise what identity formation and religious literacy entails so that pupils will have a firm grounding for their secondary experience.

Identity formation

This occurs primarily in the top half of the cycle (Communicate and Apply) where pupils are focusing on their own beliefs and values and their socio-cultural situatedness. As their learning progresses through key stages 1 and 2 with concepts that are at first less complex and then more complex, their ability to reflect on their own lives will increase and, in this way, the contribution to pupils' identity formation progresses. They become more aware of what they think, the beliefs and behaviours that is based on, and the nature of the experiences that influence them. In grander terms, identity formation is about knowing yourself, who you are and why. One teacher who is familiar with using this approach has commented:

> 'In Communicate and Apply the students can play with ideas themselves. They are liberated from "right answers". They are not frightened of expressing themselves. This allows us to get into meaningful discussion. Kids gain a confidence which allows them to open themselves up to learning.' (Wedell, 2009:25)

Another stated:

> 'The child is in the middle of everything. This is the key thing. Nothing the child says is wrong. The pupils have a voice, because there is space in the cycle for what they think. The teachers are now actually hearing what the children are saying and what they think. Children achieve because of the variety of activities, because it's about how concepts affect them in their lives, and their views on things.
>
> The pupils are involved and receptive because they know they will be listened to.
>
> Exploring what children think is an inherent part of the cycle. My pupils don't worry about what they say – [Living Difference] LD has made that difference.' (Wedell, 2009:25)

Religious literacy

Religious literacy primarily relates to the bottom half of the cycle (Enquire and Contextualise). Here, through the common concept, pupils are relating their experiences to those of others. Thus they become more aware of how and why others might behave due to their different socio-cultural and religious environments. Once pupils move from simpler concepts to more complex ones, in type A, but especially with type B concepts, literacy extends to figurative expression. We can see this with the examples given above and in the responses pupils gave in their stories from the Children and Worldviews' research. This has much in common with literacy generally. When we move to the example on resurrection, we see that religious literacy and both understanding and being able to use figurative expression (for example, simile and metaphor) are essential to pupils' progression. However, we must not think that using this form of speech and way of thinking is only the capacity of older primary children. Here is a quote from an infant school teacher on the impact of this approach:

> 'Living Difference helps pupils to focus on what they are looking for in the material – on what makes it meaningful... It was her answer, I was so gobsmacked, she's not five yet, she's not five till August and it was when we were doing Change, which was in the Spring term. We were doing Zacchaeus... and how did meeting Jesus change him. And she said "Well he had a cold heart before he met Jesus and then because Jesus loved him he had a warm one"... she was so there on board with you... and she doesn't go to church... and she went on to say: "Because if nobody loves you, you have a cold heart".' (Wedell, 2009:7)

In this example we can also see how identity formation and religious literacy come together, providing an integrated form of development. They are not two different goals but two aspects of the same goal, as reflected in both the purpose statement and the one attainment target.

The impact of conceptual enquiry

In Katherine Wedell's independent report into the implementation of the Living Difference conceptual enquiry (Wedell, 2009), commissioned by Hampshire, she quoted some of the statements teachers used in response to her questions. A few of these were used above. These matched with many other statements made by teachers who had undergone development in this approach. Below, teachers' comments from her report are selectively included to give an impression of how they interpreted the approach and its results. This may give you a further understanding of how the conceptual cycle of enquiry, presented in Figure 4.1, works in an effective way.

The teacher in the first quotation emphasises the changes in moving from content- to concept-based lessons:

'Lessons are more punchy and pacy, and clear and focused, because we're not bogged down with so much content. Discussion lessons have hugely improved since Living Difference, because we're now free to spend time on a concept. Not rushing through content. Kids latch onto the ideas better than they did in the past because there isn't the content there. For example, they can focus on Hindu ideas about reincarnation, not what happens at a Hindu burial. It's clearer. Focused on what really matters… Living Difference inspires high level discussion because we're dealing with ideas – the nitty gritty of RE, the concepts rather than the content.' (Wedell, 2009:9)

This next teacher explains the importance of Contextualise in the cycle:

'Contextualisation drives the progression. How simple or difficult the concept is depends on the context. The complication is not the concept but how it impacts on people. This is how you get the progression.' (Wedell, 2009:14)

The teacher below focuses on the value of the level descriptors:

'The level descriptors are brilliant because of the key words – identify, describe, explain, etc. These words are the learning objectives. With every other subject you have a whacking great paragraph and have to go for "best fit". The kids know that "describe" is level 3 and "explaining" is level 4 and that the way to get into level 5 is to make links between concepts from a sequence of lessons and identify issues raised.' (Wedell, 2009:15)

The next teacher refers to the skills involved:

'Enquire, Contextualise, Evaluate, Communicate, Apply: all higher order thinking skills. The skills in LD are frankly functional skills in today's world. I want them to be able to think for themselves, to state and justify what they think. The skills in [Living Difference] LD are focused. What you apply to them is open.' (Wedell, 2009:22)

Review: constructing your own cycle of enquiry

This chapter has outlined, with some illustrations, the principles and strategy for conceptual enquiry. At this point it would be valuable to construct your own cycle of enquiry based on the guidance given above. It is important to link up the main points made in each of the sections in this chapter. In particular:

- focus on the development of the learner;

- ensure that the cycle focuses on the same key concept at all stages of the enquiry;

- ensure that the Contextualise element raises issues for evaluation;

- ensure that the evaluative question is fit for purpose and sufficiently challenging;

- check that the links between the elements are clear and progressive so that the learner can recognise the connection between them but is challenged at a further level as each element is introduced, building on prior learning.

Appendix 1. Concepts

Concept type A

Here are some examples of concepts common to religious and non-religious experience. These are illustrative, not exhaustive. As with the other types of concepts they are not in alphabetical order. The important thing is to decide on how progression and continuity between concepts can best be established.

Suffering	Loyalty	Belief
Identity	Change	Good and evil
Devotion	Community	Sacrifice
Submission	Remembrance	Freedom
Wisdom	Power	Creation
Forgiveness	Justice	Peace
Love	Interpretation	Hope
Authority	Prejudice	Persecution
Justification	Hedonism	Environmentalism

Concept type B

Examples of concepts that are common to many religions and that are used in the study of religion:

God	Worship	Symbolism
Ritual	Prophethood	Sacred
Holy	Myth	Initiation
Rites of passage	Prophecy	Pilgrimage
Martyrdom	Discipleship	Stewardship
Faith	Salvation	Revelation

Concept type C

Here are some examples of key concepts that are particular to specific religions.

Christianity

■ *Trinity*: The doctrine of the three-fold nature of God as Father, Son and Holy Spirit. Three persons (or forms) in one God.

■ *Incarnation*: The doctrine that God took human form in Jesus Christ and the belief that God in Christ is active in the Church and the world through the Holy Spirit.

■ *Church*: The whole community of Christians in the world throughout time as the body of Christ or the body of believers. Also a particular congregation or denomination of Christianity. Also, the congregation of a particular church or worshipping community.

■ *Salvation*: The belief that all believers will be saved and live in God's presence.

■ *Atonement*: Reconciliation between God and humanity through Christ, restoring a relationship broken by sin.

■ *Sin*: Act or acts of rebellion against the known will of God. An understanding of the human condition as being severed from its relationship with God because of disobedience.

■ *Resurrection*: The rising from the dead of Jesus Christ, leading to the rising from the dead of all believers at the Last Day, and the belief in the new, or risen, life of Christians.

- *Redemption*: The effect of the deed of Jesus Christ in setting people free from sin through his death on the cross.

- *Repentance*: The acceptance of our unworthiness before God and recognition of the need to be saved from sin by his love.

- *Reconciliation*: The uniting of believers with God through the sacrifice of Jesus Christ. The process of reconciling Christians with one another.

- *Grace*: The freely given and unmerited favour of God's love for humanity. The means to salvation through faith in Jesus Christ.

- *Logos*: The Word. The pre-existent Word of God incarnate as Jesus Christ.

- *Agape*: The love of God for humanity, which Christians should seek to emulate.

- *Sacrament*: An outward sign of a blessing given by God (Protestant) or the actual presence of God (Catholic). In the Roman Catholic Church this represents a means to salvation.

A unit of work on Christianity, or one including the Christian tradition, would be expected to draw on some of these key concepts. Further beliefs and practices included should be related back to the key concepts.

Buddhism

- *Dukkha*: Suffering or dis-ease. The unsatisfactoriness of worldly existence.

- *Tanha*: Thirst or craving. Attachment to desiring.

- *Anicca*: Change, the continual changing nature of worldly existence.

- *Anatta*: The lack of a substantial and unchanging self, soul or identity.

- *Nirvana (nibbana)*: Enlightenment. The extinguishing of ignorance and attachment that binds one to worldly existence.

- *Karma (kamma)*: The state of rebirth through one's attachment to the world and the self.

- *Buddha*: Enlightened or awakened one. One who sees things as they really are.

- *Sangha*: The Buddhist community. Sometimes used specifically about the monastic community (arya sangha).

- *Dharma (Dhamma)*: Teachings of the Buddha. Also, the Truth about the way things are.

- *Bhavana*: Mental culture or mental development/discipline. Also, meditation/formal training. The seventh and eighth steps on the eightfold path, or middle way, taught by the historical Buddha.

- *Karuna*: Compassion, one of the two (interrelated) aspects of enlightenment.

- *Prajna*: Wisdom. The second of the aspects of enlightenment. The first three steps on the eightfold path, or middle way, taught by the historical Buddha.

- *Sila*: Ethical conduct. The fourth, fifth and sixth steps on the eightfold path, or middle way, taught by the historical Buddha.

- *Upaya*: Skilfulness/skill in means. An attribute of the Buddha. Also, the ability to adapt the teachings to an audience, and one's actions and advice to individuals and situations.

A unit of work on Buddhism, or one including the Buddhist tradition, would be expected to draw on some of these key concepts. Further beliefs and practices included should be related back to the key concepts.

Hinduism

- *Brahman*: Ultimate Reality, the formless understanding of God.

- *Avatar*: An incarnation (or descent) of God. For example, followers of Vishnu believe he was incarnated in 10 different forms, of which the most famous are Rama, Krishna and the Buddha.

- *Atman*: The presence of ultimate formless reality in a person or living being.

- *Brahmin*: The highest caste entrusted with the knowledge of the Vedas.

- *Brahma*: The Hindu God responsible for creation and creative power. One of the trimurti (the three deities who control the gunas: the three functions of creation, preservation and destruction).

- *Vishnu*: The Hindu God responsible for the preservation of creation. One of the trimurti.

- *Shiva*: The Hindu God responsible for the destructive aspect of creation. One of the trimurti.

- *Murti*: The manifestation of God in a particular form and with a particular function.

- *Darshan*: Literally *seeing*. Refers to being seen by God, and thus blessed. Hindus refer to *going for darshan* when going to the mandir (temple) for worship.

- *Samsara*: The created world, ultimately temporal and limited – even illusory. It consists of nama-rupa (name and form). It is the cycle of life, death and rebirth.

- *Maya*: The form and nature of the created world, ultimately illusory or masking the true reality.

- *Guna*: Rope or quality. Specifically refers to the three qualities that make up and influence matter: sattva (goodness), rajas (passion) and tamas (ignorance).

- *Moksha*: Liberation or release from samsara.

- *Yoga*: The paths (marg) to moksha. Literally means 'to yoke' or bind.

- *Bhakti yoga*: The yoga of loving devotion.

- *Jnana yoga*: The path of knowledge.

- *Karma yoga*: The path of ethical works or actions.

- *Karma*: The law by which one's actions result in a higher or lower rebirth according to whether one's actions have good or bad effects.

- *Vedas*: The ancient scriptures that contain the revealed knowledge of reality.

- *Dharma*: Religious duty, according to one's status or place in society (see jati). It also refers to the intrinsic quality of the self or truth (see karma).

- *Varna*: Colour. This refers to the four vedic caste sub-divisions in Hindu society. These are Brahmins (priests), Kshatriyas (ruling or warrior class), Vaishyas (merchant class), and Shudras (labouring class).

- *Jati*: This refers to the occupational kinship group to which one belongs in Indian society. It is a form of social regulation and hierarchy derived from that of varna.

- *Ahimsa*: Non-violence.

A unit of work on Hinduism, or one including the Hindu tradition, would be expected to draw on some of these key concepts. Further beliefs and practices included should be related back to the key concepts.

Islam

- *Islam*: Submission to the will of Allah, leading to peace.

- *Muslim*: One who submits.

- *Tawheed*: The oneness of God and His creation.

- *Risalah*: Prophethood, the messengers of Allah.

- *Akhirah*: Life after death, the hereafter.

- *Yawmuddin*: The day of judgement.

- *Jihad*: Individual striving toward Allah (greater jihad), preventing the corruption of Allah's creation (lesser jihad).

- *Shirk*: Forgetfulness of Allah, putting someone or something as being equal to or above Allah.

- *Umma*: The community of Muslims worldwide.

- *Iman*: Faith.

- *Ibadah*: Worship.

- *Akhlaq*: Ethics governing conduct, character and attitudes.

A unit of work on Islam, or one including the Muslim tradition, would be expected to draw on some of these key concepts. Further beliefs and practices included should be related back to the key concepts.

Judaism

- *Mitzvah/mitzvot (pl)*: Commandment in Torah.

- *Torah*: Law, teaching, God's word. The five books of Moses.

- *Shekhinah*: The presence of God.

- *Zion*: Expression of perfection in the Messianic Age.

- *Mashiach*: Messiah, the anointed one to deliver the world into the Messianic Age.

- *Israel*: One who struggles with God. This refers to the worldwide Jewish community, the land of Israel and the modern state of Israel.

- *Rabbi*: Ordained teacher of Torah (the Law). Often the religious leader of a Jewish community.

- *Kedusha*: Holiness – *You should be holy, for I, the Lord your God, am holy*.

- *Tzelem Elokim*: In the image of God.

- *Covenant*: The agreement made between God and the Jewish people involving promise and obligation.

- *Redemption*: God's promise, in the Covenant, to release the world from its fallen, sinful state.

A unit of work on Judaism, or one including the Jewish tradition, would be expected to draw on some of these key concepts. Further beliefs and practices included should be related back to the key concepts.

Sikhism

- *Niguna*: Concept of God as One and formless, without attributes.

- *Ik Onkar*: The symbol representing God as One.

- *Bani/shabad*: The word of revelation.

- *Nam simran*: Personal meditation.

- *Haumai*: The human condition of self-reliance.

- *Manmukh*: Self-centredness.

- *Gurmukh*: God-centredness.

- *Sewa*: Service as an essential response to gurmukh.

- *Guru*: God manifest, as in Guru Granth Sahib.

- *Nadar*: The grace of the Guru.

- *Panth*: The Sikh community.

- *Khalsa*: Fellowship of those who have taken amrit (both men and women).

- *Amrit*: The Sikh rite of initiation into the Khalsa. Also the sanctified sugar and water liquid (nectar) used in the initiation ceremony.

- *Jot*: The divine light indwelling everyone.

- *Mukti*: Liberation from the world and union with God.

- *Maya*: The illusion that the world has an essential reality instead of being temporary. The implication being that the soul has no true dwelling in the world.

A unit of work on Sikhism, or one including the Sikh tradition, would be expected to draw on some of these key concepts. Further beliefs and practices included should be related back to the key concepts.

Humanism

Humanism is not a religion. It does, however, share many of the values held by the world religions, such as a number of those listed below, but without a belief in God:

- *Value of life*: Seeking to make the best of the one life humans have by creating meaning and purpose.

- *Rationalism*: Explanation of human and natural phenomena based on reason, verifiable evidence and scientific method.

- *Moral values*: Derived from human knowledge and experience alone. Central to civilised living for both individuals and societies.

- *Responsibility*: Self-reliance and independence of thought. Responsibility of humans for their own destiny. Treating others in a way one would like to be treated. Care for the environment, now and for the future.

- *Evolution*: Acceptance that human beings have evolved naturally over millions of years as have all other forms of life.

- *The human spirit*: Nourished and fulfilled in the appreciation of natural beauty, in human creativity and through human relationships.

- *The human heritage*: Respect for the inheritance of human achievement – intellectual, philosophical, artistic, technological and scientific.

- *Human co-operation*: Importance of international agreements such as those on Human Rights, the Rights of the Child, and Protection of the Environment. The support for voluntary organisations which seek to help people (eg, Amnesty International, Samaritans, Citizens Advice Bureau).

- *Toleration*: Need for mutual understanding and respect between all human groups. This involves opposition to extremes of belief that seek to impose their own creeds on others and thereby deny basic human freedoms.

- *Secularism*: Impartiality towards, and equal treatment of, individuals and groups with different religious and non-religious beliefs.

(Copyright Hampshire, Portsmouth and Southampton Councils, 2004)

Appendix 2. Levels of attainment

LEVEL 1	
Enquire	Pupils can identify and talk about key concepts studied that are common to non-religious and religious experience (Type A Concept)
Contextualise	They can recognise that the concept is expressed in the practices of the religion studied
Evaluate	They can evaluate the concepts by talking about their importance to believers in simple terms, and by identifying an issue raised
Communicate	They can talk about their own response to these concepts
Apply	They can identify how their response relates to their own lives

LEVEL 2	
Enquire	Pupils can describe in simple terms key concepts studied that are common to non-religious and religious experience (Type A Concept) They can identify and talk about concepts that are common to many religions and used in the study of religion (Type B Concept)
Contextualise	They simply describe ways in which these concepts are expressed in the context of the practices of the religion studied
Evaluate	They can evaluate the concepts by describing in simple terms their value to believers and by talking about an issue raised
Communicate	They can describe in simple terms their response to these concepts
Apply	They can identify simple examples of how their response relates to their own lives and those of others
LEVEL 3	
Enquire	Pupils can describe key concepts that are common to many religions and used in the study of religion (Type B Concept)
Contextualise	They can describe how these concepts are contextualised within some of the beliefs and practices of the religion studied
Evaluate	They can evaluate the concepts by describing their value to believers and by identifying and describing an issue raised
Communicate	They can describe their own response to the concepts
Apply	They can describe examples of how their response is or can be applied in their own lives and the lives of others

LEVEL 4	
Enquire	Pupils can explain key concepts that are common to many religions and used in the study of religion (Type B Concept) They can describe some key concepts specific to the religions studied (Type C Concept)
Contextualise	They can explain how these concepts are contextualised within the beliefs and practices of the religions studied
Evaluate	They can evaluate the concepts by explaining their value to believers and by identifying and describing some issues they raise
Communicate	They can explain a personal response to Type B concepts and describe a personal response to Type C concepts.
Apply	Explain examples of how their responses to the concepts can be applied in their own lives and the lives of others
LEVEL 5	
Enquire	Students can explain key concepts specific to the religions studied (Type C Concept)
Contextualise	They can accurately contextualise them within key beliefs and practices of the religion in which they are expressed.They can explain some connections between different concepts
Evaluate	They can evaluate the concepts by explaining their value to believers and by identifying and explaining some important issues they raise
Communicate	They can explain their own response to religious concepts
Apply	They can explain significant examples of how their response does or would affect their own lives and the lives of others.

LEVEL 6	
Enquire	Students can give more detailed explanations of a range of key concepts specific to the religions studied
Contextualise	They can accurately contextualise them within key beliefs and practices of different branches of the religion in which they are expressed, and explain connections between different concepts
Evaluate	They can evaluate the concepts by giving more detailed explanations of their value to believers and by explaining significant issues they raise
Communicate	They can explain their own response to religious concepts with a justification for their response
Apply	They can give well chosen examples of how their response would affect their own lives, those of others, and wider society
LEVEL 7	
Enquire	Students can give coherent, detailed explanations of a wider range of key concepts specific to the religions studied
Contextualise	They can accurately contextualise them within the beliefs and practices of different branches of the religion in which they are expressed. They can analyse some conceptual differences and similarities across religions. They can explain how concepts within a religion are related to one another.
Evaluate	They can evaluate the concepts by giving coherent explanations of the importance of the concepts to the lives and values of believers and by identifying and explaining issues that affect the wider society.
Communicate	They can give a coherent explanation for their own response to religious concepts with a justification.
Apply	They can apply their response by giving some evidence of how their response would affect their own lives, those of others, and wider society. Students are beginning to draw on a range of sources to appropriately present and evidence their arguments.

LEVEL 8	
Enquire	Students can interpret a wide range of key concepts specific to the religions studied
Contextualise	They can accurately contextualise them within the beliefs and practices of different branches of the religion in which they are expressed, and analyse conceptual differences and similarities within and across religions. They can give more complex explanations as to how concepts within a religion are related to one another
Evaluate	They can evaluate the concepts by justifying how and why the concepts are important to the lives and values of believers and by analysing how issues arising will affect the wider society
Communicate	They can give a detailed explanation of their own response to religious concepts with a justification for their response based upon a coherent argument
Apply	They can apply their response by giving carefully selected supportive evidence of how their response would affect their own lives, those of others, wider society and global affairs. Students are drawing on a wider range of appropriately selected sources to present and evidence their arguments (Copyright Hampshire, Portsmouth and Southampton Councils, 2004)

5

Holistic and creative learning

Clive Erricker

Introduction

This chapter draws together the analyses of Chapters 2, 3 and 4 to show the implications of holistic and creative learning and the impact this can have on children's development. First let's remind ourselves of those factors emphasised so far in relation to good RE and effective learning.

Chapter 4 presented the findings of research with children that led to the construction of a methodology for conceptual enquiry. Attention was drawn to its underlying purpose of identity formation and religious literacy through the development of skills and its capacity to enhance spiritual, moral, cultural and social, or what we can also term, overall, personal development. This built upon the analysis in Chapter 2 of the vital ingredients for good RE, which were:

- a focus on significant concepts;

- exploration of religious material;

- use of religious material that reflects diversity;

- use of religious material that may raise contentious issues;

- reflection and expression of pupils' own experiences in life;

- strategies that provide experiential learning;

- an approach that is child-centred and enables pupils to express their feelings and responses and to tell their stories within a secure environment;

- an effective balance between the two dimensions of human experience and religious experience;

■ encouragement for pupils to take a critical view of what they encounter in RE lessons.

Chapter 4 also built upon the analysis in Chapter 3 of what constitutes effective learning and what needs to be addressed to make that happen. Chapter 3 emphasised using a constructivist approach to learning that created democratic classrooms; valuing the identities of pupils, diversity and difference; fostering critical and creative thinking; and building confidence and self-esteem.

The conceptual enquiry methodology for learning and teaching in Chapter 4 is a systematic way of promoting the points made about good RE and effective learning in the chapters that preceded it. This was affirmed by the teacher comments in Chapter 4.

This chapter will focus on how the conceptual enquiry methodology can be used to best effect, and how it can go wrong, with the intention of improving your own use of it. The secret to that is to think about learning as a holistic and creative endeavour and to plan learning with that in mind, always thinking from the point of view of the learning experience of the child. This builds on and develops the points made about effective learning in Chapter 3.

It is helpful to relate this to the QCA's (now QCDA) *A Big Picture* and its three aims: successful learners, confident individuals, and responsible citizens. If children are being successful in their learning they will gain confidence; if they gain confidence they are more likely to be responsible in their participation. If these things are happening then you can be sure that the learning taking place is holistic and creative in nature.

What do we mean by holistic and creative learning?

It is easier, but less effective, to plan in parts, for example by constructing a unit of work for a particular year or time of year but not also thinking about how that will connect with previous or following units as pupils progress through key stages 1 and 2. It is easier, but less effective, to plan within a subject but not take account of learning that occurs in other parts of the curriculum. It is easier, but less effective, to plan learning on the basis of what has to be learnt (instructional learning) rather than plan for learning as enquiry. Holistic learning seeks to address these problems. Also, when planning a unit of work based on a particular cycle of learning (as introduced in Chapter 4) it is necessary to keep specific principles in mind to ensure it is fit for purpose; the principles that underpin holistic and creative learning address this issue, they are presented below.

Holistic learning

Holistic learning involves:

■ Planning for systematic pupil development within and across key stages.

- Pupils' ownership of learning and their ability to connect prior learning to what they are doing now.

- Pupils being able to connect their learning to their experience and draw on their experience to progress their learning.

- Starting with an overall vision for the development of pupils' learning based on how it will contribute to developing them as young people.

This was expressed in the purpose statement in Chapter 4, which identified: supporting pupils in developing their own coherent patterns of values and principles; supporting their spiritual, moral, social and cultural development; encouraging them to interpret and respond to a variety of concepts, beliefs and practices within religions and their own and other's cultural and life experiences; developing the capacities to interpret, evaluate and respond to differing values and beliefs through extending their thinking and analytical skills and their creative, imaginative and emotional development; and fostering mutual understanding between pupils of differing religious and cultural backgrounds.

Holistic learning also involves:

- ensuring that pedagogic design has integrity – the key aspects of the pedagogy being intimately and explicitly related to each other and the levels of attainment being clearly reflected in the intended learning outcomes of the process of conceptual enquiry, so that pupils are aware of what those outcomes involve as they carry out the enquiry;

- ensuring that learning focuses on the development of skills and capacities of pupils rather than just knowledge of content or the accumulation of information.

Creative learning

Building on the points made in Chapter 3, creative learning involves:

- High levels of pupil activity, participation and engagement.

- Enquiry-based learning that involves effective and progressive questioning.

- Using pupils' responses to progress further, deeper and more complex learning.

- Asking pupils to raise issues and solve problems for themselves.

- Requiring higher level skills and active collaboration.

This can be compared with the QCDA's new descriptions of spiritual and moral development, which have been significantly revised to link directly to children's learning and development, as a result:

> 'Spiritual development may be described as young people gaining personal insights from their experience of learning, enabling them to reflect on the significance of their learning, and to connect it profoundly, creatively and healthily to themselves, other people, society and the environment.
>
> Moral development may be described as young people gaining a sense of moral values from their experience of learning, enabling them to think and act responsibly, courageously and compassionately towards themselves, other people, society and the environment.' (QCDA, 2010)

What can go wrong and what happens when it goes right?

Here we point out certain specific hindrances that can occur when teachers change from their previous practice to conceptual enquiry as a holistic and creative process and what the effect is when you get it right. These should help you to avoid some of the pitfalls involved and aspire to the achievements possible. The statements made by teachers below, taken from Katherine Wedell's independent report, indicate ways in which teachers have adapted their practice and moved forward in thinking holistically and creatively about their pupils' learning and barriers they have had to overcome to do that.

Structure and process

Holistic and creative learning are based on a process of progression into complexity. It requires a structured approach. However, if following the structure itself is seen as the means to learning rather than the structure being the way to facilitate the process, progress in pupils' learning will not occur. When teachers start to construct cycles based on the conceptual enquiry methodology they can often follow what they consider to be the structure but not engage with the underlying process. Thus, the enquiry process is substituted with particular pieces of teaching and learning within each of the elements of the enquiry. This means that there is no continuity and progression through the cycle and the learning curve is flat. Pupils just don't get it. One reason why structure may be followed without attention to process is the desire to hold on to content or a resource that teachers like using and resisting a decisive focus on the identified concept. For example, in Katherine Wedell's report she states that 'Two teachers commented that it could be hard to give up content' (Wedell, 2009:9). She includes the following teacher comments:

> 'Year 1 were doing Badger's Parting Gifts and didn't want to give it up.' (p. 9)
> 'It felt unsafe at first because we were getting rid of content stuff that had been our bread and butter for years. Now just looking at one or two concepts was quite scary.' (p. 9)

For other teachers the transition to conceptual enquiry was more easily accomplished as they started to think in a more process-oriented way. For example:

> 'I moved some units up or down [when implementing Living Difference], so that A concepts were in Year R and Year 1 and Bs in Year 2. Concepts get more abstract in each successive year. For example, Darkness to Light with the Pascal candle builds on Changing Emotions in Year 1 and Celebrating New Life in Year R. I used Living Difference to guide this.' (p. 13)

Clearly, the transition to conceptual enquiry is easier if teachers were already focused on progression in pupil learning and child development. For example, one key stage 1 teacher commented that the concept progression in Living Difference helped to make explicit what teachers were doing unconsciously: 'Living Difference did have an effect on progression, but not consciously. The hierarchy [of concepts] helped to think things through and process things' (p. 13).

Katherine Wedell comments that 'another Key Stage 1 teacher commented that the ABC concept progression relates the level of learning to the developmental stages of the children' (p. 13).

The transition to a conceptual enquiry process also required teachers to reassess the activities pupils carried out and when they did them. As Wedell records, one key stage 1 teacher commented that the learning cycle, plus the concept, gives an RE purpose to activities. The teacher stated:

> 'I had to rethink activities, for example in Harvest. Before Living Difference the pupils wrote thank-you letters (a literacy activity). Now there is an RE focus to that activity. You use literacy but focus on the concept. This activity is now used for "apply": the difference it makes to get or send a thank-you letter. The RE concept gives purpose to the activity.' (p. 13) [In this cited example the concept in focus was 'thanking' with key stage 1 pupils].

Following the concept

Because teachers may feel unsafe with planning through concepts, but wish to retain specific content, activities and resources as the basis of planning, it is possible that following the concept throughout the cycle can be lost. If you bear in mind that planning operates at different stages this will help ensure a carefully constructed enquiry:

Stage 1. Construct the conceptual enquiry in outline: concept, intended learning outcomes, evaluative question, context and then the other elements.

Stage 2. Identify the techniques (learning activities) you will use in each element and the key questions for each element at the same time.

Stage 3. Identify the material and resources you will use in each element as the vehicles for the process of enquiry into the identified concept.

Stage 4. Audit the whole enquiry to ensure it has continuity and progression and involves using higher order skills consistent with the levels of attainment at which pupils should be working.

One analogy we have used to ensure focusing on the concept is that of a coat hanger and clothes. The significance of the analogy is:

■ That the concept (the coat hanger) provides the focus for the enquiry, without which the clothes (the knowledge) would lie in a heap on the floor; ie, the enquiry would lack any obvious purpose and the material explored would be a jumble of accumulated knowledge. We could introduce religious material but not know what to do with it apart from store it in the brain, in the same way as clothes are stored in a wardrobe.

■ That exploring the concept in isolation would have little purpose, in the same way as a coat hanger without clothes on it has no purpose. The coat hanger enhances or retains the shape of the clothes you wear; in the same way the concept enhances or makes fit for purpose the value of the material you introduce in your enquiry.

■ As a result, without the concept (the coat hanger), the purpose for which the clothes are required (to be worn) would be compromised, i.e., the purpose of the enquiry is to enhance the development of the learner in the same way as clothes are worn to enhance one's appearance.

Beyond this the analogy breaks down but its purpose is to show that the importance of conceptual enquiry is its focus on providing a structured, systematic approach to the development of children's capacities and skills in reflecting on their own beliefs and values and when engaging with religions. Lose the concept and you have lost the point.

Teachers who have embedded conceptual enquiry in their practice have commented as follows (Wedell, 2009):

'The concept is at the centre. Then you've got how you want to break the concept down. Nothing more.' (p. 11)

'Living Difference focuses on the concept. It was a big thing to get this across to staff. It was a different way of teaching.' (p. 11)

'When planning, you've got to concept-crack at the start of the cycle. Unravel what the concept fully means. Then you appreciate how the secular world understands or doesn't understand the concept. It's not all just about what this means in the religious tradition… For example Trinity as a conception of God: Incarnate God, God the Father. "Do you think that only Christians could truly understand God?" would be a question that would get to the depths of the Trinity idea and how you take into consideration other views.' (p. 12)

'You have to spend time thinking about all the different manifestations and implications of a subject; eg, Umma as the global world of Muslims regardless of colour, etc. The next stage is to think "What are the implications of that idea?" You've got to do this level of unpacking before you can set the key question and the first Communicate and Apply activity.' (p. 12)

However, when dealing with concepts such as type B and C concepts, which may take pupils beyond their world of experience, attention needs to be paid as to how this is done. For the teacher below this was not successful:

'"Umma" is the least popular unit. There are lots of complaints. It's not of the children's experience. There is scepticism amongst teachers. Some of them. A few of them. They say it's hard. The Umma label – some feel it doesn't relate to kids here. In the Umma unit we start with Enquire. We brainstorm 'community'. In Contextualise we do three Pillars in three lessons. We look at prayer mats, Eid, Hajj. There is lots of Contextualise. We think about why it's important for Muslims to participate in these activities – why/why not. What if a Muslim didn't feel part of Umma? Might there be situations where you don't want to? What communities do the children belong to? Is it important to feel part of a community? There is not a great deal of response from the children. It's not a big thing for the kids. Not much to say about it. They have little experience of community. "Belonging" in Y3 does work.' (p. 11)

Diagnosis

Here we have to diagnose what is going wrong. Clearly the teacher is not thinking holistically or creatively as to how the pupils engage with the concept. When we read her description of the problem it appears curious that the pupils and teachers found that 'belonging' worked but that both 'community' and 'umma' were ideas they could not engage with. Typically this happens when pupils are not given a grounding in understanding the concept at the beginning. What techniques did the teachers use to engage them with the concept of community? This is not clear, but asking questions without using stimulus material and situations to engage with will demand only that they identify prior learning to bring to the questions asked. This will not necessarily be enough for them to engage with the concept and understand what it involves. Similarly, if we move from a concept that should be within their experience to one that is foreign to them, such as Umma, without paying careful attention to how that is done, pupils will be equally mystified as to how to respond.

Introducing three of the pillars of Islam in three lessons in contextualise suggests that the Contextualise element may be being used to cover religious material and the concept may get lost (ie, no coat hanger on which to hang the clothes). Perhaps pupils were not encouraged to consider why aspects of the five Pillars of Islam might contribute to a sense of Umma. The Pillars of Islam are lying in a heap in the bottom of the wardrobe. What are the questions being asked to further the enquiry and what issues are being raised to create complexity? The teacher's comments suggest that perhaps the cycle is being addressed in parts, as a structure not a process, that not enough attention is being paid to the techniques that need to be used for pupil engagement and that too much attention is being paid to what the teacher thinks 'needs' to be covered in terms of religious material. The fact that there is 'lots of Contextualise' is likely to be part of the problem. Contextualise appears to be misunderstood. Overall, there seems to be a lack of holistic and creative thinking in both the planning and delivery of this cycle.

What questions do you think it would be helpful to put to the teachers to diagnose the cause(s) of this problem?

Questioning

With enquiry-based learning, questioning is a key aspect. It needs to be a progressive and intrinsic part of the enquiry. Questioning is both part of what the teacher needs to do in relation to each element of an enquiry and what we need to encourage pupils to do to progress their learning. Responding to questions is a vital aspect of pupil discussion and a way forward in ensuring enquiry is effective. For some teachers this creates uncertainty because they cannot be sure how the lesson will proceed and because their planning requires a specific outcome and specific knowledge to be included at certain points. In relation to questions being an intrinsic aspect of enquiry, teachers have responded in different ways. Here are two examples. First, one in which teachers expressed concern:

'There is still an issue of people being worried about kids asking difficult questions about religion and they don't know how to answer. For some people it's about being up there giving answers. This has always been a stumbling block for RE.' (Wedell, 2009:11)

For some teachers this is a way to stop religion being controversial, and it is likely to be one reason they favour learning about religion instead. It makes it safe. However, it negates the point of learning in relation to pupil development. Also, it has to be acknowledged at the outset that religions are potentially controversial in the sense that they present different lifestyles and behaviours and differing moral positions, as well as distinctive worldviews.

In contrast, the following teacher indicates the importance of the formulation of questions in relation to the ability of pupils and the concept in focus in achieving the learning outcomes:

'Living Difference helps you formulate key questions. You focus on the concept, and on the process that makes the kids see a problem, a controversy, two or more sides. The key question needs to reflect a dichotomy. I ask 'does the key question do justice to the concept?' The plenary is kids answering the key [evaluative] question. Living Difference made me realise that I don't have to make the question controversial for controversial's sake – maybe I used to because I had less faith in the lesson. I go for a question and make it a bit more straightforward. If the question helps the kids understand the concept in its fullest implications then it's done its job. If the question is too hard you find the cycle hasn't answered it.' (Wedell, 2009:12)

Teaching not learning

The fundamental change in adapting to an enquiry-based curriculum that promotes holistic and creative learning is thinking in terms of learning rather than teaching. For example, it is learning outcomes that are important, not teaching objectives. In this respect the level descriptors are the key element. One teacher comments:

'The learning objectives [outcomes] are tied in to how the cycle works and the levels. It took a while for teachers to twig this. 'Pupils will understand...' is not a testable learning objective. Being able to explain is a testable learning objective. That is your objective and that links in exactly with the levels.' (Wedell, 2009:15).

Another teacher makes the connection between learning progression, skills, level descriptors and pupils' ownership of learning:

'The level descriptors are based on skills. The level descriptors are clear. Therefore the pupils understand where they have come from in their work and where they are going.' (Wedell, 2009:15)

The teacher below points to the assessment levels actually being the driving force of planning for progression in learning, for herself and the pupils:

'It's good for me, the assessment side of it, because I know what I'm looking for. They know what I'm looking for, on the whole. A level now means something to them. They know the skills required to move up a level. They know, when they're being taught in a lesson, that they're progressing, because the skills are getting progressively harder.' (Wedell, 2009:15)

In her report Katherine Wedell commented that:

'Of the primary phase teachers not yet using the level descriptors, one commented that measuring progression is very difficult in RE. Another commented that it is hard to use the level descriptors because you have to be clear about the learning objectives' (2009:15).

Diagnosis

For these last teachers, quoted by Wedell in her report, the issue would appear to be fairly clear. They are not incorporating the levels of assessment into their planning but referring to them afterwards as if they are disassociated from learning. However, this may be a symptom of a deeper problem. If a teacher is thinking in terms of objectives (which are the teacher's targets, perhaps simply based on whether she has achieved what she intended in her teaching) and she is not even clear about her objectives, then she is not planning on the basis of what she wants her pupils to achieve. That makes the levels of attainment of her pupils secondary to whether she has achieved *her* outcomes. This is where the gap between teaching and learning becomes dysfunctional. It is likely that the teacher does not appropriately correlate her role with advancing the development of pupils. In this case there is no holistic or creative thinking going into the planning and delivery of her work.

What advice would you give to the teachers quoted above to solve this problem?

Progression through the elements of the cycle

In Chapter 4 we included a diagram showing the spiral nature of the curriculum to illustrate progression through key stages (see Figure 4.3 on page 74). This idea has to work at the most fundamental level also, when pupils proceed through a cycle. Each element is predicated on the learning in the preceding element. As a result, each element requires a 'step up' from the enquiry in the element before because it is built upon it. When you examine a cycle you have constructed you can test it diagnostically in this way. For example, did your pupils have to do the work you gave in Communicate in order to do Apply? Did they need to do Apply before doing Enquire? How did Enquire prepare them for Contextualise? Did Contextualise provide them with the issues required in order to Evaluate? This is directly related to assessment. One teacher has commented:

> 'Before Living Difference assessment was based on fact – recall and vocabulary recall. Now in their assessment the students show understanding of why someone does something. Living Difference has upped the ante on the level of learning – especially on Evaluation. On Contextualise it has also improved. It's not just facts, but it's what people believe and key facts that reflect those beliefs, i.e., they're picking out key facts. We're getting the kids to understand why somebody does something. As a result, assessment has gone up. Much more academic, much more rigorous. The kids are grappling with key issues. For some of the kids, their assessments have improved beyond recognition.' (Wedell, 2009:18)

Diagnosis

This teacher is very positive about the improvement in pupils' assessments. But note that previously assessment was based on 'fact and recall'. Having made a radical change to how learning functions we might still ask a question about how the teacher understands the relationship between progression, attainment and assessment. Is the teacher enthused just because assessments are more positive or does she fully understand the holistic and creative potential of the cycle of learning and conceptual enquiry? The point is not only for pupils to perform better against assessment targets but to 'attain' better, that is to demonstrate a greater holistic and creative awareness in their learning.

How would you determine whether this teacher's pupils are managing to do that? What would you look for?

Another teacher comments as follows on bringing prior learning to the next concept and links that to how assessment can be done:

'With Living Difference the pupils build their learning on transferable concepts. They bring their conceptual understanding from earlier units to bear on current learning. For example, they bring their understanding of the concept of authority in the context of sacred books to understanding the concept of authority in the context of Jesus. Learning is then as it were building a wall, not just collecting bricks.' (Wedell, 2009:23)

The teacher below makes the link between the cycle as a whole, personalised learning and greater challenge and creativity:

'Contextualise is only one fifth of the circle… you're always coming back to the children and what they think about the concept. It's easier than it would have been before, because kids can achieve even if they're not high achievers in Contextualise. Using Living Difference there is more variety of task and this flags up things pupils are good at. The five elements flag up what kids are good at. A lot of assessment is what kids say. Living Difference furthers personalised learning. This was not the case before… Living Difference has separated out the learning process. This has opened up teachers and pupils to more ways of working. The pupils do more challenging work – e.g. taking photos, using computers, making clay angels. This greater variety of ways of working has resulted in higher attainment from pupils with lower ability. It suits more children's learning styles than before. It enables kids to demonstrate achievement, capturing more kids' attainment. It is the concept which enables more varied, more creative expression. Living Difference gives scope for any creative activity.' (Wedell, 2009:23)

Two teachers quoted in the Wedell report commented that in Contextualise the students learn enquiry skills – what one teacher called the 'where, what, why, who, how questions':

'[In the Year 3 unit on angels]… "We go on to Contextualise and we're then looking at Christmas cards that have got angels on and so obviously looking at angels from the Christian point of view. And they put them into categories and again that's quite interesting because I've got loads… and they'll categorise them into angels that are playing trumpets or musical instruments, or angels that are wearing party frocks, or angels that are in a white dress, or angels that are praying… it's their ideas, I don't do any input in that at all, it's their decision. And then we go on and we look at the gospel versions of the Christmas story and where angels are mentioned… and they have to highlight all the angel bits… and then they compare the different angel bits in the different gospels, which again, they can do it, they don't have to have a lot of input from me… then we go on to evaluate the purpose of the angels in the story…'. (Wedell, 2009:6)

Progression, assessment and attainment

It is clear that for teachers to grasp conceptual enquiry as a holistic and creative process, learning, progression, assessment and attainment have to be understood as integrated aspects of that process. This has altered the way teachers think about how to assess, as one of the teachers quoted above commented. Assessment has become more manageable and purposeful for many teachers, as the following comments from Wedell (2009) show:

'One element is assessed for each unit over the year. It's easier because you've not got this big thing you're assessing. You assess just one thing. It's more explicit.' (p. 20)

'Because Living Difference is so explicit about what you're after, if you're not getting the point across, then you're not getting the higher quality work from the kids, so lower quality work evaluates the teaching. You look at [for example], is this the best activity, how useful is the vehicle for assessment (eg, discussion or sorting cards). Or, is this the best place to assess, for example, Evaluate?' (p. 19)

'Assessing enquiry and application skills: I think the problem some people have here is in the nature of how they like to assess. They like to have a bit of paper in front of them. But in some elements of Living Difference there is less writing. I still assess, through noting down on Post-It notes what children say in discussion. You can assess in other elements if you're prepared to do that.' (p. 20)

'It depends on the activity how easy it is to assess. If children write you've got more to look at. You can still note on Post-Its. There is a danger of just sampling written stuff.' (p. 20)

'With Living Difference you're not thinking 'What am I going to churn out at the end?' You think 'Actually I'm going to listen to these children and question their understanding, rather than just collect in thirty sheets of paper.' (p. 20)

These comments show that assessment is now being done selectively and with discrimination. Also, assessment is being done in different ways that relate directly to what the learning is seeking to achieve and the process being implemented in order for that achievement and subsequent attainment to happen.

Making RE meaningful

Meaningfulness is about making learning directly relevant to pupil's lives. We learn if we can immediately see the value of the learning, its impact on us. Without this, whatever we do is unlikely to result in enthusiastic pupil participation. RE has always wrestled with the problem of making religious material relevant to students' interests and the result has often been seeking to find some non-religious interest that will appeal to pupils that in some way can be related to what religious people do. How can the conceptual enquiry approach help to overcome this problem?

Two key stage 1 teachers said that the concept links pupils' experience with the religion. This enables pupils to understand religious material that is beyond their own experience. One teacher comments:

'Before, the children confused the content – e.g. Jesus and Moses. Concepts give a better way in and access to the material. Gives them a way in to something that's a little bit more tricky, that demands a little bit more understanding. Gives them a handle on it. You're not teaching it in isolation.' (Wedell, 2009:21)

Seventeen of the 20 teachers interviewed for the evaluation project explicitly commented that the students are motivated to learn in RE because they can relate the concept to their own lives. For example:

'The concept really means something to the pupils. So they are interested and keen and find the work exciting and relevant and so the quality of work goes up.' (Wedell, 2009:21)

'Living Difference helps teachers to deliver interesting RE – it's got variety and point and it's linked to kids' lives, not as a religious topic. It's not six weeks on parables and you read one every week. All of it is about how those particular concepts affect children's lives and that's what I think is good about it.' (Wedell, 2009:21)

Two key stage 1 teachers commented that the pupils can apply the concept to make connections beyond RE and so extend their learning. The teacher below identifies how a type A concept can be fully inclusive of children's experience and move beyond the traditional confines of RE:

'Because RE is concept based, the pupils can make connections beyond RE. This is the other key thing. For example, they can find many examples of "change" and think about how and why things change.' (Wedell, 2009:22)

One teacher commented that 'the students are focusing on the same concept in their own lives and in the religious material and so they identify with people from the faith communities.' (Wedell, 2009:22)

Connecting learning across the curriculum

Importantly, in seeking to achieve a holistic and creative approach to learning some teachers have identified how following the conceptual enquiry methodology takes them beyond their previous understanding of the traditional confines of religious education. In Wedell's report, six primary phase teachers commented that Living Difference has strong links with PHSE and emotional literacy work and enhances those aspects of the curriculum. Five primary phase teachers said that Living Difference provides opportunities for a wider range of activities and learning styles than they had previously used. Two teachers commented:

'I plan the Rights and Respect aspect of the curriculum as well. Rights and Respect, Every Child Matters, PSE, circle time – Living Difference has made all this more coherent. RE creeps out into everything because the concept in RE enables the pupils to make connections, it takes the learning out further than RE.' (Wedell, 2009:10)

'Elements in Living Difference provide opportunities for different types of activities that perhaps previously we wouldn't have considered under the RE banner.' (Wedell, 2009:10)

The effect of holistic and creative learning on planning, the motivation of teachers and the status of RE

Some teachers, as RE coordinators or managers, reported on the effect that conceptual enquiry had had on colleagues and perceptions of RE. Katherine Wedell records that:

'All of the primary phase interviewees provided their colleagues with long- and medium-term plans for RE, using the Living Difference format. Some of these plans came from the Handbook, some from plans developed in the development groups, and some the teachers had written themselves. Twelve of the thirteen primary phase interviewees commented that their colleagues like Living Difference because the plans are clear and focused and provide good guidance. Non-specialists can see where they are going in their RE teaching and they know what they are doing at each step. Three commented that RE is now always taught, which was not the case before LD was introduced. Five primary phase teachers said that their colleagues liked the fact that they did not have to have so much subject knowledge.' (Wedell, 2009:10)

One primary teacher reports: 'RE is never not taught. It's a high priority because of the clear format. The staff come and ask me for the RE planning' (Wedell, 2009:10–11). Another speaks of a transformation in a colleague's perceptions and the effect on the children as a result:

'At first, my colleague looked at Living Difference and said there is too much chat and not enough written work. Now my colleague loves it – it's phenomenal what we've done with the children compared to what was going on before.' (Wedell, 2009:10)

We can recognise from the comments made by teachers about the progress of their pupils and the way RE has come to be valued in their schools that this holistic and creative way of approaching the subject has a significant impact, but that not all teachers can initially see the potential. To implement this approach effectively the overall idea of what we are seeking to achieve has to be grasped. In this respect, the bike riding analogy below may be helpful.

Bike riding

One analogy we have used for this promotion of holistic and creative learning through employing the methodology for conceptual enquiry is that of bike riding up a mountain (the diagram for the hierarchy of concepts, see Figure 4.2 on page 65). To continue to ride up the mountain the learning must never go flat. If it does there will be no learning curve (no challenge presented to pupils and a consequent lack of engagement). In the elements of each cycle and across units of work (subsequent cycles) this needs to be maintained. A flat cycle is like a flat tyre – hard to keep making progress. At worst, if pupils lose any sense of the point of what they are doing then the wheels fall off (they have no further motivation). At best, the learning is accelerated and pupils engage in creative thinking, they are thinking hard, and they start doing 'wheelies' and feeling proud of themselves. For example, when the teacher says, in Wedell's report, that her 4-year old states, 'Well he had a cold heart before he met Jesus and then because Jesus loved him he had a warm one' and then, 'Because if nobody loves you, you have a cold heart', we have evidence that she has engaged with the concept, understood it within the context presented and translated it into her own understanding in an original and creative way informed by her experience. That is a 'wheelie'.

Building on prior experience and creating challenge in learning are essential to this motivation. This is the way in which pupils can gain greater conceptual awareness rather than just more knowledge and understanding.

In Figure 5.1, the difference is presented between teaching to knowledge and understanding, and learning through conceptual development. The vertical axis represents conceptual development and a consequent increase in skills. The horizontal axis represents pupils' increasing knowledge. The ideal learning curve is shown as pupils progress from year 1 to year 6, from level 1 to level 5, indicated by the skills development on the vertical axis, which mirrors the skills demanded in the levels of attainment. If pupils are taught more information (more content) without attention to skills development based on increasing skills acquisition then the learning curve will be lower even though the achievement on the horizontal axis may be equivalent. Progression has to be measured by a balance of the two, but with a primacy given to the skills required for conceptual development.

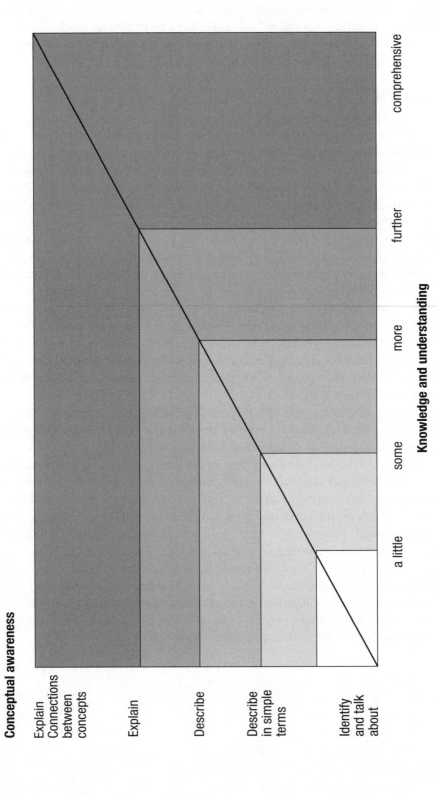

Figure 5.1 Student development

Curriculum planning within and across key stages

For planning to result in holistic and creative learning within and across key stages, attention needs to be paid to the vital ingredients for good RE, what creates effective learning and the points made that describe holistic and creative learning above. In particular, continuity and progression need careful attention in relation to:

- the complexity of the key concept employed;

- the complexity of the evaluative question;

- the complexity of the Contextualise element of the cycle.

Key stage 1

Foundation stage and year 1

In the foundation stage and in year 1 it is important that pupils can grasp the key concept in focus so that they can immediately relate it to their experience: belonging, celebrating and special(ness) are examples of concepts that can enable this connection, as was mentioned in Chapter 4. As a result of their experiential relationship with these concepts, pupils can understand better how these concepts are common to the experience of others but, nevertheless, experienced and expressed in a different way. Thus the Contextualise element may focus, respectively, on belonging to the Jewish community by attending synagogue or when a Jewish family celebrates Shabbat; celebrating Jesus' birthday and how and why Christians do that; special people that are important to them, for example the specialness of Jesus for Christians, or Guru Nanak for Sikhs.

Respectively, the evaluative questions might be:

- *Belonging*. Is it important for Jews to feel as if they belong together? If they do not go to synagogue or celebrate Shabbat would they still feel as if they belonged?

- *Celebrating*. Discuss: If someone important like the Prime Minister said 'No one can celebrate Jesus' birthday', how would Christians feel? Does it matter that Jesus can't be there (when his birthday is celebrated)?

- *Special(ness)*. Why do Christians think Jesus is special? Does it help Christians to think about Jesus being special? What if he were not special, would Christians still think about him? Why is Guru Nanak special for Sikhs? What was it about him that made him special for them?

Year 2

By year 2 the concepts will become a little more complex, for example the concepts of change, God, and remembering. Here the Contextualise element may focus, respectively, on changes to people when they met Jesus; different ways of thinking about God or Christian ideas about God's qualities; remembering Guru Gobind Singh during Baisakhi.

The respective evaluative questions may be.

- *Change*. How and why did these people change when they met Jesus? How were these changes similar or different and why? What does this tell us about how Jesus affected people's lives?

- *God*. Are Christian ideas about God important? Why might their idea of God be important to Christians? Do all Christians have the same ideas about God?

- *Remembering*. Why might it be important for Sikhs to remember the story told during Baisakhi about Guru Gobind Singh? Why might it no longer matter to some Sikhs?

When we consider the impact of the planning of this key stage 1 experience for pupils we have to ask whether it provides the right foundations for their progression into key stage 2. Were they able to talk about these concepts and were they able to respond to how these concepts are understood by others?

Key stage 2
Years 3 and 4

At key stage 2 we are seeking to build on the learning children have experienced at key stage 1 but with more challenge. In years 3–4 examples of concepts might be devotion, freedom and symbol. Here the Contextualising elements may focus, respectively, on Mahashivratri as devotion to Shiva, Passover as a way in which Jews celebrate freedom, and the empty cross as a Christian symbol.

The respective evaluative questions may be:

- *Devotion*. Which elements of the practices at Mahashivratri do you think most reflect devotion: fasting, offerings, washing or decorations? What is your opinion on devotion at Mahashivratri?

- *Freedom*. Why is freedom so important to the celebration of Passover? How important is it to celebrate Passover in order to celebrate freedom today? Is Passover more about Jewish freedom or freedom for everyone?

- *Symbol*. What is the value of the empty cross as a Christian symbol? Pupils debate on the basis of it being a symbol for resurrection or as a fashion accessory. Which is most meaningful today?

Years 5 and 6

In years 5 and 6 complexity should increase again, with attention paid to introducing more type B and some type C concepts. Examples of concepts from the three types might be interpretation (type A), prophecy (type B), Umma (type C). With Umma, the enquiry can be started with the concept of community so that pupils can then link this to Umma as a distinctive Muslim concept of community. The Contextualising element may focus, respectively, on the two gospel birth narratives and their interpretations of Jesus' birth; the Magi and the significance of their gifts in terms of what they prophesied about Jesus; the five pillars of Islam, though you may only want to select specific ones such as salat and/or hajj to indicate how the idea of Muslim community is maintained and reinforced in its practice.

The respective evaluative questions may be:

- *Interpretation*. What is the value of the different interpretations of this story for Christians? Does it matter that there are two different interpretations of this story?

- *Prophecy*. How are the gifts related to prophecies about Jesus? Would it matter if the gifts were different and why?

- *Umma*. Do you think it is important for Muslims to participate in these activities (the five pillars or selected pillars) as a member of the Umma? Why/not? Could there be a Muslim who took part in all the activities and did not feel part of Umma? How? Do you think that there might be situations when a Muslim might not want to be part of Umma? What might these be?

Points to note

The transition from one key stage to another is a traditional weakness both in RE and generally, and a lack of systematic continuity and progression results. Obviously, this can have its roots in moving from one school to another when this occurs between key stages. However, often wrong assumptions are made about pupils' prior learning when they are only based on assessing knowledge acquired as opposed to skills development and the development of the capacities of pupils. A further complicating factor occurs when pupils from different feeder schools move in to one school. Typically this is an issue when moving from key stage 2 to key stage 3 because the provision for RE at key stage 2 may be variable across different schools and there may not be any appropriate liaison between primary and secondary schools. Nevertheless, the same principles apply as with continuity and progression within a key stage and should be considered a priority for pupils' development to be effective.

Although the concepts and contexts may vary according to the religions being studied at each key stage, this should not be seen as a problem. If we return to the pupil development graph in Figure 5.1 and remember the importance of the vertical axis, then the important thing to avoid is covering too much content and too many religions such that skills development and progression are not sufficiently attended to. Pupils' development of skills enables then to engage with new material within and across key stages in an effective way.

Note that more detail on planning within and across the primary curriculum in relation to the religious traditions to be taught is provided by *Living Difference: The primary handbook* (Hampshire County Council, 2006).

In the next chapter case studies are provided to show how different schools have provided curricula that evidence continuity and progression within RE and across the curriculum using conceptual enquiry.

Community cohesion: a holistic and creative approach

In Chapters 1 and 3 reference was made to community cohesion and its relationship to identity, diversity and difference. It is possible to think of the duty to promote community cohesion as something extra that a school should attend to, but this would be to miss the point. It is also possible to think that it means telling children what their attitudes to others who are different from them should be, but this misses the point again. A school is in the business of education: that is what it is there for. So, how does the duty to promote community cohesion fit with the educational role that a school plays in society? So far we have been concerned with what makes for good education in general, and what makes for good RE in particular. In this chapter we have emphasised how learning can be holistic and creative, therefore addressing community cohesion has to be understood in this context, otherwise, like poor education, it will be ineffective.

Community cohesion and holistic and creative learning

If RE focuses upon the development of young people, for example, as stated in Chapter 4, by addressing identity formation and religious literacy, then it is bound to be laying the foundations for promoting community cohesion. To the extent that we feel confident in our identity and are able to articulate our beliefs and values, so we can involve ourselves in discussing the issues that community cohesion raises; to the extent that we know what we think and why we think it we are already in a position to address community cohesion; to the extent that, in our learning in RE, we enquire into concepts and how they may be understood and acted upon differently by others, we gain a recognition of what is entailed in recognising difference and reasons for it; to the extent that we are encouraged, in a democratic classroom, to think critically and creatively as a community, we become used to difference and how to negotiate it. Therefore, community cohesion is already being addressed within this educational process through developing the skills and capacities required within good education and the attitudes and values promoted within a democratic learning environment.

Compare the above approach to one in which RE lessons are simply learning about religions and the teaching is largely instructional and the levels of skills required of pupils was low: drawing, colouring, just writing down, just recalling information. In such a classroom the pupils are not being prepared for engaging in community cohesion. In fact what is taking place is just the opposite. However much they learn about religions it will not prepare them for engagement with difference or diversity.

Let's think of the sort of situations in which we have felt 'different' in a negative way. These will be situations in which we felt 'out of place'. Why was that? Examples include being with other people we did not know; being somewhere different for the first time (our first day at school could be one example of this); being somewhere where we feel inadequate because we don't know the rules or how to behave; being somewhere where we don't know the language people speak; being somewhere where we feel we are with people who are better than we are, for whatever reason. The effect of such experiences can be to lose confidence and want to be back somewhere where we 'feel at home'. This is perfectly understandable but we would want to think, as teachers, that we are preparing young people for dealing with these situations because they will surely encounter them, from a young age and, if we want them to achieve in life, they are likely to encounter them all the more. Therefore, when we think of community cohesion, we need to think in terms of preparing pupils for these encounters so that they are not afraid of experiencing them.

Schools sometimes ask, 'How do we address community cohesion when we are an "all white" school?' There are two problems with this perception. The first problem is reducing community cohesion to being a matter of ethnic diversity. If pupils are to be supported in their development so that they can welcome and negotiate difference then it can be found in any school. Gender differences, age differences, 'class' differences and (dis)ability differences are prevalent in most schools.

The second problem is that such schools regard their community as just the school and its children (and possibly the parents as well). As schools are being encouraged to think of children's education as taking account of the local, national and global community, community cohesion provides an opportunity to do just that.

What is striking is schools seeking to be more cohesive by eliminating as much difference as possible. We can note that this is prevalent amongst parents when exercising choice over schools for their children: oversubscribed schools tend to be ones in which it is perceived that there will be less 'difference' of the sort that will detract from their children's educational attainment. In this way, it could be argued, schools may often, ironically, hinder a wider sense of community cohesion by seeking to be more restrictively cohesive.

However, even when there is significant ethnic and religious diversity in a school this does not mean that the school will necessarily be good at promoting community cohesion. It is perfectly possible to have pupils share their different cultural differences in terms of food, music, dress, etc without addressing cohesion itself. To learn what others eat, play and wear and the festivals they have as a 'celebration of diversity' does not do much to address the values and other issues that make difference and cohesion problematic. The government language has recently changed in this respect, whereas previously 'diversity' was the only term used as a way of addressing multiculturalism we can notice the statement made by the DfES (now DCSF), also quoted in Chapter 3, that recognises there is more to be done:

'We passionately believe that it is the duty of all schools to address issues of how we live together and dealing with difference. However controversial and difficult they might sometimes seem.' (DfES, 2007:1)

The Hampshire and its Neighbours Pilot Project on community cohesion

When Hampshire Local Authority embarked on a pilot community cohesion project in 2007 it was with this question of how to deal with difference in mind. As recorded in its report:

'Headteachers began to notice and report increasing parental withdrawal of consent for their children's participation in events, especially in 2006–7. This withdrawal was especially related to visits to a local mosque in Southampton but also applied elsewhere, Sikh Gurudwaras and Hindu Mandirs. One primary school headteacher reported a 10% withdrawal rate by parents when she had previously run the visit to the mosque for several years with no parents withdrawing their children. Reasons for withdrawal could be varied but one given was that a parent was afraid of her child being bombed (there had been a recent bombing of a mosque in France). Therefore it would be wrong to conclude that it was just attitudes to Islam that were changing when the safety of offspring was also an issue.'(Hampshire County Council, 2008:1)

However, this reaction suggests both that anxiety for the safety of their children was a parental concern and that recent events and media reports had led them to think that places like mosques were suddenly unsafe. In turn, this suggests that parents, despite, for example, their children being in one primary school that had a tradition of valuing RE and visiting a mosque, had little or no knowledge of religious or ethnic groups in their local environment.

This may not be surprising if we consider the report by Sanjay Suri about his experience in Leicester, a much more religiously and ethnically diverse locality than Hampshire. As reported in Chapter 1, in one of his studies for his book *Brideless in Wembley* (Suri, 2007), Sanjay Suri parked himself on a bench in Leicester's largest mall, The Shires, to conduct a study, between 12 pm and 5 pm, concerning:

'what I dared to call myself a rough quantitative survey... I wanted to see how many came to The Shires with their ethnic own, and how many with others... the mall seemed a random enough place to see who might step out in mixed ethnic company.' (p. 23)

After five hours he concludes:

'I scanned perhaps 12,000 to 15,000 people. Through this I counted only 44 people in 12 mixed groups... Most of these mixed groups were clearly university students... If this observation was valid we were talking zero point zero zero something by way of multicultural Leicester... Leicester did not appear a multicultural city, only a city of adjacent cultures. Perhaps not even that; just variously monocultural.' (p. 25)

As noted previously, from this we might conclude that even if you live close to people who are ethnically different and share the same amenities it doesn't mean you will necessarily know anything about them. It also helps to explain why the schoolchildren's parents might have felt more informed by media reports than what was being taught in their religious education lessons. It is instructive that Suri notes that the small proportion of mixed groups were clearly university students – but why should it take going to university to bring people of different ethnicity together?

The subsequent Hampshire project's approach sought to address ways in which pupils from different backgrounds could work together and ways in which issues related to 'difference' could be addressed. In doing so it used the conceptual enquiry methodology embedded in its agreed syllabus for RE to address the concept of difference.

Of the six schools chosen to participate in this project, three were primary schools. The schools were paired to construct joint enquiries into the concept of difference as they experienced it in their lives and in relation to those differences they celebrated, were comfortable with or found challenging. Selected pupils from these schools met to carry out this enquiry, which involved creating cultural maps, questionnaires, learning walks, and research training. They were also supported in adopting the Rights, Respect and Responsibilities procedures, based on the United Nations Convention on the Rights of the Child, for the way in which they worked together. Attention was paid to ensuring that the pairings took account of diversity, especially in terms of social and cultural background and ethnicity. In the primary schools it was year 6 pupils that participated using their RE lessons to do so. The pupils' enquiries in the twinned schools developed different foci. The primary school involvement was as follows.

In the Fairfields Primary School and Costello Secondary School enquiry the main focus was the admission of new Nepalese pupils into Costello Technology College and the need for them to be socially accommodated within the school population. Pupils already in the school needed to be prepared for the arrival of the new Nepalese pupils. Since Fairfields is a multilingual school its year 6 pupils were able to work with Costello pupils in determining how best to address these issues.

In the Mount Pleasant Junior School and Kings Copse Primary School enquiry issues concerning meeting pupils from different socio-economic and ethnic backgrounds emerged and the impact of those on perceptions of identity and on pupil confidence and preparation for later life. For example, one pupil wrote: 'When I was back at (my) school I felt safe and at home' and another wrote, 'We may have differences but it doesn't mean we can't be friends.' Another said it was the scariest thing she had ever done. A strong feature of this partnership was the way in which pupils were paired across schools and the preparation for meeting up done through photographs and e-mail communication.

Findings

The schools (primary and secondary) involved presented their findings and recommendations at a conference on 27 March 2008. They are summarised below:

- that parental involvement in community cohesion would be beneficial;

- that media representation of schools and of religions can prevent cohesion amongst children and misperceptions of religion;

- that a felt lack of national identity prevents cohesion;

- that it is very easy for pupils from different schools to see each other as rivals and to initially be uncomfortable working together and make judgements based on 'race' and class. They need opportunities to share activities and experiences and to develop a project dependent on shared responsibilities and outcomes in order to enable friendships and respect to develop. For example, shared whole school days would allow for mixed team sporting and cultural activities. Working toward a shared presentation on this project increased commitment to one another;

- that the admission of new pupils of different ethnicity and mother tongue can result in tensions if pupils in the school are not prepared for this by the school.

Recommendations

- Prepare pupils for intake of new pupil admissions of minority cultural and ethnic backgrounds by educating pupils into the cultural heritage of new pupils.

- Provide a buddy system for new pupils.

- Ensure space is available for minority groups to meet together and use strategies to ensure that mixing together occurs more readily within school and class time. For example by using teamwork strategies in classroom learning.

- Support and monitor the integration of new pupils and provide opportunities for them to speak with other pupils about their cultural identity and experiences.

- Teach cohesion in and out of school.

- Address social cohesion with Years 6 and 7 as pupils transfer to a new school.

- That the Rights, Respect and Responsibility initiative should be introduced in all schools.

- Link schools with different catchments in Key Stage 2 and Key Stage 3.

- Involve parents through parent conferences/culture days. (Hampshire County Council, 2008:3–4)

Challenges and results

The pupils on the pilot project were initially hesitant about twinning with another school. It involved stepping outside their own socio-cultural space and engaging with other pupils who were clearly different in a number of ways. Secondary students were older and visiting a secondary school was bound to be a daunting experience. Visiting a different primary school with pupils who were 'all white' or 'Asian' provoked all sorts of assumptions. Two questions raised by the pupils at Mount Pleasant school, an inner-city school, about their 'all white' counterparts, were: 'Are they all Christian?' and 'Are they all posh?' The point of engaging in a community cohesion project is to break down stereotypes and cause deeper reflection on how to engage across traditional divides within society. Any work on community cohesion has to result in change. It has to make a difference, otherwise there is no point. The pupils worked together on projects with specific foci. Findings and recommendations that were to be taken seriously by their schools and the Council galvanised their efforts to succeed. It gave them responsibility to overcome the difficulties they faced and be proud of their resulting achievements. Without this, addressing community cohesion would just be a cosmetic exercise.

Further development

Since the pilot project a number of primary schools have either developed or initiated work on community cohesion. For example, in Fairfield's Primary School they were aware that only a few pupils and teachers had worked on the pilot project and they wanted to get the whole school and parents involved. To do this they undertook a number of additional initiatives, as follows:

- Working with the Hampshire Archives Service on 'memorials' linked to studying World War II in year 5, including pupils taking part in a memorial service in Basingstoke.

- Inviting older members of the community into school to share memories of World War II. This was linked with a song-writing activity.

- Inviting older community members to a tea party in school at which children spoke easily and enthusiastically with the older people.

Pupils' attitudes developed positively due to involvement with people within the community whom they might not normally meet, and participants in the project (pupils and guests) reflected on their experiences and commented on the value and importance of such activities.

Cove Junior School developed a project based on the concept of remembrance that again linked with studying World War II using memorials and artefacts from archive material. Pupils created their own memorials and reflected on feelings and responses to these memorials. This was pursued through dance, family histories, individual research projects and poetry. This resulted in a presentation for parents. They then embarked on a further project enquiring into the concept of identity and its influence on pupils with different ethnic origin in the school. This provided a case study on the Ghurkhas, who had a significant influence in the local community because of the military barracks nearby. This allowed the exploration of how and why communities change due to the different ethnic identities of members of the community. Based on issues that arose from this study, pupils were asked to recommend ways in which communities could act to ensure cohesion of diverse cultural influences.

In a questionnaire that the pupils completed there were some interesting responses. For example, in answer to the question, 'Have you been affected by racial issues?' one pupil wrote: 'Yes when I was walking alone a woman said "Go back to your own country and leave us some work".' Another said: 'Yes, when I was with my friend and we were talking and a woman said talk English you are in our country.'

Both these children are Nepalese. A non-Nepalese pupil wrote, in answer to the question, 'How have your thoughts changed as the week has progressed?': 'Before I thought that all Nepalese were bad but now I know that even though some of them are bad most are good.' In answer to the same question a Nepalese child wrote, 'A little, didn't know so [many] people were scared of us.'

In the words of the title of the Commission for Racial Equality Report, 'A lot done, a lot to do' (CRE, 2007).

Farnborough Grange Nursery and Infant School already had a cross-curricular approach embedded in the school, and its community cohesion initiative sought to build pupils' awareness of being part of a global community and having lifestyles and attitudes focused on change. They concentrated on 'Linking with philosophy for global citizenship through narratives and images, including young children's life stories' and the concept of 'transition' in liaising with a local junior school with a topic called 'conversation for change'. In this, key stage 1 pupils and key stage 2 pupils met together to share their stories.

Conclusion

This chapter has sought to show how holistic and creative learning can be achieved through the conceptual enquiry methodology. It has done so through presenting how this can be put into practice and teacher comments on planning, assessment, progression and attainment as a result. It has also shown how this can go wrong if not executed effectively. Additionally, progression was addressed within and across key stages with examples of how to introduce greater complexity into enquiries and create continuity. It has shown that it is important that community cohesion is addressed in a similar fashion to curriculum provision and that an enquiry process is used that identifies issues to be addressed and which, as a result, produces change.

We hope this chapter has shown that much can be achieved by seeking to address learning holistically and creatively in this way and that the issues such an approach reveals should be treated with real educational concern. Note also how the issues revealed in the section on community cohesion relate directly back to the comments made in Chapter 3 on community cohesion and what issues need to be addressed within and beyond the school, especially in relation to critical thinking and pupil participation. Here we can use the QCDA third aim to pose the question: 'How do we help pupils to become responsible citizens?'

6

Case studies in good practice

Judith Lowndes

Introduction

This chapter provides case studies from different schools in the primary phase to illustrate how the conceptual enquiry-based model of learning for RE informs pupils' development. The examples aim to show how the conceptual enquiry approach can be put into practice in order to promote religious literacy and confident and successful learners.

Case study 1

This case study is of an infant school in a rural location on the outskirts of a small village with approximately 170 pupils on roll. The school has an RAF base nearby and a number of pupils are from families that live on or near the airbase. There is an element of instability within the school community as a result of comings and goings of families that are stationed at the local airbase for a relatively short period of time. Some of the pupils in the school have fathers who are commissioned abroad in dangerous or threatening situations. This instability, potential fear and the sense of loss that some children experience is of concern to the staff of the school. The school aims to provide a stable and secure environment for the pupils to support pupils' sense of wellbeing and to provide positive learning experiences.

The RE manager of the school attended training in the conceptual enquiry approach to learning in RE and continued to attend a development group for RE managers. As a result she was able to evaluate and improve the provision of RE within her school and developed and implemented an RE curriculum that has considerably contributed to the emotional literacy of pupils as well as providing them with good RE, as illustrated in Chapter 2.

The curriculum planning in the school provides a unit of work for RE for every half term in each year group. The school focuses on exploring aspects of Christianity and Hinduism. The majority of concepts explored within the foundation stage and key stage 1 are type A concepts. These are concepts that are common to non-religious and religious experience. At this particular school pupils enquire into concepts such as 'remembering', 'thanking',' celebration', 'storytelling', 'change', 'special' and 'sad and happy'. Pupils in year 2 also engage with some simple type B concepts. These are concepts that are common to many religions and used in the study of religion, including 'God', 'angels' and 'the symbol of light'.

The concepts for RE learning have been located within the overall curriculum plan to make useful links with other areas of children's learning where possible. The following concepts provide some brief illustrations. For example, when children enquired into the concept of 'angels' they were able to respond to the concept whilst developing their skills and expertise in art, craft and design, looking at the work of great artists and creating their own images. Useful links were also made to learning in music as pupils explored Christian music about angels and considered and developed their own responses in music making. Pupils' enquiry into the concept of angels was enriched by the links made with their learning in understanding the arts. They had engaged with a variety of images and ideas about angels and discussed and considered what their own responses to the idea of angels might be. They were, therefore, in a more informed position to explore the two birth narratives (in the gospels of Matthew and Luke) and enquire into how the writers used the imagery of angels in the telling of the stories. Pupils were able to consider the importance of the imagery of angels at Christmas time and their significance in the nativity stories for Christians and then further reflect on their own responses to the concept. Their overall learning was reinforced by and contributed to the annual nativity play shared with parents.

It is worth making brief reference here to the traditional nativity play performed in many schools during the run up to Christmas. Participation is great fun and very popular with parents as a traditional part of the Christmas celebrations in a school. In isolation, however, it appears to have little impact on pupils' religious education. If, however, like this and many schools, the nativity play reinforces learning in RE that focuses on an enquiry into a specific concept in each year group, learning is enhanced and pupils develop a greater understanding of the significance of the nativity stories for Christians.

In this case study, 'remembering' was the concept in focus for RE when pupils explored the Hindu festival of Holi and ways in which Hindus remember Lord Vishnu during the celebrations. Within the curriculum plan of the school the concept made links for learning in RE with learning in history, in personal, social understanding and in literacy. All these areas of the curriculum contributed to pupils' holistic learning about remembering, its significance in their own and other's lives and the variety of ways in which people remember and why they remember. It is clear that there are many potential links to the history curriculum with the concept remembering. Involving children in the activity of looking back in time enables them to recognise the significance of remembering and the part it plays in people's lives. For personal and social understanding, pupils reflect on their own ways of remembering and what memories are treasured and those avoided, and emotional responses to the concept. Through speaking and listening they share their experiences with others and their points of reference are broadened and deepened. In RE pupils were enabled to explore the ways in which Hindus remember Lord Vishnu, with a greater understanding of the significance of remembering and the purpose of the festivities of Holi.

'Storytelling' was a particularly useful concept in RE to develop links with literacy. Storytelling plays such an important role within the foundation stage and key stage 1 as children explore what a story is, how it is structured and how stories convey meaning. The concept enabled pupils to explore the notion of Jesus as a teller of stories of great significance to Christians.

'Special' was a concept used within the context of special places, and learning included a local study that was part of geographical understanding. For RE the pupils considered which special places were parts of their own experience and how their own special places affected them when they went there and how they felt about them. They considered what constituted a special place and what characteristics it might have. They visited the local Church as part of the geography curriculum local study exploration of the village as a special place for Christians. What made the Church a special place for Christians? This activity contributed to pupils' understanding of the development of the local environment and their sense of place within a geographical context. Here the RE and geography curriculum were mutually supportive and a local visit enriched the pupils' experience and enhanced learning. The school also hoped to visit a Hindu temple to illustrate a special place for Hindus, but distance and travelling costs were prohibitive. Teachers have provided the pupils with virtual tours of Hindu temples as an alternative and recreated a Hindu Temple in the home corner. They then considered the value of these special places for Christians and Hindus.

The concept 'change' is one with potential links to other areas of learning. The school developed children's exploration of the concept through their learning in scientific understanding about changing materials. Part of their learning was to carry out experiments like changing bread into toast or watching jelly change from a solid to a liquid. They also consider change within their personal and social understanding, reflecting on how change can affect them, their lifestyles and their moods and emotions. Useful links are also made to learning in literacy, with a focus in this particular school on encouraging speaking and listening, which had been a skill in need of improvement. For RE the concept of change was contextualised within a unit of work called 'People Jesus Met', which focused on the Christian belief that Jesus had the ability to change people's lives. It is clear how these areas of learning are mutually supportive. As pupils explore change they develop an understanding of the wide variety of ways in which the concept can be interpreted. This helps pupils on a linguistic and philosophical level and enriches their understanding of how change affects themselves and other people and has impact on their lives. This in turn supports their learning about the Christian perception that Jesus could change people's lives.

It would be useful here to look more closely at the unit of work on the concept 'change' for it illustrates how the conceptual enquiry approach to learning benefited the children in this particular school. Learning in RE in the school follows the cycle of learning exemplified in Chapter 4, and the unit of work on the concept change was explored as follows.

Enquire

The pupils discussed in small groups what they thought the word 'change' means and what they thought about when they heard the word. Ideas were fed back to the teacher. For some pupils their responses were very simple and they thought about loose coins in their pockets as change, or what they do when getting ready for PE by changing into shorts and T-shirts. This is where learning was extended and developed over the next few days within science and personal and social education. Pupils' understanding of the concept developed. Pupils in small groups were then given large sheets of paper and discussed and wrote down what they thought the word 'change' means and what they thought about when they thought of change. Discussions within and between groups developed pupils' initial interpretation of the concept. Through careful questioning the teacher was able to challenge and refine pupils' thinking and enable them to develop their speaking and listening skills and articulate their ideas.

Contextualise

Within this area of learning the concept was contextualised within Christianity. On consecutive afternoons the teacher introduced several stories about people who met Jesus and whose lives changed as a result. These included the story of Zacchaeus, the tax collector, the story of the fishermen who became disciples, and the story of Jairus' daughter. Pupils became engaged in the stories through role play and through sequencing pictures. Attention was drawn to the concept change through the teacher's questioning and through the pupils identifying the point in the story when the person who met Jesus changed, in what way they changed and what caused the changes. A simple task was given to draw and annotate the person who changed in the story and to describe simply how they changed.

Evaluate

Within this element pupils are required to consider the value of the concept to believers. Pupils were encouraged to consider what the value or importance of change in the stories might be for Christians. The teacher retold each story briefly and added, 'What if Zacchaeus had stayed mean and greedy and had not changed at all? Would Christians still remember the story? What would they think about Jesus if Zacchaeus had not changed?' Similarly she asked, "What if the fishermen had said to Jesus, "No we don't want to come with you and be fishers of men. We don't want to change. We want to carry on fishing." Would Christians remember the story if that had been the ending? Why? Why not? What would Christians think about Jesus if nothing had changed?' In the same way she asked about the story of Jairus' daughter: 'What if Jairus' daughter had not got better and sat up? What if she had stayed lying down and nothing had changed in the story? Would the story still be important to Christians? Why? Why not? Is it important for Christians to think that Jesus could change things? Why? Why not?' Through this line of questioning pupils were encouraged to consider the value of Jesus' ability to change people's lives in the story, for Christians. Responses from pupils working on this unit are interesting. Remarks are often along the following lines: 'If Jesus couldn't change people they wouldn't think much of him.' 'They would think he was just ordinary if nothing changed.' 'They wanted him to make things better.' 'They thought he was special.' 'My gran says Jesus can make things better.'

Pupils were then provided with a picture of a Christian in Church and a speech bubble which stated, 'These stories about Jesus changing people are important to Christians because…' and pupils were asked to complete the speech bubble. Discussion followed about pupils' own evaluative responses to the change that took place in the stories. Did they think the stories about change were useful, helpful or important? Why or why not?

Communicate

In this element of the cycle pupils engaged in reflecting on their own experiences of change and their responses to change. Because a number of the pupils had experienced considerable change, this was a particularly relevant concept which resonated with their own experience. Pupils were able to share their feelings and anxieties about changes that take place in their lives that they are not able to control, and recognised and were comforted that others felt as they did. They were also able to consider how changes are frequently positive experiences and they shared their ideas about changes that were enriching or marked an achievement. Pupils were able to express their responses through pictures, simple poems or role play.

Apply

During the same day pupils were encouraged to consider how change affects their and others' lives. In group discussion pupils were asked to consider and list changes that they considered to be good and changes that they thought were bad. This was particularly beneficial in providing opportunities to develop speaking and listening skills and the philosophical approach challenged pupils to be critical and analytical when they recognised that others can have entirely different reactions to the same experiences of change. This was followed by discussions about whether the changes lasted for a long time or were followed by other changes. Will things always change?

Staff in the school found the conceptual enquiry approach to teaching and learning to have a positive impact on their pupils. The concepts identified within the RE curriculum had particular interest and significance for the children and their enthusiasm for learning increased as a result. The focus on the concept throughout each cycle of learning enabled pupils to recognise the significance of the concept within their own lives and the importance of it within the lives of religious believers. Staff felt that the approach enriched pupils' experience, improved their thinking, speaking and listening and for some units, such as change, remembering or happy and sad, provided opportunities for pupils to make more sense of their feelings and responses in difficult circumstances. The RE manager recognises the benefits of the conceptual enquiry approach and commented on the impact on pupils' learning. The feeling was that if the pupils had explored the stories about people Jesus met in isolation and without a concept with which to underpin the stories, the experience would have had little impact and be of no significance for the pupils.

Case study 2

Case study 2 features a primary school in a residential area, near a large city, with approximately 400 children on roll. The RE manager attended training on introducing the conceptual enquiry approach to learning and implemented the approach for RE across the whole school. A substantial number of the pupils are bright, confident, articulate and high achievers. The school aims to challenge pupils and extend the more able by providing a stimulating and exciting curriculum with a focus on active learning and first-hand experiences. The school is a voluntary controlled Church of England school and the RE curriculum plan ensures that units of work offer opportunities to explore aspects of Christianity and aspects of the other religions being studied within each key stage.

Within the foundation stage concepts are linked with early learning goals and pupils explore simple type A concepts such as 'special' and 'celebration'. For both key stage 1 and 2 a unit of work for RE is identified each half term. Key stage 1 pupils are introduced to type A concepts (concepts that are common to religious and non-religious people's experience) including 'teaching', 'belonging', 'community' and 'special'. Key stage 2 pupils are introduced to more challenging type A concepts such as 'freedom' and 'suffering' but they explore a number of type B concepts (that are common to many religions and used in the study of religion) such as 'sacred', 'holy', 'worship' and 'pilgrimage'. Older pupils are introduced to a few type C concepts (concepts that are specific to particular religions) such as 'resurrection' and 'incarnation'.

Members of staff have been inspired by the conceptual enquiry approach to RE and have recognised its potential for making learning more enriching in RE as well as other curriculum areas. The cycle of learning, as illustrated in Chapter 4, is shared with pupils so that they know the purpose of their activities and how their learning is progressing. They recognise that enquiry into the concept is at the heart of their learning experiences for RE and are able to explain to others how their understanding is developing. This is very empowering for them, particularly in this school where a large number of pupils are bright and articulate and they benefit from the challenge of having ownership of their learning. The following areas of learning provide a summary of the pupils' enquiry into the concept of 'pilgrimage'. This unit of work was developed by a talented teacher of a year 6 class who drew together learning in history, RE, literacy and aspects of personal and social understanding and provided some memorable experiential learning for her pupils.

Enquire

The enquire element of the cycle of learning used by the school requires pupils to interrogate the meaning of the concept. Although pupils were able to explain the meaning of a journey and the different forms a journey might take, their initial interpretations of pilgrimage were limited. The class teacher, therefore, provided an activity that enabled the pupils to role play a pilgrimage as part of their learning in history and through that experience they were able to fully engage with some historic details about pilgrims and their activities and encounter the significance of particular journeys for pilgrims. As a result they had a better understanding of the concept.

Through learning in history, pupils investigated the activities of medieval pilgrims and the purposes of their pilgrimages. The school arranged for pupils to visit a local place of pilgrimage and pupils, dressed in appropriate historical costumes, participated in a role play following the pilgrims' route and some of the activities at the appropriate sites. Pupils' learning was engaging, exciting and memorable and their understanding of the meaning of pilgrimage was extended and developed. Pupils were able to talk about a pilgrimage as a spiritual journey about which pilgrims might have a variety of emotional responses.

For literacy pupils investigated pilgrim poetry and prayers with a focus on the emotions and sentiments conveyed. They explored the language used to express those sentiments, developing their own poetry as a result.

Contextualise

Pupils in years 5 and 6 investigate aspects of Islam and Christianity in this case study school. The concept pilgrimage provided good opportunities to investigate the Hajj, the Muslim pilgrimage to Makkah. Through research into websites and books pupils investigated the activities in which Muslims participate during the Hajj and its significance for Muslims. The class teacher sought to find a Muslim visitor to speak to pupils about the Hajj and to answer questions. Pupils were engaged in a number of activities to reinforce their learning including writing postcards from an imaginary Hajji explaining his or her activities, duties and feelings during the Hajj.

Evaluate

The investigations into the Hajj in relation to pupil's previous learning about the significance of pilgrimage for medieval Christians enabled pupils to reflect on, discuss and speculate about the value of pilgrimage to Muslims. Pupils were encouraged to consider the variety of motivating factors for a Muslim to participate in the Hajj and the value of Hajj to believers. They were also encouraged to consider and express their own opinions about the pilgrimage to Makkah and what impact it has on Muslims and non-Muslims worldwide. They recognised that the Hajj can raise many issues of concern for Muslims and non-Muslims and were able to discuss potential positive and negative effects of a pilgrimage.

Communicate

Within this element of learning pupils are encouraged to consider their own responses to the concept. The teacher saw the opportunity to make links to social development and wellbeing and drew attention to events and changes in the pupils' lives so far and anxieties and fears that they may have about their future lives. Discussion in the class led pupils to consider their own and others' lives in terms of a metaphorical journey and they considered events that had already taken place that had particular impact on them, and those that they might anticipate in the future. Could the journey through life be likened to a pilgrimage? Why or why not? The teacher provided carefully chosen, thought-provoking literature to promote discussion. Pupils went on to consider what events in life might generate the wish for or the development of a pilgrimage.

Apply

This element of learning developed directly and seamlessly from the previous discussions. Pupils were encouraged to consider, in the light of all that they had learnt, how pilgrimage might affect their and others' lives. Did they consider pilgrimage to be a natural human drive for spiritual or emotional growth or does pilgrimage have little purpose in today's lifestyles?

This case study illustrates that pupils were fully engaged with their learning. It was challenging and thought-provoking and enabled the pupils to engage with the concept at their own levels of ability. Lessons were not focused on acquisition of knowledge, but encouraged pupils to take a critical and analytical view of pilgrimage and to develop a philosophical understanding of the concept and its impact on people in history and in today's world.

Case study 3

This case study introduces an infant school in an inner city. There are approximately 180 children on roll with small but growing numbers of pupils from a variety of faith and cultural backgrounds including Sikhism, Islam, Christianity and Hinduism. Some children are from families who are agnostic or atheist. The school is in a good position to develop RE and cultural education because of the rich diversity of beliefs, religions and cultures represented. There were concerns among the staff, however, about the racism in the community, and for some teachers, teaching about religion caused anxieties. They feared provoking disapproval from parents. This might be through unintentionally misrepresenting a belief or practice or by exploring religious beliefs or practices to which the parents did not wish their children exposed. In the past the RE tended to be 'light touch' with a focus on religious stories, the major Christian festivals and celebrations of other major festivals within the community such as Diwali and Eid.

A newly qualified teacher who is a religious education specialist was appointed to the school. Before long she had attended training in the conceptual enquiry approach to RE and was attending RE development groups in order to develop a curriculum plan for RE and implement it within her school. Foundation stage pupils explore simple type A concepts (concepts that are common to religious and non-religious experience) such as 'celebrating', 'remembering' and 'special'. These are linked to early learning goals where possible.

Within key stage 1 pupils explore type A concepts such as 'thanking', 'power', 'welcoming' and 'change'. They are also introduced to some type B concepts (concepts that are common to many religions and used in the study of religion) such as 'angels', 'symbol', 'ritual' and 'God'. These concepts are contextualised within learning about aspects of Christianity and Hinduism throughout the foundation stage and key stage 1. The cycle of learning also enables pupils to reflect on, contribute and discuss references to other beliefs represented in the class. In year 2, for example, pupils enquire into some Christian and Hindu interpretations of God. As well as Christian and Hindu children being involved, pupils from Muslim, atheist, Sikh and agnostic backgrounds are able to make their contributions and enrich the learning experiences of the class. Pupils, teachers and parents recognise that the enquiry is into the concept or idea of a God and how people interpret that idea in a variety of ways. Pupils are encouraged to engage in a philosophical debate, at a simple level, about the concept of God. Teachers and parents have been amazed at the sophisticated level of thinking and the children's abilities to articulate their responses and ideas as a result of the conceptual enquiry approach.

It will be useful to illustrate how learning can be developed with a year 2 class with a focus on the concept of 'God', as it was in the case study school.

Enquire

Pupils are posed the question: 'What do different people think about the idea of a God?' to lead the enquiry. On a large sheet of paper for each small group, children are encouraged to talk about and write down their responses to the question, and any words or phrases that are sparked by it. The teacher then collates the children's ideas and promotes further discussion by challenging children further with questions such as: 'That is a very interesting idea, does anyone have the same idea?'; 'Who thinks something different?'; 'Does anyone want to ask John or Jane about that idea?'; 'What do you think of that idea?'; 'Do you agree with what was just said?'; 'Why/Why not?'; 'Where did your idea come from?'; 'Do you think lots of people have that idea?'

Contextualise

The enquiry leads on to children contextualising the concept within Christianity and Hinduism. The children initially learnt about some Christian views about God. In the case study school teachers do their best to find appropriate visitors to talk to pupils. A woman vicar was skilled in speaking to young children and was able to talk about some Christian beliefs about the nature of God. Christian descriptions of God such as Heavenly Father, Almighty, Lord of all, Love Divine, Maker of Heaven and Earth and so on can be selected from Christian prayers and hymns. Pupils can hunt through the phrases and identify and highlight the descriptions they find for discussions in class. To enhance learning pupils are encouraged to consider how the Christian descriptions of God might be illustrated. How might Christians visualise God as a 'Heavenly Father' or 'Maker of Heaven and Earth', for example? This activity challenges pupils to focus on the meaning of a particular description and to analyse that description, within the capabilities of a 6- or 7-year old, and to interpret that description visually. Children really enjoy this activity and rise to the challenge. The demands on their learning are far beyond basic recall and require higher order thinking skills of analysis and interpretation. The display of children's work provides further opportunities for reflection and expression of responses. 'Do you think Tim's illustration of "Almighty God" would be a helpful one for Christians?'; 'Why do you think Sandy's picture of Almighty God is so different?'; 'Which picture do you think would be most useful to Christians?'; 'Why do you think that?' and so on. At this point in the cycle of learning pupils are moving towards the evaluate aspect of learning.

Evaluate

Within this section pupils are encouraged to consider the value of the Christian perceptions of God for Christians themselves. Again, it is helpful for pupils to ask questions of a Christian visitor at this point. Children from Christian families can provide some useful insights but teachers often wish to maintain children's privacy and avoid any direct questioning, allowing the children to freely volunteer any contributions. Another useful activity is to provide the descriptions already identified (Almighty, Heavenly Father, Maker of Heaven and Earth, Love Divine, etc) and some unlikely descriptions (such as weak, unkind, spindly, etc). The descriptions are on cards and pupils decide which descriptions are most realistic and of value for Christians. The pupils then talk about why they consider some descriptions are more important to Christians and how the ideas about God might help them. Pupils' responses can be very thoughtful, such as, 'If Christians think that God is the Maker of Heaven and Earth, that means that they believe he is so powerful he could make anything happen' And, 'If Christians think that God is Love, then there could be so much love that it gets rid of all the bad things in the world.'

Contextualise

The teacher returned to the Contextualise element in the cycle of learning at this point to enquire into some of the ways that Hindus interpret the concept of God. To convey the Hindu idea of one divine being and many manifestations, the teacher asked pupils to consider someone important in their lives and draw a simple picture of them showing something they are good at. Examples of pupils' pictures include, 'Granny holding a frying pan because she is a good cook', 'Dad singing because he has a good voice', 'Mum holding a bandage because she is like a nurse when I feel ill.' Pupils were then asked to draw the same person a few more times showing other talents. Pupils compared and discussed each other's pictures. Attention was drawn to the idea that each child's pictures depicted the same person, and their various skills and strengths.

The teacher then distributed images of some Hindu deities such as Laksmi, Krishna and Rama and pupils were asked to discuss what they thought their particular strengths might be. Pupils remark that Laksmi is sprinkling coins and that she looks as if she is kind and generous. Rama is carrying a bow and arrows and looks as if he is a good fighter, but he also looks brave. Krishna looks as if he is good at music. He looks as if he is very kind and the cow seems to like him. The teacher is then in a position to identify a parallel between pupils' drawings of one person and many talents and the Hindu view of one divine being and many manifestations.

A few Hindu stories were explored to illustrate the characteristics of some of the deities. A Hindu storyteller visited the school and this presented opportunities for literacy work and drama, music and dance to reinforce the characteristics of the deities.

Evaluate

Pupils were encouraged to consider the value of the Hindu interpretations of God, in the same way as they were within the context of Christianity. 'Why was the idea of God as a generous, kind female important for Hindus, or a brave fighter, or a kind flute player?;' 'In what ways might that be of help to Hindus?'; 'How would that idea make them feel?' With the experiences of the imagery and stories, pupils were in a position to speculate about the value of Hindu deities for Hindus. 'If God is like Rama and is kind and brave and strong, then Hindus would think that he can protect them against bad things.'

Communicate

With the richness of the exploration up to this point, pupils are in a position to reflect on and consider their own responses to the concept. What do they now think about the idea of a God? Within this case study school, teachers were careful to present the concept without any bias or assumption about the existence of God. Pupils were encouraged to express their own ideas and listen respectfully to the responses of others. Here were opportunities for pupils to formulate their own developing ideas in the light of what they have learnt at home and the exploration within school. Some pupils wrote metaphors for their ideas about God and others wanted to draw or paint pictures. (The latter activity was omitted for Muslim and Sikh pupils.)

Apply

Within this element of the cycle pupils are encouraged to consider how their response to the concept applies to their lives. Children were asked to consider what affect their responses to ideas about God made in their lives and in other people's lives? When did people think about God? Did people think about God when they were happy, when they were scared, when they were sad? Why? The teacher posed questions and pupils discussed their responses with a partner and then completed a simple writing frame.

Although not instantly dispelled, the anxieties that teachers expressed about the teaching of RE within a multicultural/multi-faith school soon dissipated. As teachers observed the level of pupils' engagement with the concepts and pupils' developing thinking and reasoning skills, they recognised the benefits of the concept-led enquiry approach to learning. The approach has provoked no anxieties from parents and many have remarked on their children's high level of discussion when they come home.

The RE manager continues to support the teachers in terms of providing useful resources and reliable information. She has also implemented a regular pattern of monitoring and evaluating pupils' development in RE through pupil conferencing and sampling pupils' work. Many pupils' attainment in RE is above expectations. This information is shared and discussed with teachers, providing them with encouraging feedback and greater confidence, and RE continues to be a high profile subject in the school.

Case study 4

This school is a junior school on the outskirts of a small market town. The intake is largely from white, middle-class families with very few ethnic minorities represented. The RE manager is a long-standing and well-respected practitioner with a good deal of experience and enthusiasm for the subject. She attended training for implementing the conceptual enquiry approach very soon after its launch through the locally agreed syllabus, Living Difference. She developed schemes of work for the school with a focus on a range of concepts including more challenging type A concepts (concepts that are common to religious and non-religious experience) such as 'community' and 'interpretation'. She also introduced a number of type B concepts (concepts that are common to many religions and used in the study of religion) such as 'holy', 'angels' and 'worship'. With year 6 pupils she has introduced some type C concepts (concepts that are specific to particular religions) such as 'dukkha' from Buddhism and 'resurrection' from Christianity. The religions covered in the RE curriculum are Christianity, Judaism and Buddhism.

Initially, when the agreed syllabus was implemented in the school, all subjects were taught separately with their own particular foci and programmes of study. RE was also planned in this way. Since then the curriculum has developed and links between subjects have been sought and exploited as teachers have felt more confident with identifying and creating common areas of exploration to aid pupils' learning. The RE manager has been diligent in improving the provision for RE in the school and, together with teachers in year group discussions, they have started to develop links, where appropriate, with RE and other areas of the curriculum. Effective connections have so far been identified with English and communication, historical, geographical and social development and the arts.

The RE manager provides strong leadership for the subject and has been effective in ensuring that RE maintains a high profile within the curriculum. She achieved this through organising staff meetings and training sessions, through displaying pupils' RE work around the school, through discussions with teachers about RE planning at formal and informal meetings and through regular monitoring of pupils' attainment in RE.

Teachers ensure that the key concept in each unit of work is at the centre of learning. They use a range of stimuli to engage pupils including images, religious artefacts, texts, visits and visitors. Many of the teachers are particularly skilled in the questioning techniques they employ to encourage pupils to be more philosophical about each concept in focus. Pupils are frequently encouraged to discuss ideas and responses in pairs and small groups and then to feed back issues openly as a class. Teachers often provoke pupils to think more deeply by providing a challenging question.

Here is an example of effective questioning within a unit about the Jewish festival of Passover. This unit of work was explored with a year 3 class. Pupils were discussing the concept of freedom and what it means as part of the Enquire element in the cycle of learning. This was the initial session for the unit of work. Pupils had been given a variety of pictures and images and were asked to discuss in small groups whether they thought the picture they had been given represented freedom or restriction. Pupils discussed their images in small groups and then shared their responses with the rest of the class. The teacher challenged pupils with questions such as: 'That is really interesting. Can you explain to us why you think that?' and, 'Does anyone agree with that idea?'; 'Does anyone think something different about this picture?'; 'Do you know where that idea came from?'; 'Does anyone want to ask this group anything about this picture?'

Teachers then asked pupils why they thought that they were exploring the idea of freedom. Responses were along the following lines:

Pupil: 'I think freedom is really important. It would be horrible being stuck in prison and not being able to do stuff.'
Teacher: 'Does that mean that everyone who is not in prison is free then?'
Pupil: 'No, there are some countries where people aren't free to say what they want or do what they want as well.'
Teacher: 'Can anyone say more about that idea?'

Discussion continued about different restrictions that can inhibit freedom with contributions from many of the pupils. The teacher asked: 'Are you saying that freedom is a good thing then?' A number of pupils said that they think it is good and the teacher asked them to explain why. Responses included:

'It makes you feel happy if you can do what you want and go where you want.'
'If you have freedom you can do a job you want and go out with your friends.'

'If you have freedom you can get a good job and make money and that's important to make you feel good.'

'People shouldn't restrict you. It's not their business. You would feel frustrated if you weren't free.'

Teacher: 'That's interesting. Now think about this. Put your hand up if you think that everyone should be allowed freedom.' A sea of hands went up.

Teacher: 'Do you think it is important to have freedom if you are 3 years old?' A hush descended on the classroom as the children then considered this new dimension that they had not thought of before. Pupils then started to contribute their thoughts about how freedom could be dangerous in different circumstances. The discussion continued at some length and included ideas such as: 'If some people express their freedom it might get in the way of another person's freedom' and, 'Perhaps complete freedom is not so good. Everybody needs rules and laws to stop them doing bad things.'

An observer of this particular lesson commented that they had not thought it possible for young children to think so deeply and articulate such sophisticated thoughts about a concept.

The RE manager of this school was keen to discover what effect the conceptual enquiry approach had on pupils' opinions about their learning in RE and their level of enthusiasm for the subject. The methodology had been implemented in the school for four years, so the year 6 pupils had experienced this approach to RE throughout their time in the junior school. She prepared a questionnaire for year 6 pupils to enable her to conduct an audit on their experiences of RE within the school:

1. Can you give your comments on the memorable RE moments from each year you have been in the junior school? Why were they memorable?
2. What do you understand about the concept of _____?
3. What do you know about some of the key beliefs of Buddhists/ Christians/ Jews?
4. Has anything you have learnt changed your views about a concept or an issue, or been particularly helpful to you?
5. What would you change/keep the same if you were starting in year 3 again?

The findings were very positive. The large majority of pupils enjoyed RE lessons and found them interesting and some said exciting. They felt that particular benefits to learning were the visits and visitors and the activities that they engaged with in class, and a number identified drama and role play. They made particular comments about how they had to 'think hard' in RE lessons and how RE lessons gave them a chance to think about things that affected them in their lives, but also were important to other people. Many particularly liked RE lessons because they 'give us an opportunity to say what we think and to listen to other people's ideas' And, 'RE sometimes makes you think about things and your ideas develop and change.'

Conclusion

In this chapter four case studies have been presented to illustrate some of the benefits that the conceptual enquiry approach to RE has had on pupils and their learning. The following questions should enable you to reflect on or discuss some issues that emerge from these case studies:

- What do you think is the most significant impact that the conceptual enquiry approach has had on creating confident and successful learners in these case study schools?

- What do you think has contributed to successful implementation of the conceptual enquiry approach in these schools?

- What qualities do you think an RE manager would need to implement the approach?

- Do you think there are any schools where this approach could not be implemented successfully? If so, what characteristics would those schools have and how might they be overcome?

- What impact do you think conceptual enquiry can have across the primary curriculum?

Transforming your practice

7

Creating an enquiry-based curriculum

Judith Lowndes

Introduction

In this chapter we provide some guidance on how to plan and deliver effective conceptual enquiry-based learning. The focus is on religious education, but there will also be guidance on how links can be made between and across RE and other areas of learning to enable learning to be more holistic and creative, as described in Chapter 5. There is guidance on how to construct useful and accessible planning and how that relates to worthwhile assessment procedures. Strategies and suggestions are supplied to enable RE managers (or coordinators or subject leaders) to implement the conceptual enquiry approach to RE across the whole school so that good quality provision of RE within the school is sustained and has real impact on pupils' learning. Within that context is guidance about effective questioning and how to achieve meaningful pupil participation in religious education activities.

Staff training

There is now a consensus among subject leaders that the overarching role of a subject manager is to raise and maintain standards in the subject and to support the teaching and learning in the school in order to achieve this. With this in mind, and assuming that the conceptual enquiry approach that this book advocates is one that you would wish to pursue, a priority for an RE manager is to support staff in the full implementation of the conceptual enquiry approach with a conviction amongst staff that it improves pupils' learning and attainment.

In our experience, this approach has provided the greatest impact on transforming RE teaching and learning in schools. When class teachers have, a) a full understanding of the purpose of the conceptual enquiry approach, and b) familiarity with the process involved, the RE curriculum takes off. The two are essential and integral to each other. Purpose without a process can lead to pupils engaging in a range of activities that can be disparate and lack a flow of progression in learning. Process without purpose happens when teaching staff are being compliant with the methodology, the cycle of learning, but have not engaged with or embraced the purpose of the conceptual enquiry approach. As a result, pupils can miss the point of their learning and they can participate in RE lessons without ever engaging with and scrutinising the concept that should be at the focus. This issue was discussed in Chapter 5.

A priority for RE managers, therefore, is to discuss the purpose of the conceptual enquiry approach with staff and enable them to interrogate it, reflect on it, and consider its implications for pupils. For some staff, the shift to an emphasis on conceptual enquiry and a move away from an emphasis on acquisition of knowledge is a big change and can cause initial anxiety. This issue has been discussed in earlier chapters. Some teachers may feel that they are in safe territory if they concentrate on acquisition of knowledge. Contentious issues don't arise, penetrating questions are rarely asked and basic recall is the skill that is developed. This might be comfortable, but it provides low level learning and lacks rigour. The conceptual enquiry approach demands higher order thinking skills and pupils find it engaging, worthwhile and meaningful. Once the conceptual enquiry approach has been explored with pupils, teachers are quickly convinced of the benefits for pupils. Chapters 4 and 5 make references to some of the feedback from teachers who have embraced the methodology with their pupils and recognise its success, as identified in the Wedell report (Wedell, 2009).

The following structure might be useful for staff training:

1. Share the pyramid diagram (Figure 4.2; see page 65) with staff and explain the three categories of different types of concepts.

2. Distribute lists or some cards of some different types of concepts for staff to discuss in pairs and decide in which category they each fit. Do all staff agree on the categories in which those concepts have been placed? Discuss their reasons for categorising them in the way that they have.

3. Discuss which concepts they consider would be accessible to different age ranges/abilities within the primary phase and whether some concepts might be best left until secondary phase.

4. Share the diagram that illustrates the methodology/cycle of learning (Figure 4.1; see page 63) explaining each of the five elements and what they are designed to achieve in relation to the key concept identified.

5. Illustrate how the five elements are applied to a unit of work by running through an example (see the examples given in Chapters 4 and 5) ensuring that staff recognise how the concept is the focus for learning throughout the cycle.

6. Staff can discuss what they consider might be the advantages or disadvantages of the approach.

7.   Provide some examples of units of work (again see Chapters 4 and 5) for teachers to try out with their pupils, arranging for a future date to share feedback and pupils' samples of work from a unit that has been taught and to discuss any issues that arise.

Developing units of work across a key stage: long-term planning

Religious education must be taught according to the requirements of a locally agreed syllabus. RE managers should ensure that they are familiar with the requirements of the agreed syllabus of their local authority. If they wish to apply the conceptual enquiry model that this book recommends, they should consider how concepts and the methodology/cycle of learning can best be applied to those requirements.

An issue to decide upon is which religions, alongside Christianity, will be explored. Some agreed syllabuses recommend particular religions for particular year groups or key stages, while others allow more flexibility. The decision the school makes, if the syllabus allows a choice, can be determined by the religious groups represented in the school and the local area. It is beneficial for the RE curriculum to reflect the interests of the local or nearby communities of which the pupils are part or to which you can make visits. This issue is highlighted in terms of RE's contribution to community cohesion in the non-statutory guidance produced by the DCSF (Department for Children, Schools and Families, 2009) entitled *Religious Education in English Schools: Non-statutory guidance*. It reads:

'Effective RE will promote community cohesion at each of the four levels outlined in DCSF guidance:

■   the school community – RE provides a positive context within which the diversity of cultures, beliefs and values within the school community can be celebrated and explored;

■   the community within which the school is located – RE provides opportunities to investigate the patterns of diversity of religion and belief within the local area and it is an important context within which links can be forged with different religious and non-religious belief groups in the local community;' (p. 15)

Teachers also need to consider which religions are being taught within the adjacent key stage or stages to ensure that pupils have access to a range of religions and belief systems as they progress through the primary and secondary phase. It is helpful to note at this point that the DCSF guidance goes on to make reference to ways in which RE can contribute to pupils' engagement with the community of the UK and the global community:

- 'the UK community – a major focus of RE is the study of the diversity of religion and belief which exists with the UK and how this diversity influences national life; and

- the global community – RE involves the study of matters of global significance recognising the diversity of religion and belief and its impact on world issues.' (DCSF, 2009:15)

To maintain coherence in pupils' learning, however, agreed syllabuses usually recommend that pupils have access to investigating Christianity in all year groups and often one other religion within the foundation stage and key stage 1, and sometimes two others at key stage 2, one of which can be introduced in years 3 and 4 and the other introduced in years 5 and 6. Some agreed syllabuses suggest introducing more religions to pupils at key stage 2. At key stages 3 and 4 students can explore other religious or non-religious beliefs to ensure that they have had access to a broad range of beliefs and worldviews throughout their time in school.

The aim of an effective RE curriculum that follows the conceptual enquiry approach is to provide a wide range of concepts that pupils will engage with, explore and interpret . Choosing appropriate concepts and placing them across a curriculum map to provide progression in learning in RE is key to a successful RE curriculum plan. Appropriate concepts are ones that:

- are of central significance within the contexts in which they are explored;

- provide opportunities for pupils to engage with the religious material required by the syllabus;

- are accessible to the pupils;

- are placed within the key stage to provide graduating challenge as pupils progress through each key stage.

Choosing a concept and the context is a little like a juggling act for RE curriculum planners. There are no particular rules that can be recommended about whether it is the concept or the context that should be selected first in order to create a worthwhile unit of work. The two are often decided upon simultaneously, although it should always be the concept that takes priority as the enquiry in which pupils engage is essentially into each key concept identified. However, a meaningful enquiry into a concept can only be achieved if it is supported by the appropriate context, which clearly illustrates the way the concept is expressed within the religious traditions or belief systems the school has chosen to study.

If you have lost the will to live at this point, an example should help clarify the issue. If an infant school RE manager wishes to create a unit of work for an enquiry into the concept of 'belonging', he or she would need to select an example from

Christianity and/or the other religion studied as a context that clearly illustrates 'belonging'. A suitable context for the concept 'belonging' therefore, might be to explore a Christian baby baptism. If Sikhism is a religion being studied, pupils might explore the wearing of the five Ks. Both these examples would provide pupils with clear illustrations of ways that some religious people show a sense of 'belonging'.

If a school needs to provide pupils with access to the Jewish festival of Passover and is, therefore, starting with the context for an enquiry, it is important that this is driven by an appropriate concept. Pupils at key stage 1 might find out about the festival through the concept 'remembering' in terms of ways in which Jews remember, during the Seder meal, the story of God helping the Jewish people escape from slavery in Egypt. At key stage 2 pupils might enquire through a concept of particular significance to Jews in relation to Passover, such as the concept of 'freedom', or perhaps 'covenant' with older pupils.

There are some concepts that are fundamentally important for pupils to engage with in order to develop a firm platform on which to explore more challenging concepts in later years. For example, enquiring into the concept 'special' in the early years and foundation stage and key stage 1 provides a basis for later exploring the concepts of 'sacred' or 'holy' at key stage 2. Enquiring into the concept 'belonging' forms the foundation for enquiring into the concept of 'community' later on. The concept 'remembering' is an important foundation on which to build an enquiry into the concepts of 'ritual' or 'symbol'. These concepts are equally important for pupils' development of their own identity formation as well as for their religious literacy.

Early years and foundation stage and key stage 1

Early years and foundation stage pupils will engage with simple type A concepts such as 'remembering', 'celebration', 'belonging' or 'special'. These are non-religious concepts that are also relevant within the experience of religious people. These might be linked to other areas of learning within the year group, but sometimes they might be taught discreetly, such as at Christmas when children will focus on the concept of celebrating (birthdays) within the context of Jesus' birthday. The concept 'special' might be linked to other areas of learning and early learning goals such as 'Special places' or 'Special clothes', which provide potential opportunities for knowledge and understanding of the world, personal, social and emotional development, creative development and communication, language and literacy. These units provide opportunities for pupils' initial engagement with very simple material from Christianity and the other religion that the locally agreed syllabus recommends or requires.

Year 1 and Year 2 pupils will also engage with type A concepts and some may be repeated. For example, as mentioned previously, the concept of 'special' is fundamentally important as a foundation for understanding the concepts of 'sacred' or ' holy' at key stage 2. The concept 'special' is potentially huge, however, and should be contextualised within units such as 'special books', 'special people', 'special times', 'special food' and so on. It is clear how religious examples in relation to these concepts can be explored within the units of work to illustrate to pupils that people of religious groups have 'special' books, people, times and food, etc.

Year 2 pupils might also explore some type B concepts. These are concepts that are common to many religions and used in the study of religion. Pupils in year 2, for example, will happily enquire into the concepts of 'God' or 'angel'. 'Symbol' is a more challenging concept suitable for year 2 pupils that can be simplified by illustrating it as a particular symbol with which the pupils can relate, such as 'symbol of bread' or 'symbol of light'.

Many infant schools establish a pattern of exploring the Christian festivals of Christmas and Easter in the second half of the appropriate terms. The conceptual enquiry-based approach provides the opportunity for pupils to engage with aspects of each festival whilst focusing on more challenging concepts as they progress through the key stage. As a result, teachers are providing different experiences for pupils and a deeper understanding of the festivals each year. For example, in the foundation stage pupils can explore the concept of 'celebrations' within the context of Jesus' birthday celebrations. In year 1 they might explore the concept of 'journey's end' whilst investigating the Christian stories about Mary and Joseph, the shepherds and the Magi, who all had a common experience at the end of their journeys when they encountered the newborn Jesus. In year 2 the concept might be 'angel' and pupils can explore how angels feature in the birth stories. Alternatively, pupils might enquire into the concept 'symbol' in relation to light, and investigate how Christians use the lights of the Advent ring as a symbol.

For Easter, pupils in the foundation stage can explore 'symbol' at a very simple level within the context of eggs as a reminder/symbol of new life. Alternatively, they might focus again on the concept of 'celebration' but this time within the context of celebrating new life. Year 1 pupils can focus on the concepts of 'sad and happy' within the context of a simple retelling of the Easter story, so that pupils can recognise that for Christians, the story has a sad part, but Christians believe there was a happy ending, reflected respectively in Good Friday and Easter Day traditions. Year 2 pupils can focus on the concept of 'welcoming' within the context of the story of Palm Sunday story and consider how there were different reactions among the crowds and onlookers to the welcome of Jesus into Jerusalem on Palm Sunday.

A locally agreed syllabus will probably require pupils to enquire into other aspects of Christianity. The concept 'storytelling' can be usefully explored within the context of 'Jesus the storyteller', enabling young pupils to encounter stories about Jesus as a person who told stories that are still remembered and treasured by Christians today. Through the concept of 'change' pupils engage with the stories about people who changed having met Jesus, such as Zacchaeus, or Jairus' daughter. Pupils might also enquire into 'authority' as a concept and that can be usefully contextualised within stories of events in Jesus' life that demonstrate his authority such as calming the storm or telling the fishermen to leave their nets and follow him. Other aspects of Christianity can be explored through the concept 'special' within the context of 'special books', with a focus on the Bible, or 'special places' within the context of a visit to a church.

Enquiries into aspects of Christianity can be accessed in isolation, through concepts as described above. However, teachers can also explore material from the other religion identified for foundation stage and key stage 1 within the same unit of work as the Christian material. For example, if pupils are enquiring into the concept 'special' within the context of 'special books', teachers might include exploring the Qur'an as a special book for Muslims, if Islam is their focus religion within the key stage, or the Guru Granth Sahib for Sikhs, or the Torah for Jews and so on. Similarly, one can see the potential within a unit of 'special places' and 'special people'.

There will also be occasions when particular concepts can be contextualised exclusively within aspects of the other religion in focus. For example, pupils may enquire into the concept 'obedience' and look at the story of Mohammed being visited by the angel Jibreel on Mount Hira, or, through the concept 'remembering', enquire into what and how Jews 'remember' during their Passover celebrations.

Table 7.1 presents an illustration of a possible long-term curriculum map for RE for the foundation stage and key stage 1 with cross-curricular links.

Table 7.1 Long-term plan for foundation stage and key stage 1 (Christianity and Judaism)

		AUTUMN	SPRING	SUMMER
Foundation Stage			**Storytelling** Jesus the Storyteller *Link: ELG**	**Special** Special Clothes *Link: ELG*
		Celebrating Birthdays Jesus' birthday	**Celebration** Celebrating new life *Link: ELG*	**Special Times** Shabbat and Sunday *Link: ELG*
Key stage 1		**Thanking** Harvest and Sukkott *Link: Science, PSHE, Literacy*	**Change** People Jesus met *Link: Science, PSHE, Literacy, History, Geography*	**Story** Religious stories *Link: literacy*
		Angels Angels *Link: Art, Music*	**Sad and Happy** Key events of Holy Week *Link: Literacy, PSHE*	**Precious** Water *Link: Geography, Science, Literacy*
Key stage 2		**Peace** Special Places – Church and Synagogue *Link: Geography, PSHE, Literacy*	**Remembering** Passover *Link: History, Literacy, Art*	**Special** Special books – Bible and Torah *Link: Literacy/Book week*
		Symbol Light as a Symbol at Hannukah and Advent *Link: Science, Literacy*	**Welcoming** Palm Sunday *Link: PSHE, Literacy, Drama*	**God** Ideas about God *Link: Literacy, Art,*

*ELG: Early Learning Goals

Key stage 2

It is at key stage 2 that pupils can more readily explore a variety of type B concepts. These are concepts that are common to many religions and used in the study of religion. It is within this age group that pupils can start to engage with and make sense of abstract ideas that form the foundation of religious literacy. We are talking about concepts such as 'holy', 'worship', 'sacred', 'ritual' and 'myth'. This is the pupils, introduction to religious figurative language and their opportunity to engage with ways in which religious belief and practice reflect those type B concepts. In years 5 and 6 they might also enquire into type C concepts. These are concepts that are particular to specific religions. Type C concepts are more often more challenging and demanding and further from children's experience, which makes them appropriate for older pupils. Through these they are enabled to recognise that religious believers interpret reality in specific ways and pupils investigate how they express these interpretations. For example, pupils might enquire into the concepts of 'dukkha', a Buddhist concept which is a specific interpretation of suffering, or 'umma', which is a particular interpretation of community that refers to the Muslim worldwide community of believers.

As with the foundation stage and key stage 1, most junior and primary schools still wish to engage key stage 2 pupils with the major Christian festivals of Christmas and Easter at the appropriate times of year. Pupils can explore different aspects of these festivals as they progress through the key stage engaging with more challenging concepts. In year 3 pupils might engage with 'symbol' as a concept within the context of light, if they have not done so in the infant years. They can explore the use of the Advent ring and what is symbolises for Christians, and they might also look at the symbolism of light for Hindus at Divali, or the Hannukah lights for Jews. Year 4 pupils can enquire into the concept of 'holy' within the context of Mary, the mother of Jesus. The focus for RE in this cycle/unit of work is on the language used in carols and prayers, and the images of Mary illustrating the Annunciation story and the birth narratives that indicate how some Christians portray Mary as holy. In year 5 pupils can enquire into the concept of 'prophecy' within the context of the story of the Magi. In the narrative the wise men visited the baby Jesus and gave him prophetic gifts of gold, frankincense and myrrh, foretelling of his kingship, his worthiness of worship and his death. In year 6 pupils can enquire into the concept of 'interpretation'. Within this year group pupils scrutinise the two birth narratives in Matthew's and Luke's gospels, investigating why early Christian writers provided different interpretations of the story.

For Easter, the concept in year 3 might be 'changing emotions', which enables pupils to investigate the Easter events at a deeper level than in the infant phase. They can consider the range of emotions expressed in the story of Holy week and Easter and remembered by Christians. Year 4 pupils might enquire into the concept of 'ritual', which can be contextualised in the rituals involved in the Easter vigil and the lighting of the Paschal candle in many churches. Year 5 pupils might focus on the concept of 'suffering' by investigating Christian art and the ways in which artists have expressed the suffering of Jesus, and the significance of that for Christians. By year 6 pupils are able to engage with the concept of 'resurrection'. This is a Type C concept, one that is particular to a specific religion, in this case Christianity. They can do this through investigating the empty cross as a symbol of resurrection.

For those who have experienced repetition of the same approaches to Christmas and Easter in each year of their primary education, the conceptual enquiry approach will provided some inspiration about how to challenge and excite pupils and provide deeper learning.

Agreed syllabuses require that pupils explore other areas of Christianity at key stage 2. That usually includes investigating Christian beliefs about Jesus. Through the conceptual enquiry approach, this can be developed through the concept of 'message', contextualised through an enquiry into Jesus' message expressed in his teachings. The concept 'belief' might be a focus and pupils can enquire into what Christians believe about Jesus and his life. The stories of Jesus' miracles can be explored through the concept of 'miracle' as a focus.

Christianity can be identified on the curriculum map as units that explore aspects of the faith in isolation. However, in some instances, features of the other religion(s) in focus within each year group can usefully be included. For example, aspects of Christianity can be investigated through the concept 'sacred', which can be contextualised within exploring the Bible, a Church building or an icon. Here it can be worthwhile to introduce examples of sacred writings, places or images from another religious tradition alongside Christianity. The same could be said for the concepts of 'ceremony', 'worship', 'prayer', 'God', 'community' and so on. In this way pupils recognise the significance of the type B concepts when they encounter them as concepts that are common to many religions and used in the study of religion.

There will also be opportunities to enquire into concepts that can be contextualised within an aspect of the other religion(s) that the pupils are studying. They may focus on the concept 'peace', for example, and contextualise that within an investigation into the image of the Buddha and its use and significance within the Buddhist community. Similarly, with the concept 'devotion' pupils could enquire into how Hindus show devotion to Lord Shiva during the festival of Mahashivratri (The Night of Shiva) or Lord Krishna during the festival of Holi.

RE in a cross-curricular setting

Whilst it is important to clearly identify continuity and progression in pupils' learning in RE, teachers might also reflect on how planning has developed for the whole curriculum over the last decade or so and consider what can be learnt from those changes and how RE might contribute to the developing curriculum.

It was in 1988/9, as a result of the Education Reform Act, that the National Curriculum was established in schools. For the first time the requirements of what should be taught in schools in the UK were centrally determined. National statutory guidance was produced by the QCA (Qualifications and Curriculum Authority) for the different subject areas taught in schools. Subject communities within each discipline flexed their muscles with these requirements. Each subject discipline had clear aims, specific subject skills identified and outlines of specific content to be covered.

Religious education was not part of the National Curriculum. There had been a legal requirement to teach RE in schools since the 1944 Education Act. RE was, and still is, determined locally by each local authority's SACRE (Standing Advisory Council for RE). The RE community also flexed its muscles in response to the National Curriculum to ensure that RE maintained a secure footing within the heavily laden curriculum over which subject managers in schools often vied for sufficient curriculum time. In Chapter 2 of this book there are details of how different approaches have influenced the delivery of RE over the past two decades alongside the National Curriculum and the impact of the non-statutory national framework for RE.

The primary curriculum, under the burden of prescriptive requirements from each subject area, continued to develop. In 2002 the QCA provided guidance for curriculum planning introducing flexibility. It stated:

'Schools are required to provide a broad and balanced curriculum and to teach the programmes of study in each national curriculum subject. English and mathematics are a priority at key stages 1 and 2 as children need to become secure and confident learners in these subjects if they are to make good progress in their education. At the same time, rich and varied activities and experiences in the rest of the curriculum are also crucial to children's motivation and progress. Schools need to take into account the interdependence of English and mathematics and the other subjects when making decisions about their priorities, and as they decide on time allocations. Beyond these considerations, however, schools have the flexibility to decide how much importance they give to each subject and which aspects they emphasise within subjects. Such decisions might apply across a key stage, to particular year groups or other groupings of children, as well as to individuals.' (QCA, 2002:7)

Subsequently the government commissioned a review of the primary curriculum in 2008/9 and as a result guidance has emerged for primary schools to develop a more flexible curriculum that is less restricted by specific subject guidance. The DCSF (Department for Children, Schools and Families) website says:

'The intention is to enable schools to have greater flexibility to meet individual pupils' needs and strengths and to reduce prescription where possible, whilst retaining the introduction to a broad range of subjects, including languages, in a way that is manageable for schools.' (www.nationalstrategies.standards.dcsf.gov. uk/node/156801)

The final reports, following the review process, published recommendations for changes in curriculum design. These are found in the Rose or Independent Review of the Primary Curriculum, cited below. A concurrent review was carried out at Cambridge University, The Cambridge Review, edited by Robin Alexander, which has also made some useful critical observations in relation to previous National Curriculum prescription, for example:

> 'as children move through the primary phase, their statutory entitlement to a broad and balanced education is increasingly but needlessly compromised by a "standards" agenda which combines high stakes testing and the national strategies' exclusive focus on literacy and numeracy. The most conspicuous casualties are the arts, the humanities and the kinds of learning in all subjects which require time for talking, problem-solving and the extended exploration of ideas. A policy-led belief that curriculum breadth is incompatible with the pursuit of standards in "the basics" has fuelled this loss of entitlement.' (Alexander, 2009:22)

Concerns had been expressed by members of the teaching profession that subjects which required time for problem solving and extended exploration of ideas, like RE, were becoming a casualty of the over-burdened and test-driven curriculum. It is, however, the Rose Review, *Independent Review of the Primary Curriculum: Final report,* that the government has adopted to provide guidance for schools. It states:

> '2.35 Areas of learning provide powerful opportunities for children to use and apply their knowledge and skills across subjects. This builds on their enthusiasm for learning from first hand investigations and researching knowledge from a range of sources to deepen their understanding.'

As a result of the guidelines of the Rose Review, some subject specialists are expressing concerns. Some fear that there is a danger of losing the specific approaches and skills developed by particular subject disciplines to a curriculum of poorly defined knowledge, like a 'porridge' of linked information. RE specialists, similarly, are expressing concerns. RE managers might consider, therefore, how to maintain the integrity of RE within a cross-curricular setting, yet seek to identify and exploit opportunities where pupils' learning can be integrated. It has been said that a successful curriculum might be viewed as muesli rather than porridge: the distinctive parts should be clearly identifiable yet combined together (where appropriate) they can provide a healthy diet.

The DCSF non-statutory guidance for RE published in 2009 states that RE can be integrated with other subjects where appropriate, or taught discreetly:

> 'schools are not required to teach subjects separately or to use their given titles, though there can be advantages in so doing. One subject can be combined with another, or it can be taught in separate lessons, or a mixture of provision used, depending on the objectives of the curriculum being followed.' (DCSF, 2009:33)

As schools move towards developing a more creative curriculum, RE managers should consult with other subject leaders or curriculum planners to consider and locate where useful links can be made with RE and other areas of learning. There is an emerging pattern of schools identifying possible avenues for developing links, all of them legitimate and worthwhile. They include the following.

Developing learning around a concept that can be meaningfully explored within several areas of learning. For the foundation stage and key stage 1 the following units of work provide useful examples. The concept 'change' has been well documented in previous chapters and for RE can be developed through the context of 'People Jesus met.' There is also plenty of scope to develop historical, geographical and social understanding with this concept as well as scientific enquiries and possibly mathematical development. The concept 'remembering' is particularly significant for RE when pupils contextualise the concept within remembering 'Guru Nanak's birthday' or 'Passover' (or any other festival) for example. The concept also has potential opportunities for historical and social understanding. Other examples of concepts that could be identified as being significant within RE and other areas of learning are 'special', 'precious' and 'welcoming'. It would be worthwhile to discuss their potential with staff with different subject specialisms.

At key stage 2 the concept of 'interpretation' provides opportunities for potential links with historical and geographical understanding, with scientific enquiry and possibly with numeracy. 'Freedom' as a concept has mileage with geographical and historical understanding and personal and social development as well as citizenship. Some other concepts with potential links with other areas of learning might be 'community', 'suffering', 'migration', 'difference' and 'peace'.

Developing learning around a context that can be meaningfully explored within several areas of learning. At foundation stage and key stage 1 the concept 'symbol' is best explored within a particular context such as 'water', 'light' or 'bread' for example. For RE, with the context of water pupils explore how water is used as a symbol in Christian baptism, at a Sikh Amrit ceremony, or for ritual washing in the River Ganges by Hindus, for example. Teachers will also recognise potential links with pupils' exploration of water within scientific and geographical understanding. The same might be said of the 'symbol of light' within the context of Hannukah lights, Divali lights or Advent lights for RE. There are also useful links to be made with a scientific enquiry in relation to the context of 'light'. The concept 'special' when explored within the context of books provides opportunities for pupils to explore the Bible, the Qur'an, the Guru Granth Sahib or the Torah scrolls. Useful links might also be explored with historical understanding and literacy.

At key stage 2 links between areas of learning can continue. For RE, pupils can explore the concept 'ceremony' within the context of death ceremonies within Christianity and perhaps Hinduism, and there can be a useful link with the study of Ancient Egyptians and their death ceremonies as part of pupils' historical development. The symbol of a tree is a potent one within a number of religious stories and a unit of work for RE requires pupils to engage with trees themselves and consider their characteristics and why they have been used symbolically in religious mythology.

Here is a useful link with areas of geographical development, such as rain forests or deforestation, or with scientific understanding in relation to habitats and plant life. Potential links can be identified with the context of other RE units such as sacred places (with geographical and historical development) and water as a symbol (with geographical and scientific development as suggested for key stage 1). It would be worthwhile to discuss potential links with other subject specialists and curriculum development managers within the school.

Developing learning around skills that can be meaningfully explored within a number of areas of learning. Skills development in RE has been discussed in previous chapters. The following suggestions provide brief examples of how skills acquired within other areas of learning such as literacy and communication, artistic and expressive development, design and technology might be utilised and linked within and across learning in RE. Within the foundation stage and key stage 1, skills developed in literacy and communication such as speaking and listening, using full stops and capital letters appropriately, instructional writing and so on can all be applied to RE to contribute to cross-curricular learning. For example, pupils may retell the story of the angels visiting the shepherds with the news of the birth of Jesus (concept 'angel') or write their own responses to the idea of angels and focus attention on the use of full stops and capital letters. Similarly teachers will find opportunities to apply their ICT skills (labels to be placed on a crib scene or a display of Christmas cards depicting angels), understanding the arts (studying different artists' depictions of angels and producing their own), drama (acting out the story of the angels visiting the shepherds), music (creating suitable sounds and simple rhythms to accompany the drama/role play) and so on.

Similarly at key stage 2, RE teaching and learning provides potential for skills development. With the concept of 'holy' pupils can explore images of Mary by looking at artists' interpretations and strategies used by artists to convey the sense of 'holy', and this could be developed through the pupils producing their own images of Mary, making a contribution to their artistic and expressive development. For literacy and communication they may look at prayers, poems and carols about Mary as a particular genre and how Christians communicate the sense of 'holy' within those writings. With the concept 'suffering' one can see the potential for linking with the creative arts and enabling pupils to engage with artistic and expressive development, including music, to enquire how Christians interpret a sense of suffering through art and music, and offer opportunities for pupils to practise their own creative skills.

In Table 7.1 an overview was provided for a long-term curriculum map in the foundation stage and key stage 1, which identified some ideas for cross-curricular links. Table 7.2 provides some ideas for a long-term curriculum map for RE at key stage 2, which identifies some ideas for cross-curricular links.

Table 7.2 Junior school: long-term plan for RE

	Christianity/Judaism		Christianity/Buddhism	
	Year 3	**Year 4**	**Year 5**	**Year 6**
Autumn	**THANKING** Sukkot and Harvest *Link: PSHE, Literacy*	**WATER AS A SYMBOL** Water *Link: Science, Geography, Literacy, Art, Music*	**PEACE** Life of the Buddha *Link: Literacy, PSHE, Art, Music*	**SACRED PLACES** Church and Temple *Link: Geography (local study), Literacy*
	LIGHT AS A SYMBOL Advent and Hannukah *Link: Science, Art, Literacy*	**HOLY** Mary Mother of God *Link: Art, Music*	**PROPHECY** The Magi *Link: Art, Music, Literacy*	**INTERPRETATION** Matthew and Luke narratives *Link: History, Literacy, Art*
Spring	**CEREMONY** Death Ceremonies (Christian and Jewish) *Link: Ancient Egyptians*	**FREEDOM** Passover *Link: History, Literacy, Art, Music, Drama, PSHE*	**DUKKHA** (Suffering) Buddhist Teachings *Link: PSHE, History, Literacy*	**MESSAGES** Jesus' Messages *Link: PSHE, Literacy*
	CHANGING EMOTIONS Holy Week *Link: PSHE, Literacy*	**RITUAL** Paschal Candle *Link: PSHE*	**SUFFERING** Easter story *Link: Art, Music, PSHE*	**RESURRECTION** The Empty Cross *Link: Art*
Summer	**CREATION** Creation Stories *Link: Literacy, Art*	**TREES AS A SYMBOL** Trees *Link: Science, Geography, Art*	**PRAYER** Christian and Buddhist	**ENLIGHTENMENT** Wesak *Link: PSHE*
	WORSHIP Jewish and Christian	**SACRED** Sacred Books *Link: History, Literacy*	**COMMUNITY** Church and Sangha *Link: Geography, History, PSHE*	**GOD** God Talk *Link: Romans/ Greeks*
	Level 3	**Level 3/4**	**Level 4**	**Level 4/5**

Summary

So far in this chapter there have been suggestions about how to implement the philosophy of the conceptual enquiry approach within a school and how RE managers might go about establishing a worthwhile curriculum map for RE within a school that makes meaningful links to other areas of the curriculum. The following questions should provide opportunities for reflection and discussion about some of the issues raised so far:

- What do you anticipate might be some barriers that emerge when introducing the conceptual enquiry approach to RE? How would you plan to overcome those barriers?

- What particular strategies or approaches do you think would lead to successful implementation of the conceptual enquiry approach within a school?

- How might staff be most effectively supported to implement and sustain the conceptual enquiry approach in school?

Medium-term planning

This section provides guidance on developing medium-term planning of units of work/cycles of learning to explore with pupils in the primary phase. Much of this material has been drawn and adapted from *Living Difference: The primary handbook* (Hampshire County Council, 2006).

Medium-term planning is usually the responsibility of the RE manager who disseminates it to all staff. In some schools the RE managers give guidance through providing the concept and context and by planning alongside colleagues in year group meetings.

Medium-term planning is fundamentally for class teachers who need guidance on how to lead pupils through an enquiry into a concept. RE subject leaders also need to keep records of medium-term planning to enable them to monitor the overall provision for RE and RE resource requirements throughout the school. Senior management and governing bodies should also have access to medium-term planning in their capacity of ensuring that the RE provision is fit for purpose and meets with the requirements of the locally agreed syllabus.

Schools have different levels of detail and different styles of format for their medium-term planning. What is particularly important is that the medium-term planning gives sufficient and succinct detail and guidance to enable teachers to provide worthwhile and effective learning in RE. The following information suggestions are for application in different schools.

It is important for teachers to have medium-term plans that inform them of:

- the key concept for each cycle/unit, the context in which it is developed and the evaluative question to focus the enquiry. In Chapter 6 you will find discussions and guidance on the development of evaluative questions about a concept within a suitable context as a starting point for medium-term planning (see pages 68, 71–72, 98).

- the estimated time allocated to the unit (in hours), the year group and the term in which the unit is to be located;

- intended learning outcomes that clarify what pupils should be able to do by the end of the unit. These should be informed by the level descriptors in the locally agreed syllabus (and with reference to the level descriptors identified in Chapter 4, Appendix 2, which relate directly to the conceptual enquiry approach);

- the sequence of teaching and learning activities planned for that unit according to the cycle of learning;

- assessment opportunities within the unit;

- the resources teachers will need; some schools also include the vocabulary that should be used specifically within the unit, and differentiated tasks or extension activities.

The following steps provide advice on how useful medium-term planning might be structured for each unit of work identified on the long-term plan.

Step 1

Write five intended outcomes for the unit, informed by the conceptual enquiry level descriptors focusing on the key concept. Each intended outcome clearly identifies what pupils should achieve by the end of the unit in relation to each element in the cycle of learning (Enquire, Contextualise, Evaluate, Communicate and Apply). If they are vague, pitched at the wrong level or do not relate to the concept or the context, they will lead to inappropriate teaching and learning. Intended outcomes should also:

- relate to the requirements of the agreed syllabus;

- be pitched at the appropriate level;

- be achievable within the allocated time;

- be measurable.

The following examples illustrate some intended outcomes that give a clear indication of what pupils should be able to achieve by the end of their enquiry. The concept is 'remembering' in the context of the Hindu festival of Janmashtami, remembering Krishna's birthday. The intended outcomes are pitched at level 1 and would be suitable for year 1 pupils.

> **Box 7.1**
>
> Pupils should be able to:
>
> 1. **ENQUIRE:** talk about 'remembering'
> 2. **CONTEXTUALISE:** recognise that Hindus remember Krishna by telling the story of his birth and by celebrating that
> 3. **EVALUATE:** talk about the importance of Hindus remembering Krishna's birthday
> 4. **COMMUNICATE:** talk about their own response to remembering someone special
> 5. **APPLY:** identify how their response relates to their own lives

Step 2

Plan a suitable sequence of activities for the pupils that are engaging, challenging, worthwhile and above all relate directly to the concept and the intended outcomes. The sequence of activities should be clearly identified within each element of the cycle of learning required by the conceptual enquiry approach. Here is an example of a sequence of activities for the intended outcomes above in relation to the concept 'remembering' within the context of Janmashtami, the celebration to remember Krishna's birth.

> **Box 7.2**
>
> **Sequences of Activities:**
>
> **Step 1: Enquire into the concept of remembering**
> - Teacher models the idea of remembering by showing something that evokes memories of someone special (such as a baby photo, a first birthday card, a first pair of shoes, etc).
> - Discuss with pupils what 'remembering' is like (thinking about things that happened, seeing pictures in your head, etc).
> - Show a picture of Krishna as a baby. Ask pupils to say what they notice about Krishna (what colour is he, jewellery, headdress, chubby). Hindus use this picture to help them remember Krishna.
>
> **Step 2: Contextualise 'remembering' within the story and celebrations of Krishna's birthday**
> - Tell (not read) the story of Krishna's birth. Pupils act out the story.
> - Discuss – which parts of the story do Hindus like to remember most? Why?
>   which parts of the story will you remember most and why?

- Tell pupils that Hindus 'remember' Krishna's birth by having a celebration. How do they think Hindus might celebrate? How do we normally celebrate? Discuss pupils' suggestions (have a party, food, drinks, presents, cards, friends, sing songs, decorate the room, etc).
- Use some of the pupils' suggestions to create a shrine for Krishna in the classroom – food offering of Indian sweets, milk offering, cards, presents, images of Krishna, lights, joss sticks.
- Explain how Hindus remember Krishna – demonstrate puja. Share the sweets, sing a song for Krishna, listen to some Indian music. Using a prepared sheet, pupils put rings around pictures that show what Hindus do to help them to remember Krishna's birthday.

Step 3: Evaluate the importance of remembering Krishna for Hindus

- Using a Hindu persona doll, or a picture of a Hindu child, explain that s/he is very upset because s/he had been on holiday, and forgotten to remember Krishna's birthday. Does it matter? How does s/he feel? Why does s/he feel sad that s/he did not remember? Why does s/he like to remember Krishna? How does s/he feel when s/he does remember Krishna's birthday? Discuss. Pupils draw the Hindu child. "I want to remember Krishna because…". Children complete.
- Do pupils think it is important for Hindus to remember Krishna? Why/Why not? Discuss with the class.

Step 4: Communicate their own response to 'remembering'. Who do we like to remember?

- Pupils bring in items/photographs, etc that help them to remember someone special. Circle time sharing (two circles using LSA support?)
- Have a 'remembering' afternoon and discuss ways that would help them to remember (eg sing songs, act out an event, make cards).

Step 5: Apply 'remembering' to different situations (continue from above)

- Discuss:
  - ➢ Do we want to remember everyone we meet? Why/why not?
  - ➢ Who do we like to remember?
  - ➢ Will we always remember special people? Why/why not?
  - ➢ Will you remember special people when you are grown up?
  - ➢ Will you remember lots of people or just one or two?
  - ➢ Do we all like to remember the same people? Why/why not?
  - ➢ How do you feel when you remember your special person?
  - ➢ Do you remember them all the time? Do you remember them on special days, or when you are sad or happy?
  - ➢ Would it matter if you forgot? Why/why not?

Step 3

Identify some assessment opportunities in terms of 'evidence can be gathered when…'. These, too, should relate directly to the intended outcomes. It is important to recognise that assessment tasks are not an added extra to the learning process, but selected from the pupils' learning activities. Evidence should be gathered that illustrates how well pupils have achieved what was initially intended.

This example illustrates how evidence can be gathered when pupils participate in the enquiry with reference, again, to the concept 'remembering' in the context of Janmashtami.

Box 7.3

Assessment Opportunities
Evidence can be gathered when:

1. pupils discuss what 'remembering' means in class discussions
2. using a prepared sheet, pupils put rings around pictures that show what Hindus do to help them to remember Krishna's birthday
3. pupils draw the Hindu child. They complete the speech bubble: "I want to remember Krishna because…"
4. pupils discuss remembering someone special in circle time activity
5. pupils discuss their responses to the questions (see activities) and own ideas during circle time

---

Step 4

List the resources teachers will need when teaching each unit such as the story of Krishna's birth, images and models of Krishna as a baby, useful websites, posters and books that illustrate how Hindus celebrate Janmashtami.

It would be useful for the RE manager within a school to provide some examples of medium-term planning to discuss with staff and for teachers to try out with their classes. As teachers begin to feel more confident with the cycle of learning they can take ownership of the planning and make amendments and suggest alternative or additional activities and potential links with other curriculum areas, in discussion with the RE manager. The RE manager would need to maintain an overview of the overall provision for RE within the school to ensure that continuity and progression in learning are sustained.

Assessing RE

The main purpose of assessment is to improve and develop learning, so it is referred to here as an integral part of the planning process. Readers may wish to look elsewhere for an in-depth discussion on assessment in education, but in this section we provide advice about how assessment can be planned to contribute to effective RE provision.

Assessment can take many forms, including pupils making judgements themselves about how well they have learnt (as part of assessment for learning), the teachers' day-to-day observations and discussions with pupils, sampling pupils' work and sometimes more formal testing. The results indicate how well pupils are learning and identifies where learning can be developed. So that these activities support pupils' progress they clearly need to be related to what pupils are expected to learn. We might deduce, therefore, that good assessment practice should:

- provide pupils with information about how well they are learning and how they can improve;

- provide teachers with information to help them plan appropriate learning activities for their pupils;

- inform teachers about the effectiveness of their planning and teaching;

- inform parents/carers and others (such as the child's next teacher) about the child's attainment and progress.

In discussion with teachers, common criteria often emerge about what are important features of worthwhile assessment procedures. They frequently say that assessment in RE should be:

- manageable;

- informative;

- useful;

- simple;

- effective.

Effective assessment depends on appropriate expectations being made explicit in planning. The importance of clear intended outcomes identified in each unit of work has already been addressed, and any assessment should be related to these. When intended outcomes are informed by the level descriptors they enable teachers to identify the appropriate challenge and pitch for learning. It is helpful to decide in advance which aspects of the learning experiences will be recorded or captured in some way in terms of assessment, as was discussed within the section above on medium-term planning. Judgements made about the pupils' performance with some of these activities or tasks will then provide indicators of pupils' progress in the subject. This process provides a coherent picture of development through the key stage.

Here are examples of intended outcomes and the related assessment opportunities from a unit for key stage 2 on the concept of 'symbol' contextualised within the symbols of the bread and wine at a Christian Eucharist. The intended outcomes are pitched at level 3.

Box 7.4

Learning Outcomes
Pupils should be able to:

1. describe the meaning of the concept 'symbol'
2. describe how and why the symbols of bread and wine are used by Christians
3. describe the importance of the symbols to Christians
4. describe their own responses and ideas about symbols
5. describe example of how feelings/responses to symbols affect theirs and others' lives.

Assessment Opportunities
Evidence can be gathered when pupils:

1. produce mind maps for the concept symbol
2. annotate some pictures of Christians participating in the Eucharist
3. complete speech bubble on picture of a Christian "The wine and bread is a symbol of … to me
4. draw and annotate symbols they use/have in their own lives.
5. discuss from above. How important is that symbol? How would they feel if it was damaged or ignored?

Schools come to their own decisions about the frequency of assessments across different areas of learning in the curriculum. It is appropriate that there should be sufficient opportunities to make judgements about pupils' attainment in RE in order to evaluate the effectiveness of the teaching and learning experiences and to identify whether pupils are making sufficient progress compared to the progress they make in other areas of learning.

Assessment of pupils' achievements in RE can take place through a variety of procedures, which include observing, listening and talking to pupils, as well as judgements about written, oral, visual and practical outcomes.

Useful assessment also provides pupils with feedback about how well they are doing. Providing pupils with constructive and specific feedback about their work will show them how they can improve. This could include both oral and written responses. Self-assessment and peer-group assessment are useful ways of developing pupils' independence and capacity for critical thinking. Approaches would need to be modelled and taught by the teacher so that pupils practise and develop the appropriate skills and vocabulary for self-assessment. As well as the formal, identified assessment task, day-to-day assessment is part of good teaching and involves the teacher in using observations to determine the appropriate pitch and pace of planned expectations for individuals, groups or the whole class.

Teachers have several opportunities to gather evidence of pupils' achievements throughout each RE unit, as assessment is part of the learning process. Teachers or RE managers can decide which of the identified activities will provide useful evidence and how frequently evidence needs to be gathered to provide a useful picture of how well pupils are learning. They might:

- provide opportunities for pupils to assess their own work, eg, by comparing their work with others or with a model example of work;

- gather evidence in relation to one intended outcome in a unit;

- gather evidence from a proportion of the class (eg, 10 pupils) in relation to an intended outcome in a unit, for example when the teacher is observing discussion, a debate or some drama;

- gather evidence from a group of pupils or a whole class that covers several intended outcomes in a unit of work, eg, through pupils creating a display or completing an assessment sheet.

Judgements about pupils' attainment need to be recorded in some way. The records provide evidence of how well pupils are progressing and achieving with different concepts in different units of work and with different teachers.

Records of pupils' attainment can be a useful diagnostic tool to enable teachers to identify where progress and attainment might not be as good as anticipated due to, for example, a concept that is too challenging, insufficient resources, inappropriate activities or insufficient focus on the concept. Alternatively, if a large number of pupils are achieving above expectations, teachers might feel that they can provide more challenge for pupils. Similarly, pupils' levels of attainment can be compared to their attainment in other curriculum areas such as literacy. Low levels of attainment in RE compared to literacy could, for example, be indicative of low expectations, or insufficient challenge in RE activities, and plans and activities can be improved as a result.

Teachers and schools often have their own methods for ensuring that these judgements are recorded in an accessible and useful format that is not overly time-consuming but is accurate. It can be useful to consider the evidence of pupils' attainment , be it oral, visual or written, in three categories:

1. Achieved below expected outcomes.

2.   Achieved in line with expected outcomes.

3.   Achieved above expected outcomes.

To obtain an overall picture of pupils' progress in all elements of the cycle of learning, it can be useful to identify one or two assessment tasks within a different element of the cycle in each unit of work. By the end of each academic year evidence has been gathered from all elements in the cycle.

There are other ways in which assessment can take place, suggested in the following list:

- Teachers keep field notes to record contributions made by pupils in relation to RE that may occur spontaneously at any time in school.

- Alternatively, select pupils to track and assess, and record their responses or achievements in short-term planning files, day books, wall charts, etc.

- Provide opportunities for pupils' self-assessment in RE, eg, a sheet inviting pupils to comment on their learning, what they enjoyed, how they learnt best and what they would like to know more about.

- Many schools find a page-a-pupil system a useful supplement to their recording framework. This might contain occasional, brief, dated comments relating to significant achievement not recorded elsewhere, providing evidence for use in reports.

It is a legal requirement to report annually to parents on RE. Reports must inform parents about how their children have progressed in religious education with reference to the requirements of the agreed syllabus. Reports might include comments on the following:

- the content and activities the child has experienced;

- the level of interest, enthusiasm and effort the child has demonstrated;

- a description of what the child has achieved in terms of knowledge, understanding of the concepts and skills – using the planned intended learning outcomes;

- any suggested targets for future work.

The report should be based on evidence gathered; for example:

- evidence of the work covered from planning documentation, schemes of work, etc;

- teachers' field notes recording contributions of children and their level of interest, enthusiasm and effort;

- children's self-evaluation, eg: 'I can now describe the meaning of the concept/idea of ___; I can describe how Christians (or Jews, Muslims, Buddhists, etc) respond to this concept; I can describe the value of that concept/idea for Christians (or Jews, Muslims, Buddhists, etc), I can describe my own experiences of and responses to ___ and I can describe examples of how the concept/idea of ___ applies to mine and others' lives';

- teacher assessment of children's oral work, written work, as evidence of progress in comparison with previous attainment.

It is not necessary to keep mountains of pupils' RE work. Selected samples, however, can serve as a useful reference point, and many teachers collate examples of work in an exemplification of standards file or portfolio as a reference for teachers so that consistent judgements can be made about standards in RE. These can also be shared with pupils as examples of expected standards, to clarify expectations.

A number of schools find it useful to collect three samples of work from each class or year group (achieved well, achieved, and achieved below expectations), which are selected by teachers and given to the RE manager at the end of each RE unit of work. The RE manager can then level the work in consultation with class teachers and perhaps provide a brief commentary for each sample to keep as exemplification of standards with planning documents. The samples should highlight any anomalies in the planning or assessment of RE. For example, if samples of work from a year 6 class are categorised as 'achieved well' but are only a level 2 standard, this might indicate that expectations are low, or inappropriate tasks have been provided for pupils. One would expect pupils achieving well in year 6 to produce work at level 4 or 5.

Maintaining standards

Having constructed a curriculum plan to implement the conceptual enquiry approach to learning in RE and potentially other areas of learning, schools will find that they wish to monitor that provision and ensure that effective teaching and learning is maintained. Subject or curriculum managers are often given the opportunity to monitor the teaching throughout the school. This can seem daunting to the observed and the observer, but might take the form of paired teaching, or the co-ordinator working with a small group of pupils. Discussions with each teacher and observations can provide useful feedback. Alternatively, conferencing with pupils about the concept they have been exploring and their responses to the activities in which they were involved can be a revealing indication of the quality of the provision. In this instance our focus is on RE, but similar questions might guide monitoring in other areas of learning:

- Is the RE planning sufficiently clear to support effective RE teaching?

- How do pupils respond to the planned teaching and learning?

- Are appropriate artefacts, books, websites, posters, etc being used – are they available and easily accessible?

- Do teachers feel competent and confident with the key concepts identified and the contexts in which they are explored?

- Do teachers feel competent and confident with the elements in the cycle of learning in the conceptual enquiry approach?

- Are the tasks provided varied, appropriately pitched and related to the identified intended outcomes?

The observations and discussions with teachers and pupils should reveal any training needs, necessary amendments to RE planning and resource requirements, and will inform the RE development plan.

Use of effective questioning

Teachers will recognise that a good deal of RE teaching involves the use of discussion and questioning. This is an invaluable tool to improve learning in RE. Effective questioning can be achieved as part of the conceptual enquiry approach when it is based on careful preparation of the possible lines of questioning before the session. This does not mean, however, that teachers should not respond to pupils' responses with further questions based on those in an impromptu fashion. Questions should be open-ended in the spirit of an open enquiry, allowing for a range of responses, asking pupils to extend their answer, or inviting other ideas. It is helpful if teacher talk is kept to a minimum to enable pupils to speculate and hypothesise about meanings and applying reasoning; this can be achieved by focusing attention on asking 'why' questions.

Teachers might also assist and challenge thinking by playing devil's advocate, when appropriate, to ensure that pupils recognise alternative viewpoints. With the conceptual enquiry approach it is important that teachers resist the expectation that pupils will provide standard answers, and avoid the 'guess what teacher is thinking you should answer' situation. The aim of the approach is that questioning encourages pupils to think for themselves. Effective questioning encourages a wide range of pupils to participate, and sometimes requires targeting questions on specific individuals.

The following list provides some examples of questions that can prompt interesting discussion within a class:

- Does anyone have any ideas about …?

- Why do you think people might do that?

- Does anyone else have a different idea?

- Can you explain that a bit more?

- But what would happen if …?

- What do you think might happen next?

- Can we think of five different answers?

- What do you think the connection might be between x and y?

- Do you think that is a good answer?

- What questions do you think we could ask about …?

- Which of these ideas, objects or pictures do you think is the most important?

- Why do you think these interpretations differ?

- Can you decide what you think we would do if …?

To support questioning techniques it is useful to draw on concrete examples to invite pupils to apply their ideas and opinions. On some occasions the teacher might set up problems or scenarios that raise issues for pupils to solve. For example, within a unit of work on the concept 'sacred' within the context of 'sacred places', pupils engage with all elements in the cycle of learning, and within the 'evaluate' section they might be asked to consider the scenario of plans for a synagogue, a church or a mosque being turned into a supermarket. How do pupils think worshippers would react to such a proposal and why? Alternatively, they may prioritise or order different ideas. For example, for key stage 1 pupils, from a list of possible answers about why the Bible is a special book for Christians (because it tells them how to behave, because it has stories about God and Jesus in it, because it is very old, etc) pupils can suggest an order of priority from a Christian perspective. In discussion pupils can give reasons for their order of priority.

Conclusion

The first half of this chapter provided a discussion and suggested guidance about strategies for introducing and implementing the conceptual enquiry approach in a school. This included ideas on how to structure a whole school curriculum plan for RE, which could usefully be linked to other areas of learning. To demonstrate how to fully implement the conceptual enquiry approach, suggestions about how to structure and create effective medium-term plans have also been provided. Closely related to this, we have discussed how effective assessment and monitoring procedures can support learning and sustain high standards for RE within a school. The importance of effective questioning techniques within RE activities has been highlighted as an integral part of the learning process.

The aim of this chapter has been to share strategies of good practice that have been observed and that have proved to be successful, and to provide readers with frameworks and ideas that they can reflect on, adapt and apply in their own teaching situations. The following questions might raise some interesting issues for reflection and discussion:

- Do you think the conceptual enquiry approach could be effectively applied to all areas of the curriculum? Why/why not?

- How might you plan to introduce assessment procedures for RE within a school?

- In what ways might the questioning techniques suggested in this chapter benefit other areas of learning within the curriculum?

8

Strategies and resources
Using the skills of the non-specialist

Elaine Bellchambers

Introduction

This chapter explores how non-specialist teachers might feel more confident in teaching effective religious education through a conceptual enquiry approach. It discusses aspects that may present problems and explores ways of tackling them. This chapter complements Chapter 7, which primarily addressed the role of the RE subject coordinator or manager, although both chapters are important for all primary teachers. Most primary teachers are 'generalists': they teach most, if not all, of the primary curriculum subjects. Nevertheless, each has different strengths in their training, specialism, interests and current expertise. In this chapter, through drawing upon specific teaching examples from the religious education curriculum, we will explore how English, drama, art, historical sources, and film and media sources can be utilised within the conceptual enquiry approach to RE.

What are the issues?

In this context we are using the term 'non-specialist' to refer to teachers without specialist academic qualifications in religious studies and with limited training in religious education, suggesting how they might draw upon their wide range of experiences across the curriculum and particular expertise in other disciplines. For the non-specialist teacher having to teach religious education there may be three particular areas that give them cause for concern:

1. Gaining appropriate subject knowledge and becoming familiar with the language and terminology of a range of world religions and their traditions, together with difficulties associated with speaking and using this language confidently and accurately, may present specific challenges. This lack of knowledge can create insecurities with regard to planning, teaching and learning.

2. Whether or not teachers have strong personal religious affiliations, they may find the requirement to remain 'neutral' difficult to sustain during teaching and class discussion.

3. Teachers may be uncertain as to the value and place that religion has in society and, therefore, its value within the education system.

Such concerns may undermine teachers' confidence and willingness to teach RE, so that they feel reluctant to actively engage with the subject matter. Nevertheless, teachers have transferable skills; they have an understanding of the complex nature of education and particularly their own individual enthusiasms for specific aspects of the curriculum. It is these existing qualities that can be incorporated effectively into the religious education curriculum, together with the key professional skills of communication, management and organisation, interpersonal relationships, planning, problem solving and decision making, research and creative thinking. These skills already exist as part of the day-to-day teaching process; rather than learning new skills, teachers need to recognise how these existing teaching skills may be developed and applied in the context of engaging with a conceptual enquiry approach to religious education.

What are the skills to be developed for learners?

At this point, it might be useful to refer back to the aim of religious education, reiterating that is not to produce believers: it is to inform young people and to give them particular skills, namely:

- *to acquire information* about religion(s), *to reflect* upon the nature of that information, and *to be able to research more information* as required;

- *to appreciate* the manner in which religion functions in the lives of individuals and communities;

- to be able *to make critical judgements* that are based upon informed awareness of religious beliefs and practices;

- *to ask pertinent questions;*

- *to reflect on the reasoning* behind their own beliefs and values and the reasoning behind those of others.

Such abilities are not subject-specific: they are all transferable and pupils are probably already applying them in other subject areas. The difference within religious education is the context, the concepts to be developed, and the enquiry methodology required.

What professional skills and experiences do we bring to religious education?

As a specialist in another area of the curriculum, a useful starting point might be to reflect upon the qualities that you bring to your own subject area:

- What is it about your specialism that excites and inspires you?

- What teaching and learning opportunities do you offer your pupils? Which strategies are the most successful?

- What challenges has your subject presented to you? How have you managed to overcome these challenges? What strategies have you employed?

Through this kind of analysis of your 'special subject' you can summarise your strengths and abilities. This in turn can highlight for you how your teaching of religious education can start from a secure professional base: your subject and skills strength.

Through your enthusiasm, confidence and knowledge of your own subject, you will have developed the skills necessary for good teaching and learning and providing a balanced approach to its curriculum, whatever your own preferences within the subject matter taught. The same is required for religious education: as with every other subject you have to leave your own beliefs outside the classroom. Pupils have the right to honest, accurate information, well-informed teaching, through a rigorous, balanced approach along with the skills they need to make their own judgements. So, religious education is not a threat to one's personal beliefs: it is enquiry-led and knowledge-seeking.

Where can we start in the classroom?

Pupils arrive in school with a range of ideas, understanding and beliefs about their world and the way it functions; ideas gleaned from their observations and experiences prior to formal education and from their enculturation. In teaching science, primary teachers draw on these experiences, trying to understand and include pupils' ideas in their teaching and helping children to refine and develop their ideas towards an understanding of scientific method. In this way, science uses a constructivist, conceptual enquiry approach (an example of this can be found in Chapter 9). Religious education differs from science, but in RE teachers will also draw upon pupils' observations, reasoning and experiences to develop an enquiry into their own beliefs and values and those of others, in their variety.

What is the approach?

As identified in Chapter 4, the conceptual enquiry approach is a constructivist approach to learning (an introduction to constructivism was presented in Chapter 3 and applied to RE in Chapter 4). Wray and Lewis (1997) identified four key aspects of the constructivist approach. Learning is:

1.   a process of interaction between what is known and what is to be learnt;

2.   a social process;

3.   a situated process;

4.   a meta cognitive (thinking about one's own thinking) process. (p. 27)

This means that pupils need to draw upon previous knowledge and understanding to learn and make new connections, and then be able to expand and critically reflect upon that previous knowledge. So, learning opportunities need an element of discussion and interaction with others so that insights may be shared. Learning contexts must be relevant to pupils and promote their thought processes. Pritchard (2005) says simply:

> 'Everything about the constructivist approach to learning, in a simple and practical way, points towards the importance of learners getting as close to the material content of what it is hoped they will learn as possible and then "doing" something with it.' (p. 37)

So it is the process that the pupil goes through that is important, so that he or she is actively engaged with, and has some influence over, the learning. The conceptual enquiry approach is very much process led, the elements of the process being: Enquire, Contextualise, Evaluate, Communicate and Apply (as explained in Chapter 4).

How does the non-specialist begin to acquire the relevant knowledge and understanding?

Talk to the subject manager. As suggested in Chapter 7, it is a priority that the subject manager talks to the staff about this approach.

Discuss the help and support you think you might need. This may mean a frank exchange of views but must also include the educational principles underpinning the teaching of religious education and what is being assessed, as required in assessing pupil progress (APP). Together, identify the best way of doing this. Perhaps you (and some colleagues) need an in-service session or two. Maybe you need some materials that will help develop your understanding and the opportunity to discuss ideas to help build your confidence.

Talk to a range of people for whom their religious affiliation is of real importance to the way they live and their understanding of the world. This may well highlight some of the differences between the understanding of religions received through media information and the lived experience of individuals. These meetings could also provide an opportunity to understand those concepts (such as type C concepts specific to a particular tradition) that appear to be more difficult. It can also clarify the accuracy of pronunciation and use of such concepts. Talking to those within religious traditions may also enable you to avoid pupils just acquiring information. Religious education is more than that.

Consider how you have tackled the acquisition of subject knowledge in other areas. It is inevitable that the acquisition of subject knowledge in religious education will touch on prejudice and preferences. The difficulties of recognising our own prejudices or preferences cannot be underestimated, but equality of opportunity is a pupil's right and our personal prejudices cannot be allowed to negate that right. You might want to refer back to comments on this in Chapter 3.

If the planning for religious education is already done for you by the subject manager, do you just have to deliver what is there (refer back to Chapter 7)? Ask questions as to the reasons behind the choice of resources, the identification of concepts to be explored and how this piece of work will move pupils forward in their thinking. A 10-minute conversation could begin the development process for you. After teaching the session, you might seek the opportunity to feed back to the subject manager your thoughts and impressions of your teaching and the pupils' responses. Through critiquing the resources, identifying pupils' misconceptions (and maybe your own), the experience of the assessment for learning process becomes part of your professional development and, of course, informs your assessment of pupils' progress.

What about remaining neutral?

If pupils are to see clearly that there is no hidden agenda to persuade them in their thinking, teaching must be objective in the sense that it is not informed by bias. This is not about apologising for, or watering down, traditions and truth claims or, indeed, the school's religious commitment (if that is relevant in terms of faith schools). It is about recognising that the school and classroom, with its compulsory attendance, is a public area where respect for the individual's rights and privacy is paramount. The faith presumptions that characterise a voluntarily joined religious group do not apply in this context.

We also need to distinguish between viewpoint and bias. A viewpoint is a consciously held opinion and, by implication, acknowledges the existence of other respectable views. However, bias can arise when teaching approaches have not been thought through so that they are influenced by unconscious ideas. If teachers do not adopt a conscious view, then education will be at the mercy of bias.

What is the value and place of religious education in the curriculum?

These issues were previously addressed in Chapter 1, examining the debate regarding the value of religion and religious education from all sides of the argument. The pupils we are educating now will, as adults, be living in a very different society from today and, as teachers, we need to give serious thought to the wider issues that may confront our pupils and that may be meaningfully explored in the context of enquiring into religion. This will include issues concerning spirituality and the way we understand ourselves; ethics, including the ethics of health and wellbeing; religious tensions; the environment and sustainability, which will have an enormous impact upon the way we live in the future (see also commentary on these issues in Chapter 9). Also, appreciating religious understandings will offer young people the opportunity to respond to other ways of looking at and interpreting the world. This is the very essence of education.

What is the educative value of the concepts underpinning a conceptual enquiry approach to religious education?

Tastard (2002) suggests that religious concepts offer another explanation of the origins of all things, that they help those seeking answers to fundamental questions. For example, within the Indian traditions there is a well developed awareness of the cycle of life, death and rebirth. Freedom from this and the suffering it causes is found through enlightenment and right living. Religious concepts offer relationality with the source of life for believers. Holy Communion in the Christian tradition enables believers to share in the life of the risen Christ through the bread and wine.

The exploration of religious concepts may provide insight into questions as to what is right and ethical behaviour. These are generally found in the commandments, laws or mitzvot within the sacred writings of each tradition. Also, religious traditions introduce pupils to the idea of transcendence: the acknowledgement of something greater than oneself that inspires the greatest good a believer can conceive. But religious concepts can be good or destructive: it depends on how they are lived.

The concepts that are identified in the Living Difference syllabus are there because they underpin religious literacy and identity formation. They are the significant nuggets of learning. To fully understand the concept there needs to be openness of enquiry and a level of emotional engagement as well as cognitive understanding. Therefore concepts should not just be presented and information given: consideration needs to be given to the emotional engagement required in an enquiry. These concepts are not just about rational engagement. Because pupils are required to take an active role in reorganizing the knowledge and beliefs they held prior to lessons, the engagement with conceptual enquiry will be affective as well as cognitive. Concepts such as celebration, remembering, belonging, death, salvation, worship, pilgrimage, identity and love, for example, all have an emotional aspect as well as cognitive. Because of the emotional engagement embedded in religious concepts, the development of the child emotionally is enabled, as well as increasing religious understanding. As Weare (2004) states:

'Emotional literacy is the ability to understand ourselves and others and to be aware of, understand and use information about the emotional states of others with competence. It includes the ability to understand, express and manage our emotions, and respond to the emotions of others, in ways that are helpful to ourselves and others.' (p. 1)

However, the teacher must focus upon the key concept and the religious context in order to promote religious literacy as an outcome, even though this will address emotional literacy. Here emotional literacy is addressed within the process applied. Emotion is response and awareness. Each response interacts with and influences the cognition as well as one's action. It is through our emotions that we become aware of ourselves as individuals and in relation to the rest of the world. Macquarrie (1972:320) says it is with our feelings that we immediately participate in the world. To illustrate how the emotions are attached to religious concepts, consider the experience of yearning and longing. From St Augustine through to today the concept of longing has always been a significant concept within religion. Think of the awareness of the numinous, the sense of mystery that causes a person to shudder with fear at the same time as feeling fascinated and attracted.

Within Hinduism the concept of bhakti is significantly emotionally charged: an intense, devotional longing and love for a personal god or goddess. It is a central feature and evident in temple worship and rituals around deity worship observed in many Hindu homes and festivals. Puja, the central ritual of devotional worship, is an important expression of emotional feeling relating to the deity. It involves the honouring of the deity through a series of steps where the image of the deity is first bathed and purified, then clothed, adorned with garlands and then fed. Finally the deity is venerated through the encircling of the arti lamp before the image. The ritual works on two levels. First, the believers' reception and honouring of a longed for, distinguished and adored guest and second, through the performance of puja, the believer momentarily transcends his or her everyday life and enjoins with the deity.

The numinous, the sense of mystery, is found in all religious traditions: the transcendent other that is all powerful, knowing and needs appeasing, that frightens us at the same time as attracting us within the concept of a god or goddess. Consider the dread that may come with understanding that life in this world is finite, that the only certainty we have is that some time in the future we will die. This dread of dying may open up a greater awareness of living, of understanding what it means to be human and give rise to a consideration of the meaningfulness of a concept of a life after death. For those who find the concept of dying difficult, religion helps by offering answers to what might otherwise be seen as a futile existence. The concept of dharma within Hinduism makes sense of the apparent chaos of life and provides an explanation. Dharma is the path of righteousness and living one's life according to the codes of conduct as described by the Hindu scriptures. The resurrection for those within the Christian tradition offers the possibility of eternal life, the idea that there is a life after death if one believes and follows the teachings of the Church or the scriptures.

The stories that contain these concepts, whatever the religious tradition, are intended for those within the tradition to engage with the emotions that are experienced as well as the arguments presented for their truth. The concepts provide pupils with opportunities to think about their humanity and to try and make sense of human experience through enquiring into and evaluating the significance of these concepts for themselves and others.

A storyteller will imagine a whole range of different voices within these stories, but pupils engaging in drama or role play will both imagine them and realise them from within their own different life experiences. Pupils bring to the role play their own emotions and visions of the world, and the subsequent dialogue is not only between the characters of the role play but also the pupil writers and the pupil actors. By engaging in these explorations, pupils also have the opportunity to develop a greater religious literacy. The conceptual enquiry approach offers ways of understanding the causes of our emotions and ways of developing an understanding of particular behaviours, needs and desires.

How might non-specialists tackle religious education from their strengths?

The English specialist

How might an English specialist begin to engage with the conceptual enquiry approach to RE? One of the English specialists' strengths lies in their understanding of and familiarity with the composition and nature of words, the ways in which they function within texts and literature and the concepts that lie behind them. The English specialist will have a well developed awareness of the value of story and mythology in developing linguistic and communication skills. Through the use of story the imagination enlarges the range of experience available to pupils and draws attention to feeling, needs, issues and interests that pupils might not otherwise reflect upon. It is through story and texts that the English specialist offers the pupil a developing awareness of different kinds and functions of language, for example metaphor and allegory as well the story genres of fable, myth, biography, poetry and legend. Themes and symbols that are found in religious stories as well as secular stories can be introduced to provoke and communicate insight through such concepts as new life, questing, pilgrimage, sacrifice, suffering and love.

The English curriculum deals with the nature of myth, the way in which it bears witness to the power of humanity to go beyond their immediate experience. Myths are the stories told to nerve oneself for adventure. They are also explanations as to why things are the way they are and what powers have determined the conditions for existence. Myths and rituals are closely connected and the story of the myth may be acted out symbolically through ritual. An example is the Rama and Sita story celebrated during the festival of Diwali. This connection is helpful as a starting point. By using the stories and mythologies from religious traditions pupils can engage with the symbolic use of ritual and so develop their religious literacy.

Similarly, but for older pupils, an enquiry into the concept of resurrection can be undertaken within the context of Easter in Christianity. Whilst an illustration of how to construct a cycle of enquiry into this concept was presented in Chapter 4, here we are considering specifically how an English specialist might approach it using his or her specific strengths. Consider the literature you are aware of that has the concept of resurrection in it, that is appropriate to the identified age range and offers quality opportunities for enquiry. Make sure you know and understand the concept of the resurrection within the Christian tradition. This is the research element you will be required to do, just as you would research for science, history, geography, art, etc. Because the approach is concept-led, you are required only to research and understand the concept within its context, not have a complete understanding of the tradition of which it is a part. The research required is tightly focused.

There is a range of secular stories in which resurrection occurs, of which English specialists will be aware, for example *Pangur Ban, The White Cat* by Fay Sampson and *The Lion, the Witch and the Wardrobe* by C S Lewis. Each offers a secular opportunity to discover the concept of resurrection occurring through sacrifice. In the example below, *The Lion, the Witch and the Wardrobe* is used. It is designed for years 5/6 within the spring term.

Box 8.1

Sequence of Activities

Enquire: Step 1.
What is resurrection? What does it mean? Discuss as a class or in small groups what they think resurrection might mean-compare ideas. In small groups try to write an agreed definition. Compare group definitions and these definitions with a dictionary definition. Keep a record of these definitions for use throughout the unit, in a class RE glossary, if appropriate.

What could symbolise the resurrection of Aslan? Show video or read extract from *The Lion, the witch and the wardrobe*, where Aslan comes alive again. If the people of Narnia wanted a symbol to represent the resurrection of Aslan, what might it be? In small groups, or individually, design a Narnia symbol which would remind people in Narnia about Aslan overcoming death.

Notice that only the relevant extract from the Narnia story is used. The focus is always tight. We are only interested in the coming alive aspect of the story.

The choice of activity to create a Narnia symbol of resurrection is laying the foundation for an understanding of the symbol of the empty cross. At this point the pupils are beginning to understand what the concept of resurrection means and have explored how the concept has been used in a story that is within their cognitive grasp. They understand the language and symbolism within a secular context. Pupils can endeavour to identify with the feelings of the characters and recognise the range of human qualities and aspirations, weaknesses and needs.

The *contextualise* element now asks the pupils to engage with this concept in a very focused and context-specific way. For Christians this concept is fundamental to their belief. It is the belief that the Jesus of history is the Christ of faith through the act of the resurrection, that through the act of sacrifice and subsequent resurrection, salvation is offered to those who believe and the attainment of a life after death in the presence of God. Pupils need to explore the gospel narratives and ask the questions that will lead to understanding why this concept is so important. Chapters 3 and 7 discuss the issue of questioning and provide suggestions as to the types of questions that may engage pupils in discussion. Questions that go beyond the text and ask pupils to synthesise knowledge and understanding and try to engage with those for whom the concept is significant, are important here.

Because the concept is resurrection, the contextualisation deals only with that aspect, not the complete Passion narratives. Hence in the example you will find questions that relate only to the empty cross. The crucifix, the cross with the figure of Jesus on it, refers to the Passion and death and is not required for the concept of resurrection.

Box 8.2

Contextualise: Step 2.
What do we think the cross means? Show the children a model of an empty cross and encourage speculation. Ask the following questions: What is it? Why is it empty? What does it symbolise? Where would you find it? Who uses it? What is it used for? Why do people wear crosses? In what rituals is it used? What significance and meaning does it have for those who use it?

What story is associated with the empty cross? Explore one of the Gospel narratives on the death and resurrection of Jesus (Matthew 27: 1–66 and 28:1–19 or Mark 16:1–8 and Luke 24:1–11). Dramatise the story and then role play in order to explore the emotions. Use hot-seating in order to pay special attention to the women visiting the tomb and consider the feelings of the women during the event. Children record these ideas in their books with thought bubbles. Discuss 'How is this event related to the empty cross?' Ask the children to draw and write labels (ICT) explaining the meaning of the cross and its significance to Christians. Feedback ideas to the whole class.

It is now necessary to include the explicitly religious texts from the Christian tradition that will contextualise the concept of resurrection for the pupils. Jones and Wyse (2004:98) argue that biblical texts represent 'unconventional' narrative structures in that they do not follow predictable genre frameworks and as such are an interesting exercise from the English perspective. Whilst this is a consideration, the specialist must remember that the focus of the session is religious education and the concept of resurrection. It is not an English exercise. Because religious education is intended to develop pupils' understanding of religion, ask yourself the question, what is the resurrection? How might it help to develop an understanding of religion for pupils? What exactly does this concept teach pupils about religion? The empty cross is a symbol of a believer's faith in the resurrection: that Jesus died and rose on the third day and has become a focus of faith for Christians. Throughout history designs of the empty cross vary and continue to do so, reflecting diversity of culture, but the empty cross unites believers in its focus on resurrection.

Having examined the Gospel narratives, the teacher now needs to *evaluate* the learning that has taken place. Can the pupils answer the question as to why Christians value the resurrection? At this point the pupils are able to offer their view and demonstrate their learning. Remember the reason we are enquiring into this concept is to further the pupils' religious understanding. It is crucial therefore that the pupils have an understanding of what this concept means and the impact it has for those within the Christian tradition. An understanding of this is the intention and aim for this element of this unit of work.

Box 8.3

Evaluate: Step 3.
Why is resurrection important to Christians? Have a class discussion about the importance of the resurrection of Jesus to Christians. You could begin by discussing the importance of the resurrection of Alsan to Narnia, as a lead into this discussion, if necessary. Consider ideas such as new life, hope, triumph of good over evil, overcoming death. Invite a Christian visitor to answer questions about resurrection and pupils produce a speech bubble for a Christian: 'The idea of resurrection is important to me because …'.

Also they can evaluate whether the concept of resurrection with Aslan is the same as the concept of resurrection with Jesus.

In the light of this understanding, pupils are then asked to consider their ideas about the resurrection. They are asked to *communicate*. This is offering the pupils an opportunity for personal reflection, engaging with the insights and thoughts of others, asking creative and challenging questions and generally responding to the learning that has taken place. It is not about believing or agreeing. Rather it is about developing the skills of thinking, critiquing and being reflective. Pupils are bound to ask questions that the teacher is unsure of. If you do not know the answer, say so – you cannot know everything. Say you don't know, but will find out and then return to the question and answer it another time. It demonstrates to the pupils the fact that you value them, take their questions seriously and offer them a good learning model.

Box 8.4

Communicate: Step 4.
What are our responses to the concept of resurrection? Children discuss in groups what they think about the concept of resurrection. Use these questions as prompts throughout the discussions. Can it happen? Is our view of whether resurrection is possible affected by our views of death? Is death the end? Or do we go to sleep, only to be awoken again? What about animals/plants? Groups feedback to the whole class. (NB: the empty cross is a sign for the risen Christ. Christians believe that Jesus came alive again after his death; there is a theological point in resurrection – the overcoming of sin – reconciliation – not just living on beyond death).

Apply: Step 5.
How does our response to resurrection affect our lives? Discuss – continue from above. When people believe in resurrection, how does it affect the way they live? Does it make any difference? Do people who believe in resurrection live better/more careful/worse lives? Does everyone believe in resurrection? Why/why not?

The drama specialist

For teachers who have the confidence and skill the teaching of drama involves an experimental approach. Through drama, teachers can use artefacts, images, words and movement to create a tangible reality for children, and this offers a learning environment that provides potential for change. Within drama, a teacher is able to offer pupils the freedom to ask questions, to take risks and discover new insights: skills that are at the heart of all learning and particularly religious education. Nevertheless, because drama has a structure and rules, it should offer a safe environment for the exploration of sensitive issues, for both pupils and teachers. As a medium, drama has the potential for allowing more than one voice to be heard, for the exchange of opinions and points of view.

An example of the use of drama might be for younger pupils (key stage 1) to enquire into the concept of remembering, and for older pupils (key stage 2) to enquire into the concept of remembrance (the collective and ritual act of remembering at a specific place and time); for example, contextualised within Easter, Wesak, Christmas or Baisakhi. The Sikh festival of Baisakhi is a remembrance of the founding of the khalsa, the 'pure ones'. The initiation ritual into the khalsa is by the pouring on of sugared water called Amrit. Those who receive this initiation and take the oath are called Singh (lion) if male and Kaur (princess) if female. The five Ks are the symbols of khalsa commitment.

In the case of the Passover (Pesach) in Judaism, the situation needs to be presented so that it resonates beyond the actual event and the pupils become involved because they are both intrigued and informed. The purpose is for pupils to recognise the significance of what is being performed and its connection to the concept of either remembering or remembrance. There is a freedom to this type of learning: there is no finished end product and there is always ambivalence and uncertainty about the learning. It is a way of teaching and learning that produces knowing and understanding, that allows for constant debate and, in so doing it has the power to change thinking, as pupils arrive at differing interpretations. Below is a cycle of learning based on enquiring into the concept of remembering using Passover as the context and utilising drama and role play. It is designed for year 1.

Box 8.5

Sequence of Activities
Communicate: Step 1.
What is remembering? Discuss as a class. What do we use to help us to remember? (Teacher models using photos, letters, postcards, souvenirs etc). Pupils respond with their own examples and discuss what, who, when and why they remember and why particular objects help them to remember. This can be done as a show and tell activity.

Apply: Step 2.
What if we stopped remembering? Talk about what would happen if they lost these objects that help them remember and if they stopped remembering. How do we ensure we remember and what things do we think are worth remembering? Are there some things we can't help remembering? Do we all remember the same things? Why? Why not?

Enquire: Step 3.
What do Jews remember at Passover? Show Seder plate. What is it? What is it used for? Where is it used? Who uses it? Invite children's responses in open speculations/guesses. What do they think it might help people remember?
This plate helps Jews to remember a special story.... Tell story of Passover (Exodus 7 v.17 Ch.12). Role-play in groups to show different parts of the story or draw picture story / cartoon or sequence story or pupils retell story.

Contextualise: Step 4.
How do Jews remember? Show a picture of a family celebrating the Seder meal at Passover. Role-play the meal with children, explaining how Jewish people use the Seder plate to help them to remember this story.
Taste some foods, eg, Charoset, Matzah. Create a classroom display with the pupils showing a Jewish family around a table for the Seder meal. Pupils produce pictures and labels for the display

---

The example uses role play to *contextualise* the concept of remembering through the Seder meal eaten during the Passover (Pesach) celebrations. This ritual meal reminds Jews of the experience of being freed from slavery: the Exodus. The Israelites (Jews) are freed because of God's intervention on their behalf and Jews today remember this event as confirmation of the covenant relationship with God, the hope for freedom and equality. The act of remembering reminds Jews of what God has done for them and the freedom they have as a result. So the evaluative question that pupils need to be able to answer is: 'Why is it important for Jews to remember Passover?'

Box 8.6

Evaluate: Step 5.
Why do Jews remember? Watch video about Passover – discuss what they are remembering and why .Is it important for them to remember things that happened? How do these Jews feel at the Seder meal? Do they think the items used and the celebrations are a good way of remembering? Why is remembering important on this occasion and what effect would not remembering have? Discuss as a class. Pupils complete speech bubbles for a Jewish family saying what they like to remember at Passover and why.
How is the Jewish act of remembering similar or different from our own and why?

The pupils enjoy and develop skills during the role play but the point of the lesson is the concept. We are not exploring the techniques of role play or drama, neither are we going to evaluate their effectiveness. We are interested in the effectiveness of the Seder meal as a form of remembering, the expression and ritual around the meal, and the symbols and emotions attached. The pupils need to be able to evaluate this. The concept of remembering in this example is explored within a historically specific time but, 'It can make visible the roots, the causes, the implications and effects of our actions. It can involve us deeply and engage us critically' (Jones and Wyse, 2004:98).

Using visual sources to teach religious education

The importance of the visual to religion has long been recognised. Historically, within forms of Christianity, religious images have given a focus to and informed piety. Yet, as a society today, we do not generally get our informing images from the walls of sacred places in the same way as religious people have done. We get them from the media culture in which we live. Examining religious art can reveal a great deal about the society from which it came, just as exploring media images tells us about the preoccupations of our society. But television and video are among the first cultural experiences of most children in the UK today. The British Film Institute (2003) states that:

'by the time a child is three years old, most children have learned another language in addition to their spoken mother tongue: they have learned the codes and conventions through which moving images tell stories... this sets them on the brink of an amazing world of images and sounds. Wild fantasy, gritty realism, scenes from yesterday and from hundreds of years ago, live events from across the world are all available for children to see and understand through the moving image media.' (p. 3)

This is just one example of how the beliefs and experiences children bring into school are acquired and from which the conceptual enquiry approach might start. Teachers understand the dangers of indiscriminate use of visual materials in the context of ICT. They know that using imagery brings with it a raft of issues. Clips of films can be used effectively in primary schools to offer lessons about accepting ourselves for who we are, but some films may suggest improbable scenarios and distortive values that are not educationally helpful. Such material needs to be evaluated and handled carefully so that misconceptions are not promoted or developed. Giroux (2004) supports the British Film Institute's view when he says that:

'Media culture has become a substantial, if not the primary educational force in recognising the meanings, values and tastes that set the norms, that offer up and legitimate particular subject positions – what it means to claim an identity as a male, female, white, black citizen, noncitizen.' (pp. 2–3)

So films and media material are not value free and that is the point to enquire into. They should be viewed closely and critically to be used effectively, not just to explore concepts but to develop pupils' awareness that such material is deliberately constructed and may serve a variety of motives. Stereotyping, racist and gender attitudes may discretely underpin the film or imagery. Freire (1993) in his book *Pedagogy of the Oppressed,* advocates that the relationship between the pupil and teacher should be one of mutual respect, one in which the pupil's experience is valued so that a dialogue that is a genuine exchange of knowledge can exist. Media education lends itself well to dialogue as pupils will have experienced many hours of media exposure. This dialogue does require the teacher to suspend his or her own judgements and values and the urge to give his or her perceived 'right answer'. Chapter 3 of this book deals with this in the development of the community of enquiry.

Research from the Commercial and Industrial Security Corporation (Fadel, 2008:11) suggests that pupils remember a lot more through pictures and words than just from words. They learn more readily when words and pictures are presented simultaneously and from animation and narration rather than text. For pupils for whom English is an additional language, film can be significant for active and autonomous learning because of its inclusive nature. Therefore it is an effective resource for use within a conceptual enquiry approach.

As a medium for enquiry, film and visual imagery are effective if the level of questioning that surrounds any extract used is focused and challenging. But remember to keep the concept in mind: it is not about using the video or DVD as a text, with pupils answering questions about the extract that do not pertain to the concept. Questions must be focused upon the concept. For example, if an extract from the film 'Ice Age' (this is a film that illustrates an understanding of love between the main characters and their understanding of the way love might work within another community) is used to illustrate the (type A) concept of love, in *Enquire* the key question is, what is love? How is it represented in the film? Then explore the concept more widely. Can you love things as well as people? Is it the same kind of love? Could you be in love with (or love) everyone? This would then move the teaching and learning process to *Contextualise* within the religious tradition.

For example, how is the concept of love understood within Christianity? Pupils could, first, look at Matthew 22:36–40 where we are told that the greatest commandment of all is to love the lord your God with all your heart, your soul and your mind. The second greatest commandment is to love your neighbour as yourself. The parables of 'The Vineyard Workers', 'The Prodigal Son' and the birth of Jesus all illustrate for the Christian the nature of God's love which is freely given to those who seek it and cannot be earned.

If the concept being enquired into is 'community', an A type concept most appropriate for years 3 and 4 in the primary school, then an extract from the film 'An Antz Life' might be a suitable starting point. The film illustrates the frustration felt by a worker ant in having no freedom of choice or expression. His life is viewed solely in relation to his work for the ant community, a community whose ethos he finds difficult to accept and whose power structure allows for no individuality. Starting from the *Enquire* point in the methodology, extracts from this film raise issues to do with the conflict of the individual's need for identity and self-expression and the constraints that societies and communities may impose. The first set of questions that need to be asked is: What is a community? Are there a variety of communities? What communities do the pupils belong to? What were the problems living in the community for the ant? Why? What sort of community was it? How does it differ from or have similarities to our own?

Extracts from this film offer the pupils real opportunities to begin to understand the nature and construct of a community and an individual's place within it. The evaluation question for this aspect of the methodology might be to describe or explain the good and not so good aspects of living in a community. The contextualisation of this concept might be to look at community within Islam, Sikhism or the community of the Christian Church. The evaluation question for this aspect of the methodology could focus on the significance of belonging to their community for Muslims, Sikhs or Christians.

The art specialist

Continuing the theme of visual imagery introduced above, but using the painted image as a stimulus within *Enquire* and *Contextualise,* the concept of Holy Communion could be chosen. This is a C type concept from Christianity and the resource material would be appropriate for year 6 pupils. The art specialists within the primary phase will recognise how they can bring the strengths of their expertise to enable pupils to analyse and interpret religious imagery and to examine the techniques artists use with colour, line and form to convey meanings.

The images referred to below are those of 'The Last Supper' painted by both Leonardo Da Vinci and Ghirlandaio. Respectively, they can be found on the following websites: (http://www.google.co.uk/search?hl=en&source=hp&q=leonardo+da+vinci&meta=&aq=0&oq=Leonard) and (http://www.google.co.uk/search?hl=en&q=Ghirlandaio+last+supper+picture&btnG=Search&meta=&aq=f&oq=).

The painting of 'The Last Supper' reflects an event believed to be initiated during the Passover meal that Jesus shared with his disciples before his death: the symbolic sharing of his body and blood, a ritual that is appropriated in the Church today and referred to as Holy Communion. This genre of painting was usually found in monasteries where communal meals were eaten in refectories. The monks would eat at one end of the room, look towards the other end where the picture had been hung and so understand themselves to be a part of that meal. Ghirlandaio's fresco replicates the architecture of a refectory showing Jesus handing the bread to Judas, signifying that he would be the one to betray him. Leonardo's painting is of a humbler dwelling and depicts the moment when Jesus says that one of them will betray him and the disciples look at one another uncertain of whom he is speaking. These pictures work on two levels. First, they depict the occasion when Jesus foretold of his betrayal by Judas and, second, they represent the event that initiated the rite of Holy Communion.

The *Enquire* stage explores the event and asks the question, what is so significant about the meal in the picture? Questions to be asked have been explored in Chapters 3 and 7, but you might start by getting the pupils to look closely at the figures, asking what they notice and what interests them. Could it happen today? What makes a meal special? Why would a painter paint this particular meal? We are looking at Holy Communion, not the Passover meal, so it is inappropriate to explore the Passover (but, actually we are seeing Jesus celebrate the Passover meal with his disciples, which later becomes understood, doctrinally, as Holy Communion). The point of *Enquire* is to explain the concept so pupils need to recognise how artists interpreted the Passover meal Jesus undertook with his disciples such that it later became understood as Holy Communion. Pupils need to investigate the gospel stories Matthew 26:26–28, Mark 14:22–24, Luke 22:19–20 and John 6:53–54. What were the words Jesus said? Why did he say them? What does a Christian understand them to mean?

To *Contextualise* the concept the questions that need answering are: what is the purpose of Holy Communion and why do Christians observe it? Pupils need to refer to 1 Corinthians 10:16–17 and 11:24–28. There are three main Christian views. First, the bread and wine miraculously become the actual body and blood of Christ. The Roman Catholic term for this is 'transubstantiation'. Second, the bread and wine are unchanged elements, but Christ's presence through faith is made spiritually real in and through them. Finally, the bread and wine are unchanged elements, used as symbols representing Christ's body and blood in remembrance of His enduring sacrifice. Bread symbolises life, because it is the nourishment that sustains life (John, 6:35) and wine represents God's covenant in blood poured out in payment for mankind's sin. A visit to a church may be the best way to extend the exploration of this element. Pupils may engage with the ritual aspects of the gospel words.

The *Evaluate* element of the methodology could be a discussion as to the significance of this concept for Christians and how it translates into their lives. *Communicate* and *Apply* can focus on pupils being asked to express a personal response to the concept of the Holy Communion. Here, with the expertise of the Art specialist in mind, the response to the concept of 'communion' in the lives of the pupils can be explored and depicted. With whom is 'communion' for them most meaningful and why? In what place and how can this be best depicted to convey its significance? Depicting their scenes can be the *Communicate* element, and discussing the various depictions and the captions given to them can be the *Apply* element, including discussing the various ways in which responses to 'communion' have been interpreted and why they are meaningful to pupils.

The history specialist

The history specialist will be very familiar with the idea of using a conceptual approach, because history is divided into three orders of concept. The overarching ones are chronology, period, change, continuity, cause and effect, and evidence and interpretation. These are followed by the concepts of society, monarchy, democracy, class, the Church, and then finally concepts that are specific to historical period, such as The Middle Ages, The Feudal System, The Renaissance and The Enlightenment. Religious education, given the conceptual enquiry approach, is similarly concept-led and enquiry-based, though the types of concepts are different. A-type concepts are concepts common to religious and non-religious experience. Type B concepts are common to many religions and are used in the study of religion, and type C concepts that are particular to specific religions.

History has a process of enquiry. It is the search for evidence, examination of the evidence, the recording and interpretation and weighing of different sources and types of evidence. Religious education's process of enquiry described in Chapter 4 of this book focused on a specific concept: is a process involving an open-ended key evaluative question that students seek to answer. RE too, with this approach, examines sources, develops interpretation and utilises a range of evidence bases. Both religious education and history are involved in the interpretation of artefacts. The history teacher understands that if pupils can learn to interpret artefacts they can make links between themselves and people in the past who had similar and different needs and feelings. Religious education parallels this understanding in that pupils are encouraged to make links between differing cultures that exist today. History requires that artefacts are investigated in context; so does religious education. Additionally, in religious education this would mean engagement with members of a faith, for example through a visit to place of worship.

The historian uses a range of visual imagery, paintings of scenes, portraits, images of artefacts and still images from video or film. One technique is to enter into the picture and use the imagination to empathise with what the scene might have meant to the people who were alive at the time. Then, using a range of sources, find out more. The religious education approach is similar provided the focus is on the key concept and questions related to this. Below are two examples of enquiries in RE that utilise techniques with which historians will be familiar.

Key stage 1: Ganesh and the concept of power

An enquiry focusing on the Hindu God Ganesh and the concept of power might be done as follows.

Starting with *Enquire,* focus on the questions: What is power? What sorts of power are there? Are the pupils as individuals powerful? Who or what do they think are powerful? How is power demonstrated? Following this discussion, the pupils might look at a range of pictures and images and sort into powerful and not powerful. In *Contextualise,* introduce the God Ganesh. Lord Ganesh is the Hindu deity in a human form but with the head of an elephant, representing the power of the Supreme Being that removes obstacles and ensures success in human endeavours. It is for this reason that Hindus worship Ganesh first before beginning any religious, spiritual or worldly activity.

The large head of Ganesh symbolises wisdom, understanding and the capacity to think. His ears are large and therefore he possesses a great capacity to listen and assimilate ideas. Elephant eyes are small but focused, ensuring concentration. The trunk of the elephant can uproot a tree or pick up the tiniest of objects. It is highly efficient and adaptable. The two tusks, with the left tusk broken, represent the wisdom and emotion within a human personality. The right tusk represents wisdom and the left tusk represents emotion. The broken tusk conveys the idea that one must conquer emotions with wisdom to attain perfection.

The four arms indicate that Ganesh is omnipresent (present in all places at the same time) and omnipotent (having unlimited power). The left side of the body symbolises emotion and the right side symbolises reason. The axe he holds and the lotus on which he sits signify that in order to attain spiritual perfection one needs to cut worldly attachments and conquer emotions. The lotus flower grows in dirty water but remains unpolluted by it. In a lower hand he holds a fruit or vegetable or bulb representing the bestowing of wealth and prosperity upon his devotees. The lower right hand is shown in a blessing pose, which signifies that Ganesh always blesses his devotees. A human body with a large belly enables the digestion of all the good and bad in life. Ganesh's body is usually portrayed wearing red and yellow clothes. Yellow symbolises purity, peace and truthfulness. Red symbolises the activity of the world. The mouse sitting at the foot of Ganesh is his vehicle: it represents the ego and desire and unless this is under control it can cause havoc. You ride the desire and keep it under control and don't allow it to take you for a ride. The right foot dangling over the left foot reminds the devotee that in order to live a successful life a person needs to utilise knowledge and reason to overcome emotions. The food at the foot of the image is prasad, indicating that the world is at your feet and you need only to ask.

The *Contextualise* element of the cycle applies the concept of power to Ganesh. Introduce the pupils to Ganesh by providing them with the opportunity of exploring the image of Ganesh through the 'slow reveal' technique. This is usually a three-stage process whereby the image is slowly revealed, offering pupils the opportunity to make deductions from observations, then as more of the image is revealed to combine and revise those deductions and draw different conclusions, while at the same time posing questions. Images of Ganesh are easy to find on the internet; a starting point might be: http://groups.ku.edu/~kuindia/lordGanesh.jpg.

The first stage of the 'slow reveal' process is to show the pupils the top third of the image and ask them to talk to the person next to them about what they can see. Encourage them to take it in turns to mention one or two things that they can see. Suggest they comment on the symbols they can see: crown, axe, lotus, and size of ears, the eyes and any decorations on the forehead. The concept under scrutiny is power. Are there any clues as to whether the character in this part of the picture is powerful? Log their ideas on a whiteboard for later reference. Reveal the second section of the picture. From this the pupils should be able to see most of the image with the exception of the feet, the mouse and prasad. They should now be able to comment on the new aspects of the image, other symbols, for example the trunk, belly and decorative aspects, as well as the predominate colours. Conversations may well start from the idea of the elephant. What do they know and understand about elephants? Are elephants powerful? Where does their power lie? Can they remove obstacles that humans alone cannot? Do humans need to be frightened of elephants? If so why, if not, why not? Why might the elephant head be combined with a human body? Do humans and elephants have different sorts of power?

Reveal the final section of the picture. The image is now complete. What other observations need to be added to those already highlighted? Ask the pupils to consider, on the basis of this picture, whether they think that this image is a good representation of power. Ask them to speculate about why and how the symbols that Ganesh has might contribute to his power.

Support this 'slow reveal' technique by exploring the stories that surround Ganesh that illustrate his power. Be sure to focus on the concept of power Hindus believe this figure to have. At this point in the approach, pupils should be able to identify and talk about why Ganesh is understood as being powerful.

The *Evaluate* element of the cycle explores why Hindus worship Ganesh as the one who helps to overcome obstacles through his power. When and why is Ganesh important for Hindus? Can they talk about the influence or importance of Ganesh in the life of a Hindu? Next, pupils are asked to reflect on the value of Ganesh as a powerful figure. Do they think that an elephant is a suitable representation of power or would a whale or tiger be better? Why is the power of the God not represented by a tortoise? What sort of power do they think Ganesh has? Is it just a physical power or more than that?

The approach then moves on to the *Communicate* and *Apply* elements. The communicate element asks the pupils to consider their own experiences of power. What is powerful to them? Is it the natural elements? Could it be people that they know? For the apply element you can ask how does power affect me and other people? Can we use power in both a good way and a bad way?

Key stage 2: The Christian birth narratives and the concept of interpretation

Another technique that both historians and English specialists and primary teachers in general share is that of analysing texts. At the top end of key stage two (years 5 and 6), textual analysis of the birth narrative stories found in Matthew and Luke would build upon previous skills developed in literacy and religious literacy, and focus on the concept of interpretation. Alongside the textual analysis might also be a 'slow reveal' technique exploring a range of birth narrative pictures (the Nativity) and the different interpretations of this event by the artists.

The *Enquire* element develops the pupils' understanding of the concept 'interpretation'. Starting outside the religious material this might be approached visually by using an image of a child standing in a corner facing the wall with his or her head in his or her hands (or a similar ambiguous image) and asking pupils to say what they think is going on here. Is the child in trouble, frightened or playing hide and seek? Equally, a snippet of film that has some ambiguity about it might be open to interpretation. Look at newspaper articles of an event from a range of papers to get an idea of how events may be differently interpreted and why. What might be the factors that lead to a range of interpretations? By the end of this element of enquiry pupils should be able to explain the meaning of interpretation.

Contextualise now focuses on the different interpretation of the birth narratives as evidenced in Matthew (1:18–25 and 2:1–23) and Luke (2:1–20 and 2:39–40). The aim of this element is for pupils to be able to explain the value of the different interpretation of the birth narratives and identify some of the reasons for variation. It is important that teachers have undertaken some research into these two gospels in order to understand that they were written for different audiences and with different interpretations in mind. Print off enlarged copies of the two narratives and stick them in the middle of a large sheet of white paper, allowing space for pupils to write comments around them. Start with one account and let pupils identify aspects they think are or may be significant and any queries about the narrative. Repeat the process with the other account and begin to identify the similarities and differences. What would be an explanation for the similarities? Why might these differences have occurred? Could one be right and the other wrong? If the authors were writing for different audiences, how might this affect the interpretation? Would the emphasis and details be different? Would they include small details that might be persuasive for their particular audience? Here draw out how Matthew was writing for a Jewish audience and Luke for a Gentile one. How is this reflected in the two different sources? The groups share their responses and consider further questions they might need to pursue and how they can find answers to them.

The *Evaluate* element asks pupils to explain the impact and value these varying interpretations may have for the Christian and the Christian community. For the Christian, does it matter that there are variations of interpretation? Is one interpretation more accurate than the other? Why are both these accounts in the Bible? What is the Christian supposed to make of the variation in them? Is it just a matter of which one they prefer? Can such difference of interpretation lead to tension or conflict? Could it lead to a split within the Christian community? It would be helpful here to have a range of Christian sources that comment on the importance of the birth of Jesus and the narratives for them. Also, you may be able to provide Christian speakers to do this.

The *Communicate* element explores the question of what interpretation means to the pupils. When/what do they 'interpret' in their lives? They may have different interpretation of rules or behaviour. They may view images and actions quite differently from their friends. Why is this? You might provide the pupils with an opportunity to create a documentary about the concept of interpretation. You can use cameras to create a range of interpretations. Camera angles and lighting will affect the interpretation. A range of photographs of commonplace objects viewed from unusual positions will affect interpretation. Discuss the outcomes.

Finally, the *Apply* element engages pupils with situations in which an interpretation may be highly significant and asks them to explain how their interpretation may affect their lives and the lives of others. Through drama pupils can create situations that are relevant to today and their lives; for example, an eyewitness to an accident, a playground scenario or getting lost on a trip. Their dramas can be shared and a discussion may follow as to the implication of their judgements.

Conclusion

This chapter has explored ways in which teachers who might initially lack confidence in teaching RE can begin to apply their many strengths and skills to it and employ their familiarity with resources and strategies for teaching and learning in this context. The intention is to encourage teachers who are not RE specialists to have confidence and realise that the strength of the approach is its focus. It does not require vast swaths of subject knowledge, just the ability to research thoroughly concepts being enquired into, to understand them and be creative in their application and the way they are related to assessment, as is the case for every other curriculum subject.

What next for RE and the primary curriculum?

Clive Erricker and Elaine Bellchambers

Introduction

In this book we have presented ways in which religious education has moved forward and can improve in its attention to children's development, how that is related to effective learning and the development of capacities and skills, and how it can be understood as an integral and necessary aspect of the development of young people in a democratic society. Sixty-six years ago, in 1944, the Education Act, commonly known as the Butler Act, was introduced. Since then the world has changed in significant and unpredictable ways. When you review the provision for religious education it introduced at that time it bears no comparison to what is in place today and, we might predict, what is in place today is as unlikely to be relevant to what is required in 50 years from now. Therefore, how do we plan forward for relevant provision? Whilst prediction is likely to be unreliable we can suggest what might be a way of planning for the futures of children today such that they inherit something that they can then change to their advantage. What might that planning look like?

In 20 years who will be here? Reviewing the purposes of the primary curriculum

As teachers it is vital to recognize that today's 5-year olds will be 25 in 20 years time and to keep that in mind. It is not that we do not know this, but it can slip from view. We then think of ourselves as teachers of 5-year olds rather than being also teachers of the next generation of 25-year olds. Add to that the knowledge that the younger the child, the larger the impression on their experience, the shaping of their identity and their memories, and the influence on their future we are likely to have. This we know from research already available to us within and beyond education. It also impacts upon research into religious and spiritual experience. In an ongoing research project carried out by the Alister Hardy Religious Experience Research Centre, the question was asked: Have you spiritual or religious experience or felt a presence or power, whether you call it God or not, which is different from your everyday life? In the responses submitted it is significant how many of them refer to experiences early in life. Even more forcefully this was apparent in the work of the Children and Worldviews Project (Erricker *et al*, 1997), some of which was introduced earlier in Chapter 4, in which children spoke with conviction about their experiences and the impact these had had on their lives and the resilience that resulted.

The significance of teaching with this awareness in mind is that when we view our 5-year olds as future 25-year olds, we are influential in shaping the identities they will own in later life – thus the attention paid to identity formation within the design of religious education in Chapter 4. It follows that the purpose of primary education, and indeed secondary education, is the development of young people in the present for them to take over our responsibilities in later life. The notion of 'development' is much abused, often in the sense that 'we develop them (children)' as passive agents. Not only should this not be the case but it cannot be the case. The importance of having this professional awareness is brought out in the latest reviews of primary education (comments on which were made in Chapter 7 in relation to an enquiry-based curriculum, but which are augmented here): the Rose Report (Rose, 2009) and the Cambridge Review (Alexander, 2009) but more explicitly in the latter, where it states:

> 'A recent gain is the growing respect for children as agents, valuable people and citizens in their own right. Children who feel empowered are more likely to be better and happier learners. In recognition of this, the power relations in many schools are beginning to shift, but the picture is still mixed and children are far from uniformly regarded as young citizens with important and insightful things to say about their education.' (Alexander, 2009:12)

This sort of language and the sort of approach to the curriculum that underpins it is seen by some as reminiscent of the 'progressive' education championed in the 1970s. Is this a return to the past, from prescription to progressive ideas? We should be wary of this sort of slogan. Progressive educational ideas have been much derided in later decades due to overall changes of attitudes in society as it has moved to the Right. Also, there is no return to the past: that context is gone and what has replaced it are often distorted memories and myths constructed through the lens of different subsequent social and cultural attitudes. The Cambridge Review, again, aptly comments on this:

> 'The belief that after 1967 primary schools were swept by a tide of progressivism is untrue. In its 1978 primary survey, HMI reported that only 5 per cent of classrooms were fully "exploratory" and three-quarters still used what HMI called "didactic' methods".' (Alexander, 2009:10)

What is most shocking about this statement, beyond the implication that progressivism was in need of defence, is the identification of 95 per cent of schools using didactic methods. This gives cause for reflection since, if this were the case in 1967, how much more likely is it that didacticism is presumed as appropriate today in a less 'progressive' climate heavily reliant on centralised statutory guidance and compliance? Also, why should it be assumed that didacticism is an appropriate educational norm and progressivism is a name for 'non-didactic' education, and somehow radical? Both the new reviews and reports on primary education react against this, but whilst the Rose Report positively (and conservatively) claims that:

> 'Our best primary schools already demonstrate that [the] priorities – [of] literacy, numeracy, ICT skills and personal development – are crucial for enabling children to access a broad and balanced curriculum' (Rose, 2009:2)

the Cambridge Review negatively states that:

> 'In many ways, today's primary schools would not look unfamiliar to the Victorians. Even some of the anxieties are similar. As Matthew Arnold, the eminent poet and schools inspector, reported in 1867: "The mode of teaching in the primary schools has certainly fallen off in intelligence, spirit and inventiveness. It could not well be otherwise… in a country where everyone is prone to rely too much on mechanical processes and too little on intelligence".' (Alexander, 2009:10)

Extrapolating from the reports as a whole, when the Rose Report includes findings and recommendations from the Cambridge Review it does so to show compatibility. When the Cambridge Review does likewise it emphasises difference. Beyond that we can note that, though titled as the *Independent Review*, the Rose Report was commissioned by the government and, in its findings and recommendations, emphasises a 'next steps' agenda building on present good practice. The Cambridge Review is more far reaching and critical, calling for attention to be paid to the need to change government policies to issues beyond educational practice that have a direct influence on its effectiveness, such as inequality and child poverty and, within education, the need to revise teacher training priorities and emphases to improve practice. Also, the Rose Report still emphasises the importance of literacy, numeracy and ICT as a core curriculum priority distinct from other subjects whilst, still prioritising these skills, including oracy, the Cambridge Review does not see these as distinctive components of curriculum time but emphasised across the curriculum.

However, what they have in common is the emphasis on the personal development of the learner through more creative, holistic and personalised learning. For example, the Rose Report makes the following statements:

> 'the new curriculum must be underpinned by an understanding of the distinct but interlocking ways in which children learn and develop – physically, intellectually, emotionally, socially, culturally, morally and spiritually – between

the ages of 5 and 11. ... Among other things, a well-planned, vibrant curriculum recognises that primary children relish learning independently and co-operatively; they love to be challenged and engaged in practical activities; they delight in the wealth of opportunities for understanding more about the world; and they readily empathise with others through working together and through experiences in the arts, literature, religious education and much else... primary children must not only learn what to study, they must also learn how to study.' (Rose, 2009:9)

This leads to these key features of a new primary curriculum:

- recognise the continuing importance of subjects and the essential knowledge, skills and understanding they represent [but recognise there is too much prescribed content in the current curriculum (Rose, 2009:2)];

- provide a stronger focus on curriculum progression;

- strengthen the focus on ensuring that, by the age of 7, children have a secure grasp of the literacy and numeracy skills they need to make good progress thereafter;

- provide a greater emphasis on personal development through a more integrated and simpler framework for schools;

- build stronger links between the EYFS and key stage 1, and between key stage 2 and key stage 3 (Rose, 2009:11).

The Cambridge Review emphasises similar features but is broader, deeper and more radical in its analysis, leading to a more extensive commentary on what needs to be done, for example, in the following respects:

'There needs to be a new set of aims that drive the curriculum, teaching, assessment, schools and policy. The aims and principles proposed by the Review unashamedly reflect values and moral purposes, for that is what education is about. They are designed to empower children to manage life and find meaning in the 21st century. They reflect a coherent view of what it takes to become an educated person.

'These aims are interdependent. For instance, empowerment and autonomy are achieved in part through exploring, knowing, understanding and making sense, through the development of skill and freeing of imagination, and through the power of dialogue. Should such a set of aims be statutory? The Review leaves this question open for debate.' (Alexander, 2009:19)

This reads very differently to the Rose Report's three aims: successful learners, confident individuals, responsible citizens, and the commentary on them, which is largely exemplification but not analysis. These now are incorporated as the statutory aims of both the new secondary and primary curricula. Acceptable as they are, who could disagree with them? They do not have the philosophical underpinning and therefore principled rigour associated with 'empowerment', 'autonomy', 'values and purposes' and 'find[ing] meaning' proposed in the Cambridge Review. The latter's 12 aims are identified as follows:

'well-being; engagement; empowerment; autonomy; encouraging respect and reciprocity; promoting interdependence and sustainability; empowering local, national and global citizenship; celebrating culture and community; exploring, knowing, understanding and making sense; fostering skill; exciting the imagination; enacting dialogue. (Alexander, 2009:23)

However, there is no problem in interpreting the aims of the two reviews such that they are consistent with each other (the Rose Report aims can be enriched by those of the Cambridge Review), the main issue comes with how they are achieved. It is possible to conceive the aims of the Rose Report being achieved through the aims (thus acting as objectives) of the Cambridge Review: Successful learners are those who make sense of their learning, are skilful and imaginative. Confident individuals experience wellbeing, empowerment and autonomy. Responsible citizens value respect and reciprocity, interdependence and sustainability, citizenship, culture and community and enacting dialogue. This alignment is effectively the way in which the Rose Report presents its compatibility with the Cambridge Review. Is this the way in which we ensure that those who will be here in 20 years' time, as the next generation of adults, will be equal to the tasks that confront them? That is the fundamental question.

The purpose of the school

Changes to the primary curriculum that the two reviews offer could result in the role of RE being reconceived and radically reappraised. However, for this to happen it is necessary to interpret these proposed changes in a holistic and creative way, which does not start with thinking in a compliant fashion or with giving first consideration to subjects. Starting with the aims, presented above, allows us to consider what a primary curriculum is for. What does it add to children's experience? How does it help them to learn? How does this affect their overall development? In Chapter 3 we considered what constitutes effective learning and that is directly relevant here. It cannot begin with what is taught: it should begin by considering the conditions that are put in place to ensure that there is congruence between the experiences children bring to their learning in school and what is provided by the school. In other words, the school has to be conceived as a significant and integral part of the community. In simple terms, all children should want to come to school, want to learn in school and want to tell their parents about their learning and why they value it. Additionally, of course, this should mean that parents value the school's contribution to the development of their children. Wellbeing, engagement, empowerment and autonomy (in the words of the Cambridge Review) are what it is all about. When these are absent something is (humanly) wrong and something has to be done about it, which is why, of course, the Cambridge Review is so concerned about government policy in relation to poverty and wealth.

As teachers we can also formulate our task and our school's task in relation to the idea of capital (which is what must underpin these aims). Poverty and wealth are aspects of economic capital. The school can do little to remedy lack of economic capital for parents, but what can it do to enhance the opportunity of future greater economic capital of 5-year old children? One of the reasons schools in poor catchment areas can find themselves fighting against the negative attitudes of parents toward schooling is the lack of social and cultural capital of those parents. This lack produces a defensive attitude toward the school, as an institution, that represents a privileged sense of social and cultural capital: it seeks to imbue their children with new attitudes that will separate their children from them. Actually, these parents can be said to be correct: schools do need to enhance the social and cultural capital of all their children – they are there to do that. For example, encouraging respect, developing literacy and oracy, the appreciation of the arts and visiting museums and religious communities, should all contribute to these forms of capital but that does not mean they have to represent encouraging different, elitist, values as some of those parents might think.

Of course we know that aptitude and having certain innate capabilities play a part in the development of these forms of capital as well, and that some children come from homes where these forms of capital are valued and inculcated and others do not, but when we consider all children in our schools we need to attend to children where this is absent in their upbringing, even if they also lack 'talent' as well. To recount my own experience, I am 'tone-deaf', as the expression goes. In primary school we were selected for the choir by singing the first verse of 'Bah, bah black sheep' accompanied by the piano. In my case I only managed the first line before the music teacher stopped me. I didn't know if I was so good I didn't need to go on or so bad that I was a lost cause. Having not made the choir didn't stop me singing as loudly as I could when I relished the sentiments of the song. Later in my 'primary career', as a class, in our music lesson, we were singing 'And Shall Trelawney Die?', a Cornish rebel song. It was my favourite. When we got to verse three the teacher asked me to stop singing so the others could sing in tune. I have come to terms with my 'disability' but still wish I could sing and play an instrument. It is not surprising I developed no confidence in learning musically but, on reflection, my school experience did not help. Fortunately I can do other things quite well. What if I could not write, for example? Educational capital is what schools exist for. It underpins the development of economic, social and cultural capital and, I would suggest, spiritual capital. This is what wellbeing is all about. Its opposite is poverty in every sense. If you want to address community cohesion you must address this.

Curriculum: the contribution of subjects as disciplines

Subjects such as RE have to understand themselves as effective and complementary contributors to the overall purpose of the school, otherwise the value of schooling in education is severely compromised by a dysfunctional curriculum. However, it is necessary to think in terms of the contributions of disciplines, rather than subjects, to the development of young people. 'Subjects' connotes content and the acquisition of knowledge; disciplines are about the development of skills, are defined by concepts and based on enquiry. If we consider history, a subject that has a strong sense of itself as a discipline, its skills and conceptual base are clearly grounded, for example, in chronology, evidence and sources, cause and effect, significance and interpretation. The idea of historical enquiry is therefore taken for granted. One example of the effect of this is in the use of texts. A study carried out by the Association of Religious Education Inspectors and Advisers (AREIAC) compared the use of texts in history and RE, with the following results:

History – tasks tend to require pupils to:

- Read multiple source materials

- Make decisions and choices about the material they are reading

- Work with original texts

- Handle challenging text material

- Process reading so that their writing output is significantly different from the material they have read.

RE – tasks tend to require pupils to:

- Rarely use multiple texts

- Simply recycle their reading

- Use second-hand rather than original texts

- Engage with over-processed simplified language

- Read for understanding doing little with the original: too much emphasis on low-level comprehension and recall. (Stern, 2006:8)

Whilst these results clearly reflect practice in the secondary curriculum as well, rather than just primary, it would also apply to the way in which artefacts, photographs, pictures and images are used. The message is clear: when a subject fails to identify what it is about as a discipline its contribution to pupils' progress and the level of engagement it requires from learners suffers significantly.

Yet RE, as the educational equivalent of the academic discipline of religious studies, is polymethodic. In other words, it draws on a number of disciplines as a field of study: philosophy, ethics, theology, sociology and anthropology, history and psychology. This is, perhaps, part of the problem since, in being reduced to the study of world religions, it has forfeited its rich possibilities to descriptive accounts of the representation of religions (in the QCA attainment target 'learning about') and the nebulousness of somehow being enriched by religion (in the QCA attainment target of 'learning from') as analysed in Chapter 2. If we consider religious education (within which, as the QCDA – the Qualifications and Curriculum Development Agency – has now recommended, we include the study of both religious and non-religious worldviews expressed in the form of beliefs and values) the rich opportunities for philosophical, ethical, theological and socio-anthropological enquiry provide enormous possibilities for RE's contribution to pupils' development. One of the reasons this is part of the problem is that it demands much from primary school teachers, but if you review what has been embedded in the previous chapters you will find elements of these different disciplines in the enquiries presented.

Concepts as a way of focusing children's learning

In the non-statutory guidance, the QCDA presents the scope of religious education within the secondary curriculum as 'concepts'. In the non-statutory guidance for RE in the primary curriculum, however, the areas for enquiry are under the heading of 'essential knowledge', probably to maintain consistency with other subjects. It might be helpful to consider these six areas of essential knowledge, as fields of enquiry. They are:

1. beliefs, teachings and sources;

2. practices and ways of life;

3. forms of expressing meaning;

4. identity, diversity and belonging;

5. meaning, purpose and truth;

6. values and commitments.

As we write this book, the QCDA is in the process of suggesting that within locally agreed syllabuses, these areas of essential knowledge are broken down into concept-driven enquiries. The conceptual enquiry methodology that this book recommends provides just such an approach. The cycles of learning enable teachers to support pupils in their enquiry into different concepts (A, B or C concepts) that clearly contribute to the fields of enquiry (six areas of essential knowledge) as they progress through the primary phase. Some examples are given below. You should be able to identify which concepts you would use with which year groups across the primary curriculum, thus covering all six 'fields of enquiry'. You will see that some concepts can be placed under more than one of these fields:

1. *Beliefs, teachings and sources*

    Type A: change, wisdom, authority, interpretation

    Type B: God, salvation, scripture, miracle

    Type C: redemption, resurrection, incarnation, torah, Covenant, moksha, nirvana

2. *Practices and ways of life*

    Type A: giving, charity, celebration, ceremony, commitment

    Type B: initiation, discipleship, stewardship, pilgrimage, prayer

    Type C: mitzvot, amrit, communion, eucharist, darshan, covenant

3. *Expressing meaning*

    Type A: hope, thanking, love

    Type B: symbolism, ritual, myth

    Type C: sacrament, holy matrimony, samskars (Hindu ceremonies)

4. *Identity, diversity and belonging*

    Type A: belonging, community, identity, diversity, difference

    Type B: ceremony, ordination, worship

    Type C: baptism, church, umma, sangha, khalsa, Israel, varna

5. *Meaning, purpose and truth*

    Type A: truth, specialness, purpose, power, destiny, fate, free-will, chance, change

    Type B: revelation, faith, transcendence, prophesy

    Type C: dharma, maya, omnipotence, dukkha

6. *Values and commitments*

    Type A: toleration, justice, forgiveness, freedom, compassion, obedience

    Type B: sacred(ness), holy(ness), prophethood, martyrdom, repentance

    Type C: reconciliation, agape, jihad

The purpose of religious education and attitudes towards it

Chapter 1 considered some attitudes to religion and RE, especially in the context of democracy and a secular curriculum and changes that have taken place historically. When the QCDA was consulting on its new primary curriculum under the auspices of the Rose Report, RE was originally included within one of the six areas of learning called historical, geographical and social understanding, along with citizenship, history and geography. Now it is absent from this and every other area of learning. It is on its own and it is a struggle to find any reference to it and its purposes within the report. A reason given for its final absence from this or any other area of learning was the withdrawal clause. RE, like collective worship, whilst compulsory, is subject to parental withdrawal. Parents can withdraw their children from RE without having to give any reason. This historical anomaly was originally provided on the basis that parents of Christian persuasions other than that of the Church of England could, according to conscience, be given the right of withdrawal. The clause remains, and is not infrequently used by Jehovah's Witness, Muslim, Pagan and Christian, as well as atheist parents, all for differing reasons. In some cases it is due to the fundamentalist and iconoclastic attitudes of parents, in some cases it is due to not wishing their child to learn about a specific religion such as Islam. In all cases it is due to the fundamental purpose and value of a properly taught religious education not being understood, wilfully in many cases. At root it is about ignorance, wilful or not, and that is not so surprising. Present day RE and collective worship have completely different intentions, but they are both subject to compulsion and withdrawal. Logically, they are both, as a result, optional.

In continental Europe the problem is overcome in a different, and no more helpful, way. Religion is not on the educational agenda, but culture is. Yes, religion is taught in Germany, for example, but under the auspices of either the Lutheran or Catholic Church, depending on the school. In France it is simply not taught (the revolution put paid to that). Interestingly, in the Rose Report, culture is also clearly in evidence, in a way that religion is not. Learning about different cultures is important, but this is not directly referenced to the curriculum purpose of RE. Such shying away from religion compounds the public perception of RE as something different. The report quotes one primary school thus:

'Our curriculum provides a context for real-life learning through local, national and international partnerships that support learners' development as global citizens and members of a culturally rich community.' Darran Lee, Head, Mills Hill Primary School, Oldham (Rose, 2009:92)

Also, diversity of culture is in evidence in the images and photographs used throughout the report. It is interesting to note, amongst these, the conspicuous number of those of women and children in hijab. Is hijab just cultural or is it religious? Hijab is based on the concept of modesty, identified in the foundational texts of Islam and expressed in various ways in the socio-political expansion of Islam, through till today, in which in the case of women it can manifest itself in a range of ways from headscarf to burkha. This is not just about diversity, it is also about difference, and it is not just about culture but about religion. Avoiding these deeper ramifications of religious influence and emphasising cultural diversity is an example of the superficial obfuscations that multicultural policy and strategy have always dealt in. There isn't really any problem, so don't introduce religion and, if you do, represent it as presenting common values that we can all agree with and 'learn from'. No, it is not like that, and, yes, there is an elephant in the room; but once you admit that, you are into a whole new set of problems, so don't go there. That is the history of the last 30 years of RE and there is no political will to change that situation. But it won't wash in the longer term and it should not be continued with now.

Try this argument:

- Religious education is about developing and supporting one's own beliefs and values and enquiring into those of others.

- In doing this we gain a greater understanding of ourselves and the world we live in.

- As a result we make more rational choices and come to recognise how and why others choose to live in ways different from our own.

- Therefore the subject makes a significant contribution to negotiating our collective futures and dispelling ignorance.

- Finally, therefore, democratic forms of education should value the subject as a way of critically reflecting on our own and others' worldviews in relation to the development of humankind.

The problem? This brief for the subject is beyond the title of the subject: religious education. What should we do about that?

In the Cambridge Review, two particular domains are significant in the delivery of what we call RE: faith and belief, and citizenship and ethics. Respectively, it makes the following statements:

'Faith and belief
Religion is so fundamental to this country's history, culture and language, as well as to the daily lives of many of its inhabitants, that it must remain within the curriculum, even though some Review witnesses argued that it should be removed on the grounds that England is a predominantly secular society or that religious belief is a matter for the family. Non-denominational schools should teach about religion with respect and understanding, but they should also explore other beliefs, including those questioning the validity of religion itself. The place of the daily act of worship, required by the 1944 Education Act and now seen by many as anomalous, deserves proper debate.

Citizenship and ethics

This domain has both global and national components and includes the values, moral codes, customs and procedures by which people act, coexist and regulate their affairs. It stems in part from widespread concern about growing selfishness and material greed. It intersects clearly with a number of the aims: encouraging respect and reciprocity; promoting interdependence and sustainability, celebrating culture and community and exploring, knowing, understanding and making sense. In relation to the aim of enacting dialogue, work in schools on dialogic teaching and philosophy for children are examples of this domain in action.' (Alexander, 2009:24)

If you combine these two domains you have (in the Rose Report's parlance) a significant area of learning (or, better put, area of enquiry). The Cambridge Review reinforces the separateness of RE by providing a distinct domain of faith and belief. As is quoted, some Review witnesses argued that England is a predominantly secular society. However, if you are really concerned with children having a developing global understanding of the world you will recognise that secularisation is not a global phenomenon, for better or worse. Nor is religion likely to go away, but the issue may be that we wish it would; we promote its opposite.

Here we arrive at a knotty problem that bedevils not just RE but education as a whole in Western Europe and, it could be argued, the Anglo-Saxon-influenced part of the world. The reason why people oppose religious education, even though it is an academically-based subject, is because they oppose religion. Equally, the reason why many defend religious education is because they have an affinity with religion. In both cases they believe religion is either bad or good for us. Neither view can be a basis for supporting RE in the curriculum or removing it. It is an old, redundant argument that has been maintained for too long and it must go, as must RE's separation from the rest of the curriculum. Whilst, on the one hand, inclusivism is preached, on the other it is denied. The safety patch applied is called 'culture' by some and 'secularization' by others. It is no more than first-aid applied in a culture of denial. It is a sign of an impoverished democracy that will not look beyond its own national horizons at a fast-changing globalizing world in which what happens in Africa or China connects with our own society in unpredictable ways. Within this, beliefs, values and religions play a significant shifting role. In the next 20 years and beyond we are likely to experience a tsunami of change. I don't think it is adequate to teach our 5-year olds either how to put their fingers in the dyke or to pretend that there is no issue to be attended to.

A new vision of primary education and RE?

The Cambridge Review quotes an example of a science lesson that exemplifies good practice in assessment for learning, as follows:

'The nine and 10-year-olds were learning about changes in materials. The teacher's goal was to enable them to recognise the origin of some everyday materials and the ways they have been changed to reach their familiar form. She began with fabrics. The teacher asked the children to think about what the clothing they were wearing was made of, but she did not want answers just yet. What they would be doing in this and the next lesson, she told them, was to find out more about the different materials used in making their clothes and shoes. She wanted to explore the children's initial ideas about one of these materials and at the same time show them a way in which they could report their work. Holding up a silk scarf, she asked the pupils to produce four sequenced drawings of what the scarf was like before it was a scarf, what it was like before that, and again before that, and before that (as suggested in Nuffield Primary Science materials). The children worked in pairs, discussing their ideas and working on their drawings for about 20 minutes. Then the teacher asked them to pin their drawings on a large board she had prepared for this purpose. The children looked at each other's drawings and thought up plenty of questions to ask in the ensuing class discussion.

Meanwhile, the collage of drawings gave the teacher an immediate overview of the children's way of tackling this work as well as of their ideas about the origin and changes in this particular material. She noticed that most recognised that the material had been woven from a thread and had been dyed before or after weaving, but few had an idea of the origin of the thread from a living thing, a silk worm. Since the children's drawings were not self-explanatory, she discussed with them how they could make them clearer; for instance, she showed them other drawings which had labels that clarified what was being represented. Groups of four then worked with a different material, using equipment such as magnifying lenses and information books and other sources. The teacher listened in to their discussions, at times asking questions to help them advance their ideas. If necessary, she reminded them of the aim of their work and to record it in a way that would best help others understand it when they came to report to the class.' (Alexander, 2009:1, adapted from Harlen *et al*, 2003)

The key point to note in the teacher's approach is the constant reference to change, which is identified as the teacher's goal, informs her aim and determines the progression of the enquiry, the questions asked, the activities undertaken, the outcomes achieved and the diagnosis undertaken. Change is the *concept* upon which the enquiry was based (it wasn't just a theme or topic). We have referred to the concept of change in earlier chapters and here we find it being used to promote assessment for learning within a science enquiry. Certain concepts, such as this, lend themselves to developing learning across disciplines and, as what we might call 'umbrella concepts', are pertinent to use across the curriculum. If we construct 'cross-curricular' learning on this conceptual basis it is far more meaningful for children and much more integrated, progressive, creative and holistic. Also, it does not compromise the rigour or integrity of disciplines. This provides the basis for meaningful interdisciplinary collaboration.

When we consider the role RE can play in interdisciplinary collaboration we first have to consider the way in which its potential is transformed through the methodology for conceptual enquiry. RE is no longer isolated as a separate subject about religious things and religious people. Its purpose is enquiry into beliefs and values. The scope of the enquiry should cover religious and non-religious manifestations of these. Its *prime* intention is to encourage and support the development of the beliefs and values of pupils.

In the science example above, the concept of change is used to consider the link between everyday materials and scientific changes that have resulted in them. In history, the concept of change can be enquired into in relation to historical change or changes over time. In 'religious' education the concept of change will be enquired into in relation to how and why beliefs and values change. In all three, the purpose is enquiry into the concept of change so that the learners gain a deeper interdisciplinary awareness of this fundamental concept and its effect on our lives and our world. Other disciplines can obviously be involved, so the point is not what subjects we can include in this topic but what disciplines can best inform our enquiry into this concept.

To decide what other concepts might be the focus for enquiry we need to ask what concepts are fundamental to our understanding of ourselves and the world. In this way a meaningful interdisciplinary curriculum can be constructed. For example, concepts such as belonging, remembering, celebration, change, authority and interpretation lend themselves to this purpose by virtue of their relevance to children's experiences and the breadth of the concepts, which can accommodate a number of subject disciplines. In this way the curriculum takes full advantage of the potential of a conceptual enquiry approach to learning and children's development. Nevertheless, sensitivity is required to ensure that the integrity of the subject discipline is not compromised by placing it within an umbrella concept. This can be addressed by ensuring that concepts within a subject discipline are aligned rather than just accommodated. For example, in history, migration and settlement can be a conceptual focus under the umbrella concept of change. In other subject disciplines, RE being one, similar alignment can be applied. What has to be appreciated is that the key subject-specific concept needs to contribute to an enquiry into the overall conceptual focus in the curriculum plan, otherwise pupils will not see the connection in terms of the development of their learning. Further discussion about making links within learning across the curriculum can be found in Chapter 7.

Just as teaching a subject addresses the question, 'What do we know?', so enquiry within a discipline addresses the question, 'How can we learn or find out?' Beyond both of these, however, conceptual enquiry, by using the methodology employed in this book, reflexively asks the enquirer to consider the value of the learning for understanding ourselves and the world. It addresses the questions, 'How is this learning useful to us?' and, 'How does it change our understanding of ourselves and our world?' In this way it deepens the potential and meaningfulness of assessment for learning and promotes the further question, 'How can we find out more?' Because new questions will arise as a result of the learning in our enquiries that could not have been posed previously, we are able to measure the success of learning by the new questions we are able to pose and engage with. To suggest that a conceptual enquiry constructed curriculum should not include enquiry into beliefs and values, I hope, by now, sounds preposterous.

Beliefs and values in the 21st century curriculum

'Education is the point at which we decide whether we love the world enough to assume responsibility for it and by the same token save it from ruin which, except for renewal, except for the coming of the new and young, would be inevitable. And education, too, is where we decide whether we love our children enough not to expel them from our world and leave them to their own devices, nor to strike from their hands their chance of understanding something new, something unforeseen by us, but to prepare them in advance for the task of renewing a common world.' (Arendt, 1961:196)

With Hannah Arendt's comments in mind, this section attempts to look into the future and in the light of scientific and technical advancement today and other factors, present some of the issues that will be confronting society, religion and the pupils we currently teach in their adult lives. It will offer some thoughts on the current issues to do with climate change and ask questions about sustainability. Also under consideration will be health and the quality of life, cyborg technology (the integration of a human and electronic technology) and religious tensions. It is not written with the intention of creating a specific programme of study to be used in school; rather it is to raise the awareness of teachers and educators in general of the need to create a curriculum that has relevance and depth and is holistic and creative.

The worlds of children

For the primary school child it is not too early to begin to lay foundations for them to engage with issues in later life. Conversations with children as young as 7 have indicated that they are well aware of them. They are intrigued by implants and bionic humans. The films they watch often include this element, as do some of their games. The Olympic Games features aspects of this technology in the Paralympics. Adverts constantly refer to healthy lifestyles, how we should all live and what we should value about being human. Children are not immune from these messages and influences. They also are aware that there is tension in the world between different beliefs and values systems involving different religions and different cultures. You may consider these issues too advanced for primary pupils, but according to a recent review of the primary curriculum by the Department for Children, Schools and Families, conducted by Sir Jim Rose:

'deep societal concerns about such critical matters as drug abuse, obesity, sex and relationship education, violent behaviour, e-safety, financial capability and so forth, press for an educational response in primary schools with children at an even earlier age'. (Rose, 2009:6)

The Rose Review's concerns don't include the ones mentioned above specifically but there is a good case for saying they should. None of these concerns, one might argue, is primary material however, and this may be a discussion that staff need to have. Nevertheless, there is a perception, held by government policymakers, that primary children need to begin to have greater understanding of issues that will prepare them for later in their lives. It is important to add that they need to gain the enquiry skills and develop the capacity for evaluative judgement to make up their own minds on issues such as those raised above. We need to prepare pupils for making informed choices based on having secure knowledge, plus the necessary critical thinking and questioning skills, and an awareness of the complexity of the issues involved and the variety of possible responses and consequences. At the heart of this is a need to address our beliefs and values and how we support children in developing theirs.

The principle behind presenting this change of perspective on primary education is to prepare pupils for those issues they will face in later life, those new questions they will have to face and the responsibilities they will bear. One way in which we can approach this task is by, again, focusing on conceptual enquiry and deciding on the broad concept that would allow us to identify what issues matter and why. Presented below is a way of using the conceptual enquiry approach as a pattern for teacher training that might help primary teachers to take that step back from everyday matters and reshape the fundamental principles and purposes upon which they will base their curriculum planning, incorporating reflection on beliefs and values within it, but not restricting that to what we presently regard as religious education. This should not be regarded as a short developmental input to present practice but as a fundamental revisiting of the school's primary curriculum shape and aims over time. As a staff development activity, the conceptual enquiry cycle for discussion and debate might look like this.

Box 9.1

Humanity and Life in the 21st Century
Concept: Humanity

Enquire
What are the most important issues facing humanity in the 21st century that our children will confront? This element of the enquiry introduces the issues facing humanity in the 21st century. Exploring these issues provides an opportunity for staff to reflect upon the dilemmas we face as humans and how and why we interact with each other and the world in the way that we do. In a school setting this element of the overall enquiry would take an introductory twilight session and a day closure with at least four weeks between them to provide reading time. Students involved in initial teacher training might approach this over several consecutive sessions.

Contextualise

What do different sources and traditions (including religious ones) say about the nature of humanity and the issues we face? Staff would need to have some subject knowledge input at this point in order to understand the complexity of the chosen issues. It would not be possible to cover all the issues. A choice would have to be made as to the sources and tradition/s chosen (from various disciplines and viewpoints) in relation to the issues discussed.

Evaluate

How useful do we think particular sources and traditions' (including humanist, scientific and religious ones, such as Christian, Muslim, Jewish, Hindu, and Buddhist) views of the concept of being human are in addressing the issues identified? Do they offer strategies or courses of action that offer insight as to how the issues have arisen or ways of tackling them? (In the sections below specific issues have been identified and some sources given that can inform this element of the enquiry.)

Communicate

What do we think are the issues and sources to which we should introduce our pupils as a way of addressing their development in being human? Each of the issues raised in the enquiry can be presented, followed by discussion.

Apply

How can we, as teachers, incorporate addressing the concept of humanity/being human and issues we face as humans into our planning for the curriculum? This is the 'nitty-gritty' task of what goes where, when and how it is to be done. This should end with a review of whether it fulfils the holistic and creative purpose that it was intended to achieve.

Of course, the practical question is how to create curriculum time for incorporating an endeavour of this kind. This takes us back to the re-planning proposed earlier in this chapter through 'umbrella' concepts and fields of enquiry led by key concepts to which the subject disciplines contribute. How do you incorporate the concept of 'Being human' within the primary curriculum? The answer has to be that you address it progressively, within and across key stages, through the way in which you approach the concepts you put in place. Understanding what it means to be human and the issues and responsibilities to be addressed as a result becomes the underlying purpose of the primary curriculum in relation to the development of pupils' beliefs and values beyond simply doing discrete RE.

Examples of important issues that could be addressed

Issue 1: Humanity, global climate change and sustainability

The issue of global climate change and, by implication, sustainability is readily addressed within the science and geography curriculum, which engages pupils with ideas about taking responsibility for their environment. The non-statutory guidance produced by the QCDA for the religious education curriculum at the time of writing does not address this issue. It should, as it may be argued that the current view of the world, particularly within the West, is due in some part to the Christian tradition, that the Western world has distanced itself physically, mentally and spiritually from the natural world, and that the concept of 'progress' is understood mainly in terms of belief in economic and industrial progress and the creation of material wealth.

Thomas Berry, in his paper on Christianity and ecology, identifies three phases of the loss of connectedness with the natural world within the development of Christianity. The first separation he suggests occurred during 'the meeting of early Christian spirituality with Greek humanism to form the basis of a strong anthropocentrism' (Berry, 2009:60). Anthropocentrism is about humanity seeing itself at the centre of all things. He goes on to say that this anthropocentrism developed so much that humankind forgot it was only one component in the world picture. The second loss of connectedness he puts down to the Black Death. Between 1347 and 1349, a third of the population of Europe died from the plague. At a loss to explain why this was happening to them, Berry suggests that 'They could only conclude that the world had become wicked and that God was punishing the world' (Berry, 2009:61). People therefore felt the need to repent, withdraw from the world and look for redemption. Berry then suggests that, 'The spirituality that developed involved detachment from worldly concerns and found expression in a new devotional intensity directed towards the saviour personality' (Berry, 2009:61).

In other words, the world is put aside and the focus of attention becomes salvation through the figure of Jesus Christ. The Christianity that subsequently developed becomes a redemptive experience of salvation – a salvation that implies that the sensuous qualities of the natural world are seductive and distracting and should at all costs be avoided. So humankind lives *on* the world, but detached from it. The emphasis is placed upon the soul not the body. Berry continues by saying this detachment from the natural world left room for a scientific perception of the world that was ushered in with the Enlightenment, a world that was mechanical. No longer viewed as a living organism, the world is increasingly perceived as a machine that may be technologically controlled by humanity for our use. This leads to the final separation, the abandonment of working with and alongside the natural world, 'in favour of an industrialised, extractive economy' (Berry, 2009:63).

This third phase of separation brought with it the second aspect, that of the Western societies' understanding of progress. Progress began to be seen purely in terms of economic growth, brought about by the Industrial Revolution. Technologies began to develop and science made great strides. Science increased the understanding of the structures and workings of nature and in so doing gave humanity a sense of having the power to control them. Today, science informs us about the problems of global climate change and the language of science is now firmly in our vocabulary and we frequently use it.

Primavesi highlights that underpinning this language are certain presuppositions we need to be aware of and that also inform our understanding of 'progress'. She identifies these suppositions as:

> 'our entitlement to handle global resources as though they are nothing but an inexhaustible supply of material for gratifying our desires – or indeed our curiosity. It has also presupposed that we have the competence to do so without damaging our future.' (Primavesi, 2009:11)

She explores this idea by saying that in the Western world particularly, we are so used to hearing about and accepting market growth and forces, a need for a growing economy to support lifestyles, travel and global communication that any threat to this is seen as hostile. This, she says:

> 'is enforced by government regulations, defence systems, border controls and tariffs that rely on surveillance techniques and, ultimately, on weapons whose lethal impact is sufficient to wipe out whole communities.' (Primavesi, 2009:11)

Where will this understanding of and implementation of progress lead humanity? Radford-Ruether argues that it will lead to environmental devastation, economic destitution and war. If the population of the world increases considerably, then humanity will suffer from malnutrition, disease and unclean water, as the cost of providing the necessary infrastructure would be too great. The burning of fossil fuels significantly increases air pollution and acid rain, global warming, melting ice caps and the threat of rising sea levels. Radford-Ruether also identifies that:

> 'Soil erosion and pollution of soil and water from industrial and domestic wastes, are also major causes of decreasing fertility of the soil, toxic water supply and diseases conveyed to humans and animals through such pollution… world food supply is threatened by a corporate agricultural system which is destroying the variety of species of foods, whilst demanding high levels of irrigation, pesticides and petroleum fertilizers.' (Radford- Ruether, 2007:270)

Points to consider

- If these are accurate views, what are the implications for the pupils we teach? What do we need to be teaching today to help change, alleviate or cope with these historical and contemporary attitudes and possible events?

- What do I, as a professional educator, need to be doing to develop my knowledge, understanding and teaching?

- What subject disciplines can contribute to helping primary pupils enquire into this issue?

Issue 2: Humanity, quality of life and wellbeing

Following on from and linked to the idea of 'progress' discussed above is the concept of 'quality of life'. This is a concept that permeates Western culture financially and politically to encourage developed societies that are capable of producing the means to satisfy basic needs to go further and aspire to a particular interpretation of 'wellbeing'. This requires a level of social security, health care, enjoyment of wealth, the improvement of the ecological environment and the satisfaction of certain desires. The peoples of the West in the main expect 'wellbeing' as a right. It supports the image of a significant individual, affording him or her status. It is a utilitarian principle elaborated by the philosopher Jeremy Bentham that has over time become a fundamental idea, that is, ethical good will produce pleasure and eliminate pain, so a political programme based upon the 'quality of life' becomes an ethical obligation. We are sold the dream of 'wellbeing' wherever we turn: it can be achievable for us, in fact it is part of realising our human potential.

It is unfortunate that the consequences of this concept may produce human beings and cultures that do not understand each other, value or wish to mix with those who are unable to lead a life that goes beyond basic needs. Whilst we probably immediately think of the vast numbers of people living in the developing world and quite rightly so, it is a global issue. But also, it is much closer to home. The implications for 'community cohesion' are highly significant. This is connected to the idea of sustainability we considered above. We need to ask at whose expense is our 'wellbeing'? Is the sustainability we all talk about threatened by a level of living above basic needs? Does our 'wellbeing' threaten the sustainability of different life forms? If sacrifices need to be made the question is, will it be the developed world's lifestyle that is sacrificed, or rather modified, or does sustainability really refer to maintaining the status quo of the developed world's 'wellbeing' and sustaining the current inequalities of human life? Radford- Ruether, from her research in this respect, concludes that the disparities of wealth and poverty today are vast:

> 'some 20 per cent of humanity control 55 per cent of world resources, much of it concentrated in the top 1 per cent. This means that 80 per cent of the world shares about 15 per cent of the wealth and the poorest 20 per cent a mere 1.3 per cent, living in dire misery'. (Radford-Ruether, 2007:268).

Points to consider

- What different views do different individuals and groups have of 'wellbeing' and sustainability and why do they hold them?

- What are the implications of 'wellbeing' for sustainability, community cohesion and 'developing' societies?

- How might religious education work alongside science and geography in enquiring into this issue? What other subject disciplines and curriculum areas can support primary pupils in enquiring into this issue?

Issue 3: Humanity, the cyborg and body perfect

Alongside the issue of 'quality of life' is that of the ethics surrounding the cyborg. Ethics is a broad philosophical field of enquiry that goes beyond the concepts of right and wrong and looks towards 'the good life'. Mizrach (2008), when talking of the need for a cyborg ethic, identifies that 'the computer, more than any other device in history, is now making possible the augmentation of the human being' (p. 1).

For the first time, through electronic technology, human biology no longer creates our destiny. Through bionic prosthesis, bio-implants and bio-chips, electronic technology can be integrated into the human organism. The computer now seems to offer the human species the opportunity to transcend limitations of intellect, strength and longevity previously programmed into its DNA by evolution, or by being God-given. The ethical question this raises is whether human beings should be doing this? Should there be limitations on the integration of technology into human life and what will the social consequences be of not doing so? Mizrach (2008) suggests that:

> 'It may be disturbing, but it is at least acceptable for humanity to face the fact that they might have a large degree of kinship with the other forms of life on the planet and that our genes might be interchangeable with its myriad species. Bio-electronic technology would seem to be suggesting that it is possible for kinship between humans and computers. The integration of biological and electronic processes suggests that they may be similar in the way they function and the only difference is based on the physical constituents.' (p. 2)

So the key question here for both Mizrach and us is, 'What does it mean to be human?' Most people assume that they have attributes machines do not: possibly free will, emotions and a soul, for example, but what will happen if the electronic technology becomes 'hard wired' into human organisms? How much of the human can you replace and still preserve its 'essential' humanity? As conflicts develop around the world, medical science is resorting to using electronic technology to patch up those who have been injured, through the use of artificial limbs and prostheses; biological implants and electronic devices for restoring sight are becoming commonplace.

Perfection is one of the oldest of utopian dreams. But will it become humanity's downfall? In society today many look to science and technology to provide the dream in the here and now as a physical dream. In Western society there is an interesting perception of perfection that is changing, at least with regard to disability. The Greeks and Romans, from where a large number of our cultural concepts are drawn, had an attitude to the body beautiful, particularly amongst the patrician class, which is personified in their sculptures. The Renaissance painters idealised the human form even though it was a time when many people had impairments or were scarred by smallpox. By implication the beauty of the body came to represent the beauty of the person. Beautiful bodies were also representative of what was good and acceptable and what should be aspired to. Ugly, misshapen or deformed bodies, by contrast, represented the opposite. Is this a belief still held by some today? Is this view inherent in our culture, is it still being promoted? Could cyborg technology be seen as a further means of pursuing the ideal of the body beautiful or the perfect human rather than just repairing the disabled?

Disability Equality in Education (2002) explores this idea. It tells us that the folklore of Britain and Europe, as presented by the brothers Grimm, who collected the oral stories from northern Europe and made them into fairy tales, illustrates this dualistic portrayal in which physical ugliness or beauty are respective representations of human badness or goodness. Physical imperfection is routinely portrayed as evil. There are ugly sisters, stepmothers, deformed, blind and ugly, as is the witch in *Hansel and Gretel*. In *Peter Pan*, the pirate Captain Hook is deformed. Generally pirates are characters who have eye patches, hooks as hands, wooden legs and are shown as corrupt or evil. The English curriculum requires that pupils analyse fairy tales; would this be an appropriate point in the curriculum to discuss this form of representation and its implications and to what extent we have perpetuated it today? What role could religious education play?

Points to consider

- Is this technology likely to result in greater social inequality and make society less cohesive?

- Are there risks to human health and safety? Do procedures already carried out such as silicone implants and the use of steroids suggest this may be the case?

- Will this technology have a negative effect on our ideas of beauty and human attractiveness if only wedded to physical attributes?

How can we as teachers begin to lay foundations for our pupils to prepare them for these types of dilemmas? This technology may have significant consequences for religion in relation to the idea of the intrinsic sanctity and integrity of human life. Within many religious traditions is the idea that humanity is made in the image of God and/or has the divine within them. Even those not religiously inclined nevertheless possess the feeling that there is something within humanity that is not found in animals or machines which makes us uniquely human. These beliefs can lead to the concern that the 'essence' of our humanity will be lost. Could the idea that human beings are worth something, no matter how flawed or infirm, be relinquished through an obsession with human bio-technological improvement?

Certainly this is an area in which personal, social and health education is relevant and in which beliefs and values are prominent, and in which the English curriculum can play a part, as mentioned previously. What other subject disciplines and curriculum areas can support primary pupils in enquiring into this issue at their own level?

Issue 4: Humanity and religious and non-religious tension

A further issue that will present itself to our young people, possibly with a greater impact than it currently has, is that of religious and non-religious tension; that is the tension between the various religious traditions and between religion, secularism and other ideologies. It is the fundamentalist aspects of these traditions that cause concern for democratic societies. Herriot (2007) describes fundamentalism as follows:

> 'the term fundamentalism refers to a discernible pattern of religious militance by which self styled " true believers" attempt to arrest the erosion of religious identity, fortify the borders of the religious community and create viable alternatives to secular institutions and behaviours'. (p. 6)

He goes on to identify five features that distinguish fundamentalism from other religious and secular movements:

1. *Reactivity*: hostility to the secular modern world;

2. *Dualism*: the tendency to evaluate in starkly binary terms as good and bad;

3. *Authority*: The willingness to believe and obey the Sacred Book of the movement and/or its leaders;

4. *Selectivity*: The choice, from the Sacred Book or the movement's tradition, of certain beliefs and practices in preference to others;

5. *Millennialism*: The belief that God will triumph in the end and establish his kingdom on earth. (Herriot, 2007:6)

He continues:

> 'The central and defining feature of Fundamentalism is reactivity against Modernism. Modernism is defined as the set of secular values and beliefs derived from modernity (the organisational and technological developments which underpin modern societies). Fundamentalists perceive modernism, and the secular societies which express it, as being hostile to their religion and intent on destroying it.' (Herriot, 2007:7)

Therefore social pluralism, individual freedom of choice and liberal politics are fundamentalism's enemies. It goes without saying that Liberalism is an enemy. Liberalism within religion would wish to place the emphasis upon the inclusiveness of the tradition. For example, within Christianity, this would mean the inclusiveness of God's love and also the Church. Within Humanism's stress is placed on our common humanity. The present conflicts in the world are often underpinned by varying fundamentalist ideologies. Whilst we are not suggesting that primary children need to understand the complexity of this, it is helpful if their teachers have reflected on the issues and considered their implications when teaching RE. Some pupils will have parents in the armed forces and they may ask questions about the conflicts in which their parents are involved. Many pupils will hear, at least at second hand, of the regular news broadcasts and newspaper coverage of conflicts at the heart of which these issues are to be found. A lack of development in pupils' learning in addressing causes of tension and conflict because of differing beliefs and values and types of beliefs and values will not enable them to interpret, understand and respond to these in an informed way in adult life.

Points to consider

- As a staff, what are your views? Do you think it appropriate to consider these types of tensions in the light of the pupils attending your school?

- In what ways can you prepare your pupils for dealing with these sorts of issues so that they are informed and capable of discernment?

- What subject disciplines might be involved?

Conclusion

This chapter has reviewed the possibilities for RE within the primary curriculum and the nature of the primary curriculum overall in the light of the Rose Report and the Cambridge Review. It has suggested ways in which the primary curriculum can be reconceived and that religious education can have a more significant role to play by being focused on a more inclusive understanding of beliefs and values, rather than just religions. We have highlighted the way in which a conceptual enquiry approach to learning, based on the methodology explored throughout Parts 2 and 3 of this book, is able to provide a coherent and effective pedagogic model for producing an integrated and creative curriculum, focused on the development of young people that will be relevant to them and meaningful for them. Finally, we have asked you to consider the issues that they are likely to face and be responsible for as the next generation of adults, and regard the primary school curriculum as the vehicle which will prepare them for that role. We hope this has given you a better sense of the importance of employing an effective pedagogy and the purpose for which it can be employed. Now it is over to you.

References

Chapter 1

Ali, A.H. (2006) *The Caged Virgin: A Muslim woman's cry for reason,* London: Pocket Books.

Barnard, H.C. (1961) *A History of English Education,* London: University of London Press.

Bowker, J. (1996) 'World religions: the boundaries of belief and unbelief', in B. Gates (ed.) *Freedom and Authority in Religions and Religious Education,* London: Cassell.

Bunting, M. (2008) 'Faith schools can best generate the common purpose that pupils need' *The Guardian,* 4 December.

Dawkins, R. (2006) *The God Delusion,* London: Bantam Press.

Debray, R. (2004) *God: An itinerary,* trans: Jeffrey Mehlman. London/New York, Verso.

Department for Children, Schools and Families (2008) *Toolkit for Schools,* London: DCSF, www.dcsf.gov.uk/publications/violentextremism/toolkitforschools.

Department for Education and Schools (2007) *Guidance on the Duty to Promote Community: Draft guidance for schools and consultation response form,* London: DfES.

Green, J.A. (1905) *Educational Ideas of Pestalozzi,* London: University Tutorial Press.

Marples, R. (2006) 'Against faith schools: a philosophical argument for children's rights', in H. Johnson (ed.) *Reflecting on Faith Schools,* Abingdon and New York: Routledge.

Omaar, R (2007) *Only Half of Me,* London: Penguin Books.

Owen, R (1813) 'Fourth essay on the formation of character', in *A New View of Society.*

Pullman, P. (2004) 'The art of reading in colour', in *Does God Love Democracy? Index for free expression,* 33 (4), 213: 156–63.

QCA (2006) *A Big Picture of the Curriculum,* London: Qualifications and Curriculum Authority, http://www.qca.org.uk/qca_13575.aspx

Reiss, M. (2008) 'Science lessons should tackle creationism and intelligent design', *The Guardian,* 12 September.

Smart, N. (1999) 'Foreword' in P. Connolly (ed.) *Approaches to the Study of Religion,* London and New York: Cassell.

Suri, S. (2007) *Brideless in Wembley: I search of Indian England,* Chichester: Summersdale.

Walinets, S. (2008) 'Faith schools and the community', *The Guardian,* 3 September.

Chapter 2

Brent Council (2002) *Living with Beliefs: The Brent agreed syllabus for RE,* London: London Borough of Brent Education Standards Service.

Bruner, J. (1977) *The Process of Education,* Harvard: Harvard University Press.

Cooling, T. (2000) 'The Stapleford Project: theology as the basis for religious education', in M. Grimmitt (ed.) *Pedagogies of Religious Education: Case studies in the research and practice of good pedagogic practice in RE*, Great Wakering: McCrimmon, 170–87.

Donaldson, M. (1978) *Children's Minds*, London: Fontana.

Erricker, C and Erricker, J. (2000) *Reconstructing Religious, Spiritual and Moral Education*, London and New York: Routledge.

Erricker, C and Erricker, J. (2000a) 'The Children and Worldviews Project: a narrative pedagogy of religious education', in M. Grimmitt (ed.) *Pedagogies of Religious Education: Case studies in the research and practice of good pedagogic practice in RE*, Great Wakering: McCrimmon, 188–206.

Grimmit, M. (1973) *What can I do in RE?*, Great Wakering: Mahew-McCrimmon.

Grimmit, M. (1987) *Religious Education and Human Development*, Great Wakering: McCrimmon.

Grimmit, M. (2000) (ed.) *Pedagogies in Religious Education: Case studies in the research and development of good pedagogic practice in RE*, Great Wakering: McCrimmon.

Grimmitt, M., Grove, J., Hull, J. and Spencer, L. (1991) *A Gift to the Child: Religious education in the primary school,* Cheltenham: Stanley Thornes.

Hammond, J., Hay, D., Moxon, J., Netto, B., Raban, K., Straugheir, G. and Williams, C. (1990) *New Methods in RE Teaching: An experiential approach*, Harlow: Oliver and Boyd.

Hay, D. (1979)'Religious experience amongst a group of postgraduate students: a qualitative study', *Journal for the Scientific Study of Religion,* 18 (2), 164–82.

Hay, D. (1982) *Exploring Inner Space: Scientists and religious experience*, Harmondsworth: Penguin Books.

Hay, D. (2000) 'The Religious Experience and Education project', in M. Grimmitt (ed.) *Pedagogies of Religious Education: Case studies in the research and practice of good pedagogic practice in RE*, Great Wakering: McCrimmon, 70–89.

Hay, D. and Morisy, A. (1978) 'Reports of ecstatic, paranormal or religious experience in Great Britain and the United States: a comparison of trends', *Journal for the Scientific Study of Religion,* 17 (3), 255–68.

Hay, D. and Morisy, A. (1985) 'Secular society/religious meanings: a contemporary paradox', *Review of Religious Research,* 26 (3), 213–27.

Hay, D. with Nye, R. (1998) *The Spirit of the Child*, London: HarperCollins.

Hay, D. Nye, R. and Murphy, R. (1996) 'Thinking about childhood spirituality: review of research and current directions', in L. Francis, William K. Kay and William S. Campbell (eds) *Research in Religious Education,* Leominster: Gracewing Press.

Hull, J. (2000) 'Religion in the service of the child project: the gift approach to religious education', in M. Grimmitt (ed.) *Pedagogies of Religious Education: Case studies in the research and practice of good pedagogic practice in RE*, Great Wakering: McCrimmon, 112–29.

Jackson, R. (2000) 'The Warwick Religious Education project: the interpretive approach to religious education', in M. Grimmitt (ed.) *Pedagogies of Religious Education: Case studies in the research and practice of good pedagogic practice in RE*, Great Wakering: McCrimmon, 130–52.

Ofsted (2007) *Making Sense of Religion: A report on religious education in schools and the impact of the locally agreed Syllabi*, London: Ofsted.

Read, G., Rudge, J., Teece, G. and Howard, R.B. (1992) *How do I teach RE?,* The Westhill Project, RE 5–16, 2nd edn, Cheltenham: Stanley Thornes.

Rudge, J. (2000) 'The Westhill Project: religious education as maturing pupils' patterns of belief and behaviour', in M. Grimmitt (ed.) *Pedagogies of Religious Education: Case studies in the research and practice of good pedagogic practice in RE*, Great Wakering: McCrimmon, 88–111.

Wright, A. (2000) 'The Spiritual Education project: cultivating spiritual and religious literacy through a critical pedagogy of religious education', in M. Grimmitt (ed.) *Pedagogies of Religious Education: Case studies in the research and practice of good pedagogic practice in RE*, Great Wakering: McCrimmon, 170–87.

Chapter 3

Baldock, J. (1990) *Christian Symbolism,* Dorset: Elements Books

Bigger, S. and Brown, E. (eds) (1999) *Spiritual, Moral, Social and Cultural Education,* London: D Fulton.

Broadbent, L (2004) 'Creativity through religious education', in R. Fisher and D. M. Williams M. (eds) *Unlocking Creativity: Teaching across the curriculum,* London: D Fulton.

DCSF (2007) *The Children's Plan,* Norwich: TSO.

DCSF (2008) *Personalised Learning – A practical guide,* Nottingham: DCSF.

Dewey, J. (1909) *Democracy and Education: An introduction to the philosophy of education.* New York: Macmillan, cited in Fisher, A (2001) *Teaching Children to Think,* London: Simon and Schuster.

DfES (2003) *Excellence and Enjoyment: A strategy for primary schools,* London: DfES.

DfES (2004) *Every Child Matters,* London: DfES.

DfES (2007) *Community Cohesion: A draft guide for schools and consultation response,* London: DfES.

Fisher, A. (2001) *Critical Thinking: An introduction,* Cambridge: Cambridge Press.

Fisher, R. (1990) *Teaching Children to Think,* London: Simon and Schuster.

Fisher, R. and Williams, M. (2004) *Unlocking Creativity: Teaching across the curriculum,* London: D Fulton.

Freire, P. (1993) *Pedagogy of the Oppressed,* London: Penguin.

Gale, T and Densmore, K. (2000) *Just Schooling: Explorations in the cultural politics of teaching,* Buckingham: Open University Press.

Giddens, A. (1994) *Beyond Left and Right: The future of radical politics,* Cambridge: Polity Press.

Grainger, A.J.T. and Wray, D. (2006) *Learning to Teach in the Primary School,* London: Routledge.

Halliday, M.A.K. (1978) *Language as Social Semiotic,* Baltimore MD: University Park Press.

Howard, C. (1995) *Investigating Artefacts in Religious Education: A guide for primary teachers,* London: RMEP.

Jacques, K and Hyland, P. (2004) *Professional Studies: Primary phase,* London: Paul Chapman.

Jones, R. and Wyse, D (2004) *Creativity in the Primary School,* London: D Fulton.

NACCCE (1999) *All our Futures: Creativity, culture and education,* London: DfEE.

Paul, R. (1993) 'Workshop on critical thinking strategies, Sonoma State University, CA. Foundation for Critical Thinking', cited in Fisher, A. (2001) *Critical Thinking: An introduction,* Cambridge: Cambridge University Press.

Perkins, D.N. (1994) 'Creativity: beyond the Darwinian paradigm', in M. Boden (ed.) *Dimensions of Creativity,* London: MIT Press.

Pritchard, A. (2005) *Ways of Learning,* London: D Fulton.

QCA (2004) *Creativity: Find it, promote it – promoting pupils' creative thinking and behaviour across the curriculum at Key stages 1, 2 and 3,* London: QCA.

QCA (2006) *A Big Picture of the Curriculum,* London: Qualifications and Curriculum Authority (http://www.qca.org.uk/qca_13575.aspx).

Rose, Sir J. (2009) *The Independent Review of the Primary Curriculum: Final report,* Nottingham: DCSF Publications.

SIFRE (2003) *Interfaith Handbook,* Ipswich: SIFRE.

SIFRE (2003a) *Diversity Game. Interfaith resource,* Ipswich: SIFRE.

Sung, J. (2007) *Desire, Market and Religion,* London: SCM.

Topping, T. and Maloney, S. (2005) *A Reader in Inclusive Education,* London: Routledge Falmer.

UNESCO (1994) *The Salamanca Statement and Framework for Action on Special Educational Needs,* Salamanca: Ministry of Education and Science, Spain.

UNICEF (1990) *The United Nations Convention on the Rights of the Child,* London: UNICEF.

Vygotsky, L.S. (1978) *Mind in Society: The development of higher psychological processes,* Harvard: Harvard University Press.

Walker, J. (2003) *Nature of Belief,* London: Hodder Gibson.

Wallace, B., Maker, J., Cave, D. and Chandler, S. (2004) *Thinking Skills and Problem Solving: An inclusive approach,* London: D Fulton.

Chapter 4

Atherton, J.S. (2009) *Learning and Teaching: Bloom's taxonomy,* online: http://www.learningandteaching.info/learning/bloomtax.htm.

Bagley, K. (2009) *Resurrection,* Winchester: RE Centre.

Erricker, C., Erricker, J., Ota, C., Sullivan, D. and Fletcher, M. (1997) *The Education of the Whole Child,* London: Cassell.

Grimmitt, M. (2000) 'Introduction: the captivity and liberation of religious education and the meaning and significance of pedagogy', in M. Grimmitt (ed.) *Pedagogies of Religious Education,* Great Wakering: McCrimmon.

Hampshire, Portsmouth and Southampton Councils (2004) *Living Difference: The agreed syllabus for Hampshire, Portsmouth and Southampton,* Winchester: Hampshire County Council.

Hampshire, County Council. (2006) *Living Difference: The primary handbook,* Winchester: Hampshire County Council.

Lowndes, J. (2006) 'Remembering', in *Living Difference: The primary handbook,* Winchester: Hampshire County Council, 134–6.

Ofsted (2007) *Making Sense of Religion,* London: Office for Standards in Education.

Patten, B. (1985) 'Looking for Dad', in *Gargling with Jelly,* London: Puffin.

QCA (2004) *The Non-Statutory Framework for Religious Education,* London: Qualifications and Curriculum Authority.

QCA (2006) *A Big Picture of the Curriculum,* London: Qualifications and Curriculum Authority, http://www.qca.org.uk/qca_13575.aspx.

QCDA (2009) *Curriculum Reform Consultation,* London: Qualifications and Curriculum Authority, http://www.qcda.gov.uk/22256.aspx .

Rose, Sir J. (2009) *The Independent Review of the Primary Curriculum,* http://publications.teachernet.gov.uk.

Webster, R.S. (2009) 'The educative value of Dewey's religious attitude for spirituality', *International Journal of Children's Spirituality,* 14 (2), 93–104.

Wedell, K. (2009) *The Living Difference Evaluation Report,* http://hias.hants.gov.uk/re/course/view.php?id=42. See also Wedell, K. (2010) 'Evaluating the Impact of the Hampshire agreed syllabus: 'Living Difference' on teaching and learning in religious education'. *British Journal of Religious Education,* 32: 2, pp. 147–162.

Chapter 5

CRE (2007) *A Lot Done, A Lot to Do: Our vision for an integrated Britain,* London: Commission for Racial Equality.

DfES (2007) *Guidance on the Duty to Promote Community: Draft guidance for schools and consultation response form,* London: DfES.

Hampshire County Council (2006) *Living Difference: The primary handbook,* Winchester: Hampshire County Council.

Hampshire County Council (2008) *Is Difference Good For Us? A report on the Hampshire and its neighbour's social cohesion project, UK,* Winchester: Hampshire County Council.

Qualifications and Curriculum Development Agency (2010) *Spiritual and Moral Development,* London: QCDA.

Suri, S. (2007) *Brideless in Wembley: In search of Indian England,* Chichester: Summersdale.

Wedell, K. (2009) *The Living Difference Evaluation Project Report,* http://hias.hants.gov.uk/re/course/view.php?id=42. See also Wedell, K. (2010) 'Evaluating the Impact of the Hampshire agreed syllabus: 'Living Difference' on teaching and learning in religious education'. *British Journal of Religious Education,* 32: 2, pp. 147–162.

Chapter 7

Alexander, R. (2009) *Introducing the Cambridge Primary Review,* Cambridge: University of Cambridge, www.primaryreview.org.uk/Downloads/Finalreport/CPR-booklet_/ow-res.pdf.

Department for Children, Schools and Families (2009) *Religious Education in English schools: Non statutory guidance,* London: DCSF.

Hampshire County Council (2006) *Living Difference: The primary handbook,* Winchester: Hampshire County Council.

Qualifications and Curriculum Authority (2002) *Designing and Timetabling the Primary Curriculum: A practical guide for key stages 1 and 2,* Suffolk: QCA Publications.

Rose, Sir J. (2009) *Independent Review of the Primary Curriculum: Final report,* Nottingham: DCSF Publications.

Wedell, K. (2009) *The Living Difference Evaluation Project Report,* http://hias.hants.gov.uk/re/course/view.php?id=42.

Chapter 8

British Film Institute (2003) *Look Again: A teaching guide to using film and television with three to eleven year olds,* London: BFI Education.

Fadel, C. (2008) *White Paper: Multimodal learning through media – what the research says,* San Jose CA: Global Lead Educations.

Friere, P. (1993) *Pedagogy of the Oppressed,* London: Penguin Press.

Giroux, H. (2004) 'Pedagogy, film and the responsibility of intellectuals', *Cinema Journal,* 43 (2), 119–26, Texas: University of Texas Press.

Jones, R. and Wyse, D. (2004) *Creativity in the Primary School,* London: D Fulton.

Lewis, C.S. (1950) *The Lion, The Witch and The Wardrobe,* London: Harper Collins.

Macquarrie, J. (1972) *Existentialism,* Harmondsworth: Penguin.

Pritchard, A. (2005) *Ways of Learning,* London: Fulton Press.

Sampson, F (1983) *Pangur Ban, The White Cat,* London: Lion Hudson.

Tastard, T. (2002) *World Religions,* London: Pitkin Guides.

Turner-Bisset, R. (2005*) Creative Teaching: History in the primary classroom,* London: Fulton Press.

Weare, K. (2004) *Developing the Emotionally Literate School,* London: Paul Chapman, http://www.ltscotland.org.uk/healthpromotingschools/practitioners/topics/emotionalwellbeing/emotionalliteracy.asp

Wray, D and Lewis, M (1997) *Children Reading and Writing Non Fiction,* London: Routledge.

Chapter 9

Alexander, R. (2009) *Introducing the Cambridge Primary Review: Children, their world, their education,* Cambridge: Esme Fairbairn Foundation.

Arendt, H. (1961) *Between Past and Future,* London: Faber and Faber.

Berry, T. (2009) *The Christian Future and the Fate of Earth,* New York: Orbis Books.

Disability Equality in Education (2002) http://www.bfi.org.uk/education/teaching/disability/

Erricker, C., Erricker, J., Ota, C., Sullivan, D. and Fletcher, M. (1997) *The Education of the Whole Child,* London: Cassell.

Harlen, W., Macro, C., Reed, K. and Schilling, M. (2003) *Making Progress in Primary Science,* London: Routledge Falmer.

Herriot, P. (2007) *Religious Fundamentalism and Social Identity,* London: Routledge.

Mizrach, S. (2008) *The Ethics of the Cyborg,* www.fiu.edu/~mizrachs/cyborg-ethics.html.

Primavesi, A. (2009) *Gaia and Climate Change: A theology of gift events,* London: Routledge.

Radford-Ruether, R. (2007) *America: Elect Nation and Imperial Violence,* London: Equinox

Rose, Sir J. (2009) *The Independent Review of the Primary Curriculum: Final report,* Nottingham: DCSF Publications.

Stern, J. (2006) *Teaching Religious Education,* London: Continuum.

INDEX